# Database Modeling in the PC Environment

# Database Modeling in the PC Environment

**Bradley D. Kliewer**

BANTAM BOOKS
NEW YORK • TORONTO • LONDON • SYDNEY • AUCKLAND

*DATABASE MODELING IN THE PC ENVIRONMENT*
A Bantam Book / May 1992

ISBN 0-553-08952-8
Library of Congress Cataolg Card Number 92-70974

*Published simultaneously in the United States and Canada*

Bantam Books are published by Bantam Books, Inc., a division of Bantam Double-
day Dell Publishing Group, Inc. Its trademark, consisting of the words "Bantam
Books" and the portrayal of a rooster, is Registered in U.S. Patent and Trademark
Office and in other countries. Marca Registrada, Bantam Books, Inc., 666 Fifth
Avenue, New York, New York  10103.

PRINTED IN THE UNITED STATES OF AMERICA


0   9   8   7   6   5   4   3   2   1

*To Wes and Cheryl*

# Contents

# Preface

The electronic spreadsheet was a critical factor in the establishment of the PC as an important business tool. Since the early days of the IBM PC, spreadsheets have remained one of the top-selling software categories. However, if one talks to people who use minicomputers and mainframes, it quickly becomes apparent that databases are one of the primary business applications on these larger systems. In fact, the database is often central to the operating system of minicomputers and mainframes.

Because a database requires large, fast disks for data storage and retrieval, the early PC database systems were limited in both performance and capacity. As PC disk capacities increased to hundreds of megabytes, even gigabytes, databases have played an increasingly important role in the PC environment. PC networks allow several computers to share files, representing another feature that mimics the capabilities of the larger database systems. While many PC prognosticators foretell the replacement of the minicomputer and mainframe with ever more powerful PC-based systems, proponents of the larger systems contend that they will always retain performance and security advantages over desktop systems. In either scenario, it is clear that improvements in PC technology will continue to converge on territory once firmly held by central systems.

Occupying the middle ground are those who believe that the overlap in computer systems will result in new software based on cooperative processing. In this scenario, the PC's responsiveness and easy-to-use interface create a quick, friendly access path to central information stores. Additionally, the PC's processing power acts as a preprocessing engine, handling many time-consuming tasks and allowing the minicomputer or mainframe to devote full performance to the central storage tasks for which it was designed.

In all three environments many of the database systems have at least a partial basis in the relational model. Although the commands may vary from system to system (or even between different software packages on the same hardware), there are many concepts which apply to a number of different systems.

Whatever the future holds for your business—migration from large systems to small, from small systems to large, or cooperative processing—an understanding of relational database systems in the PC environment will be a valuable tool.

# Introduction

Most readers probably are familiar with flat file databases: programs such as PC File, PFS:File, and Lotus 1-2-3, among many others. In a flat file system, most of the data is arranged in one file or in the case of 1-2-3, one continuous set of columns and rows. The program lets you select data by particular properties such as numeric range and then prints reports based on those selections. These operations, queries and reports, are at the heart of any database system.

Many people move from a flat file database to a relational database because they have heard that it is more powerful. The relational database may support larger files, more functions, or run faster. Others may change to a more popular system to find better support. The relational model for database management was designed in the late 1960s. It is often abbreviated RDBMS (Relational Database Management System). In 1985, E. F. Codd, the creator of the relational database, published the 12 requirements or rules of a fully relational database. Among them are the ability to define data structures, as well as the storage and retrieval operations that can be performed upon them, and the provision of integrity constraints upon the data. Although the term "relational database" is used rather loosely to describe several PC databases, two of the most popular systems, dBASE and Paradox, have at least a partial basis in the relational model.

Many of the reasons why people select a relational-based system have nothing to do with the relational structure of the database. Accordingly, applications ported from a flat file system into a relational system frequently fall short of the full potential available.

If you have been working with a flat file system and want to get the most from a relational system, you must make a major conceptual shift. You must learn to look at data differently. Rather than lumping all data into one large file, you must recognize smaller groups, organize data into these groups, and understand how each group relates to the others. Finally, you must learn the operations that combine these groups into a larger whole. Mastering these skills and applying them to the design and use of a database can be very frustrating. At first, it will seem to add a new layer of complexity to the process.

But once mastered, these skills will reap many advantages. Most important, your applications will be much more adaptable to new tasks.

Codd devoted considerable effort to maintaining consistency throughout the relational model. In theory, a few fundamental skills should give the user a reliable method for performing all operations on a database. Such consistency means more efficient work. In addition, relational methods can save storage space and improve the performance over more traditional flat file approaches.

This book will work through some of Codd's theories and see how they apply to (or fall short of) the two most popular database systems for personal computers, dBASE and Paradox. Although there are several other products that more closely match Codd's relational database model, these two were selected because they are more widely used and, in some cases, much easier to learn than other systems. While the emphasis will be on practical application of skills, it is hoped that a basic understanding of the theory behind a relational database will enable readers to improve their skills.

# 1

# Building Relations

E. F. Codd based the relational model on mathematical theory. Indeed, readers with a background in set theory will have a much fuller understanding of relational databases by reading his book, *The Relational Model of Database Management, Version 2*. Anyone interested in developing a more technical understanding of the logic behind RDBMS should read Codd. This book will not attempt to go into as complete a description as Codd, but it will at least try to cover the important points and a few of their practical implications to the PC database user. Because of its basis in set theory, it is difficult to describe or understand a relational database without starting with the basic underlying structure derived from a set—the *relation*.

Relations are collections of *rows* and *columns* of data typically called *tables* or *files*, although this is not technically correct. Conceptually, relations are similar to files with records (rows) and fields (columns). But don't be misled. The relational model does not specify storage methods at the operating system (e.g., DOS) level—a file could contain several relations, or (more likely) a relation might be constructed from several files.

Furthermore, relations have special properties that do not apply to tables and files. For example, a relation does not have identical information in two or more rows. Each relation also has a primary key—a column (or a combination of columns) of data that uniquely identifies it. With few exceptions, the key for a particular row cannot be changed once it is entered, which is one of the integrity constraints an RDBMS provides. Other rules may apply to the data within a column; allowing only the values "red" or "blue." When you are inside the database system (for example, running Paradox) the rules may be stored in one file and the raw data in another. But the system will present the table in the menu as a single file selection. It's apparent that an RDBMS adds a great deal of complexity to the underlying file system. Fortunately, it also adds tools to hide these complexities from the user and simplify your work.

When you start working with a database system, you should learn to manipulate all data from within the system and be wary of making changes at the DOS level. If you use DOS to erase a file, for example, you might unintentionally destroy or corrupt data used by another file. A complete RDBMS should let you perform all necessary maintenance functions (copy, delete, rename, etc.) from within the system. In a few cases file manipulation from within the RDBMS may be a bit more awkward than DOS, but it is certainly much safer.

So, what's the use of an RDBMS if the file system becomes more complicated? Power and flexibility. And, as just stated, while the underlying structure is more complicated, the system provides tools to simplify management while working within the RDBMS. In addition, links (or *joins*) between relations may be designated. A join may be implemented in one of two ways: a query or a view. Queries and views let you break data into smaller and more manageable chunks. When structured properly, queries and views based on joins can reduce storage requirements and simplify queries. A simple example should clarify the point. Consider a list of clients, addresses, and phone numbers. The list might include:

| Business | Address | Phone | FAX |
| --- | --- | --- | --- |
| Frank's Franks | 345 Weiner Way | (612) 555-4859 | (612) 555-4860 |
| Bob's Kabobs | 978 Grill Lane | (812) 555-7455 | |
| Robin's Robins | 888 Egg Drive | (212) 555-8888 | (212) 555-8889 |
| Chuck's Chucks | 555 Bit Ave | (507) 555-2288 | (507) 555-8822 |

This is a very typical structure for an address list. Note that Bob's Kabobs doesn't have a FAX number. This wastes some storage space, although it's not unreasonable. But what happens when you need other numbers such as modem, home, or private lines? Do you add columns? With four columns of phone numbers, a business with a single phone line could waste more storage space than the actual data for the business occupies.

With a relational database, the data can be separated into two or more relations. First, a *primary key* is required. The name of the business might work, unless two cities have companies with the same name. Using both the name and address is another possibility. But this becomes unwieldy. Usually, you'll create your own keys—a client number, for example. In this example, let's create two relations: a client list and a phone number list. The first would resemble this:

**Relation 1**

| Client Number | Name | Address |
|---|---|---|
| 1 | Frank's Franks | 345 Weiner Way |
| 2 | Bob's Kabobs | 978 Grill Lane |
| 3 | Robin's Robins | 888 Egg Drive |
| 4 | Chuck's Chucks | 555 Bit Ave |

The primary key of the second relation requires at least two columns. The Client Number is not sufficient because a single client may have more than one phone number. The combined columns, Client Number and Phone Number, will be used as the primary key. The second relation would look like this:

**Relation 2**

| Client Number | Phone | Description |
|---|---|---|
| 1 | (612) 555-4859 | work |
| 1 | (612) 555-4860 | FAX |
| 2 | (812) 555-7455 | work |
| 3 | (212) 555-8888 | work |
| 3 | (212) 555-8889 | FAX |
| 4 | (507) 555-2288 | work |
| 4 | (507) 555-8822 | FAX |
| 4 | (507) 555-2828 | modem |
| 4 | (507) 555-8282 | direct |
| 4 | (507) 555-2882 | home |

Now, a link must be established between the two relations. The common column is Client Number. In Relation 2, the Client Number is a *foreign key* with its target in Relation 1. In other words, to include a Client Number in Relation 2, it must exist in Relation 1.

By establishing a link between Relations 1 and 2 through the Client Number, the RDBMS can find the phone numbers for each client. Have you ever placed a want ad in the newspaper? Many advertising sales representatives will first ask for your telephone number, and then use the number to find your name and address. In a similar way, the RDBMS can also use the join to find the address in Relation 1 that matches a phone number in Relation 2.

Now, imagine using a flat file database for this application. You ask Chuck for his phone number, and he gives you his direct line rather than the main business number. If the RDBMS searches just one column, it may not find the number and you might add Chuck's Chucks to the database again. If you program the RDBMS to search every phone number column, the program will be more complicated, and may be slower.

In a flat file database the structure of the file is determined by its intended use. Thus, in this example, the original flat file database is designed in typical phone directory form; given a name, you can look up an address or phone number. In a relational system, the independence between the data structuture and its intended use is maintained. Data is gathered into similar categories or groups, and each group is stored as a separate table. An identifier (the primary key) allows matching between various groups. This process of breaking a file into its constituent groups is called *normalization*.

The idea is that, if given any one fact about an item, you should have a file that will uniquely identify it by a key value. Then by applying the key to other files, or even the same files, you can retrieve additional information. The retrieval method is more complicated because it requires more work. Likewise, the structuring process (normalization) requires more planning and effort. The payoff comes when you need the data for several different projects or objectives.

It can be argued that a particular database will be used for only limited projects. But data is a very valuable commodity, and once the effort is made to organize and enter data, frequently other uses for the data will be discovered that had never been intended. Or perhaps someone in your office will hear about your file and need something similar for a slightly different project. With a flat file system, it may be difficult for him or her to obtain. In the long run, the extra time spent designing, building, and learning a relational system is a valuable investment.

While the preceding examples showed some key differences between relational and flat file databases, they are by no means complete. Despite popular terminology, a database requires much more than multiple file support and relational operators to be truly relational. In his book, Codd describes 333 features of a Version 2 RDBMS (the original, 12-rule definition includes about 40 of the Version 2 features). The features are encompassed in three broad categories: structure, maintaining data integrity, and data manipulation. As noted, this book will examine dBASE and Paradox to see how they measure up against several of Codd's features and rules for RDBMS.

A very important part of the relational model is its versatility and ease of use. The features are designed for minimal programmer intervention once the database is defined. It should be easy to use in an interactive manner without sacrificing programmability for more complex tasks. In a true RDBMS the distinctions between programs and objects, such as table definitions and queries, are not as clear cut as with the more traditional programming languages such as BASIC, C, and Pascal.

None of the PC database packages used in this text follow the relational model very closely. The emphasis will be on developing databases using the packages. Codd's features can act as guidelines in your development and are useful for avoiding pitfalls in a package weak in its relational capabilities. They also can help plan for features that may be added later to the package, or convert the database to another system that more fully supports relational capabilities.

At times, you may think this book is picking nits. After all, many of Codd's rules place severe restrictions on how data is used. To many people, this makes the system too inflexible. But there are two very important reasons for such restrictions. First, Codd intended an RDBMS to have an interactive mode for novice users. Thus, someone unfamiliar with programming concepts can easily retrieve and alter the underlying data. However, you must have a way to protect the data against corruption, such as illegal values or inadvertent duplication of critical data. An example is catalog number reassignments. Second, an RDBMS may be shared by several users. It must be capable of handling the demands of everyone, and yet appear consistent. This consistency in operations is important for obtaining reliable results, and achieving it in a multiuser environment is not a trivial task. It should not become the responsibility of the programmer, if adequate tools are available to prevent such problems, and novice users should not be required to know such technical details.

## Codd's Twelve Rules

A look at Codd's original 12 rules for a relational database is in order here. While the Version 2 rules are far more extensive (and they will occasionally be referred to), the original rules form a sound basis for understanding a relational system. In fact, it is these original 12 rules that most people use as the standard, and which most databases still do not meet.

## Rule 1—The Information Rule

- All data in an RDBMS is accessed through values in base relations.
- Record numbers are prohibited (see Rule 2).
- Duplicate rows are not allowed.
- The system may present the data in any arbitrary order.
- The system will also provide indirect access to the base relations through *views* (Codd uses the term *derived relation*).
- Views resemble base relations, but retrieve their contents from one or more base relations and allow user-defined ordering (sorted results).
- Base relations include not only data entered by the user or application programs, but information about the database itself (see Rule 4).

## Rule 2—Guaranteed Access

- Every value stored in an RDBMS may be retrieved by specifying a base relation name, column name, and its associated primary key value.
- The primary key is defined by the user and consists of one or more columns. Note that this addressing method is entirely independent of the table structure and record storage order.

## Rule 3—Missing Information (RS-13/RM-10)

- The database must be able to designate missing information through the use of *marks* (also called *nulls* or *null values*). Codd's original definition included only one type of mark. Version 2 includes two different marks called *missing-and-applicable* (A-mark) and *missing-and-inapplicable* (I-mark). Consider a relation with a column for middle names: If a person's middle name is not known, an A-mark is used. On the other hand, a person may not have a middle name—in this case an I-mark is selected (the data does not apply to this person).

## Rule 4—Active Catalog

- A relational database stores data about itself in the database. Such information could include relation names, column names, domains, creation dates, etc.
- The data describing the database is called the *catalog* and may consist of several base relations and views.

## Rule 5—Comprehensive Data Sublanguage (DSL)

- A relational database includes a data manipulation language that uses four-valued logic (True, False, Maybe/Applicable, Maybe/Inapplicable). This language is frequently called the query language. SQL (Structured Query Language) is a well-known example.

- The data sublanguage is used for data retrieval, view definition, row insertion, row deletion, row update, and defining integrity constraints. (See Rule 7 for further details about these operations.)

## Rule 6—View Updateability

- A view may be created directly from a query, and will act like an interactive query (when the base data changes, the contents of the view will change).

- As long as a user or an application program does not attempt to alter the contents of a view, it will behave exactly like a relation. However, there are some cases where it would be impossible to update or modify the contents of a view in a consistent manner. For example, two users might keep separate lists of names that share an indentical structure. A view could display the combined list as if it were a single relation. But should you attempt to add a name to the view, where would the database put the data? Does the database put the new name in the first table, the second, or both? This is only one small example of a very complex problem.

- There are many views that can accept changes safely and unambiguously. The database should attempt to determine which types of changes a view can accept when the view is defined well before the user ever attempts to modify data in a view. These modifications include row insertion, row deletion, and/or updates to existing data. The database may disallow one or more of these operations if necessary

## Rule 7—High-Level Operations

- The database sublanguage (see Rule 5) is designed to work with entire data sets rather than single records. As an example, consider a file (relation) that stores information about all orders received at the shipping dock. At the end of the day, this information is merged with the current inventory data. With a language such as C, Pascal, or BASIC, you might read a record from the RECEIVED relation, write a record to the INVEN-TORY relation, and repeat the process until all data had been transferred. This program would require several lines of programming. With a relational database, a single command would update INVENTORY with the contents of RECEIVED. These operations should also work with multiple relation sources and destinations.

## Rule 8—Physical Data Independence

- The database should allow physical changes to data storage without affecting programs that access the data. For example, some systems support an *index*. The index is a special set of data that helps the database find information more quickly. The presence of an index should not affect the methodology of database operation. Thus, if a column were indexed, it should not suddenly disallow duplicate values. Or, if an index is dropped, it should not compromise the integrity of the data.

- Database operations should be unaffected by changes in the storage method. If the records are reorganized (different physical storage order) or the files are moved (a different subdirectory), programs and user instructions should not require changes.

## Rule 9—Logical Data Independence

- The database should allow certain types of logical changes to the database structure without affecting users or programs. For example, two relations accessed through a view might be combined into a single relation. If the new table has the same name as the former view, users or programs should not notice an operational difference.

- If a single relation can be split into multiple tables and a view with full modification rights can be generated, you or your programs should be able to use the view transparently.

## Rule 10—Integrity Independence

- The database should allow definition and enforcement of integrity constraints (rules) at the database level.

- These rules are defined within the catalog and may be examined or changed by the database administrator.

- Rules that define acceptable data or prevent corrupted links between relations cannot be circumvented by writing data through another method.

    There are two common situations covered by this rule. The first is when one relation references another. For example, an invoice may reference a customer. It should not be possible to delete a customer record if that customer is referenced by an invoice. This is known as *referential integrity* and is built into the database system.

The second situation involves changing policies or laws. For example, a business may require a minimum order of $5. If the policy later changes to a $10 minimum order, a simple change to the rule definition (stored in the database catalog) should enforce the new rule for all programs and interactive users.

## Rule 11—Distribution Independence

- The RDBMS sublanguage will be designed in such a way that the data in the base relations can be redistributed without affecting user or programmed operations.

- Redistribution might include moving base relations from a single network server to multiple network servers or even moving data to several different physical sites assuming there is a sufficient communication link between them.

## Rule 12—Non-subversion

- It is possible (although not required) that a database may allow access to programs written in languages other than the data sublanguage. For example, the database might allow access to C, Pascal, or BASIC programs.

- The database must keep such programs from bypassing integrity constraints (see Rule 10).

## Practical Applications

The database rules are designed to ease maintenance tasks so that data maintains its value. If every change to the structure or content of that data requires rewriting the programs that access the data, more time will be spent revising programs than using them (or writing new applications). Data from an invoicing application may be used in a number of other programs: sales analysis, general ledger, accounts receivable, inventory, etc. If a billing program needs a new field for credit limits, wouldn't it be nice to add such a field without reprogramming the other modules? That is the intent of a relational database.

There is some ambiguity to the term *relation* when applied to a database. As shown, a relation is simply a collection of rows and columns, which most PC users call records and fields. But, because the comparison here will be between database and RDBMS systems, the more commonly accepted term, rows and columns, will be used. There will be some reversion to record/field notation to clarify certain points, as when discussing screen formats where position is referred to as rows and columns. Rows and columns are also a very convenient notation since the default view of a table is typically in a spreadsheet-like format. Codd frequently calls rows *tuples*, so you may see this term appear from time to time, also. Thus, the rows represent the elements of a set, or table.

Creating a relation from a table requires the restriction cited earlier: The rows of a relation may not be duplicated. Of the two databases presented here, only Paradox partially implements this feature (it is an option, rather than a requirement). Because none of the packages *fully* implement this feature, the more appropriate term, *table*, will be used when referring to the basic structure created by these programs. If the text refers to a relation, it is implied that the table has no duplicate rows.

A new table is created by defining the name and data type of its columns. Technically, the column should be assigned a *domain* name rather than a data type. A domain consists of a data type with optional restrictions such as minimum or maximum values. Comparisons between relations should be restricted to columns from the same domain. Unfortunately, none of the databases referenced in this book use domains. But the concept is important enough that you should at least be aware of its implications.

Consider three tables: VENDOR, CLIENT, and INVENTORY. Both may have a six-digit ID number. Perhaps the INVENTORY references both a primary vendor and a primary client. In the early design phases, you may have overlooked the ambiguity and named the columns [ID1] and [ID2]. If you change column names to something more reasonable, like [Vendor ID] and [Client ID], you must change all programs (and user instructions) that reference those columns. But domains offer built-in protection from such situations— [ID1] might be from the domain VENDOR# and [ID2] from the domain CLIENT#. If you should attempt to reference [ID1] to the CLIENT table, the database would issue a warning, "The domain VENDOR# does not match the CLIENT# domain."

After defining the table structure (assigning data types or domains to each column in the table), data may be entered in the various rows. The data types of the databases used in this book fall into two classes, alphanumeric and numeric. In the future, additional types such as image and sound data will probably be supported as multimedia applications gain popularity.

Numeric data is manipulated with mathematical operations such as addition, subtraction, multiplication, and division. Familiar examples would be unit price and quantity. Anything else should be alphanumeric (even if it consists only of numbers). For example, names, addresses, and telephone numbers are alphanumeric. Even part or invoice numbers that have no symbols or letters should be defined as alphanumeric, because such numbers are not normally used in arithmetic.

Numeric data is sometimes divided into subclasses such as date, floating point, currency, logical, and/or integer. Some, such as floating point and integer, can make more efficient use of storage space. Others, like currency and date, may require special output formats, but are frequently used in mathematical operations such as totals or determining days between dates. Alphanumeric data is usually defined with the maximum amount of data that may be placed in the column.

The first step is to create a table called ADDRESS for storing a name, address, and phone number. The table will have separate columns for first name, last name, street address, city, state, zip code, and telephone number. All are alphanumeric fields, so as they are defined, convenient sizes will be set. Whenever practical, the menu systems will be used rather than working at the programming level.

As defined by Codd, the underlying database language would make provisions for table definitions. Thus, in SQL, the command **CREATE TABLE Address (Client_Num Char(6), AddNum Char(2), FirstName Char(15), LastName Char(15), Address Char(25), City Char (15), State Char(2), Zip Char(5))** would create an ADDRESS table. Most modern database programs have a more convenient, visually driven table definition method. While the underlying effect is the same as a command-driven system (in fact, some programs simply translate the screen design to the appropriate command), the menu system is much simpler to use and understand.

In dBASE IV, the Control Center is used as a menu-based system. Many dBASE systems start running the control center as soon the dBASE program is loaded. But if your system does not, you will see an empty screen with a dot. To enter the control center from this *dot prompt*, type **assist**. To use the dBASE menu system, you first select the object, and then the action. The control center lists the objects that are available by category: Data (tables), Queries, Forms, Reports, Labels, and Applications (programs) (see Figure 1.1).

To design a table, select **<Create>** under the data column. After selecting **<Create>** a screen with the column definitions will appear. Simply enter the names and data types. A filled-in table definition form for the ADDRESS table appears in Figure 1.2. Note that the index attributes are N (no) for all columns.

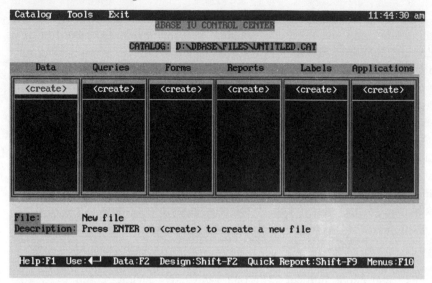

**Figure 1.1   The dBASE control center. The selection is set for table Create.**

A dBASE index is purely performance oriented—if the values in a column are highly varied, an index will help the database find a particular value faster. Now hit **F10** and select **Exit/Save changes and Exit** from the menu. The system will prompt you for a table name (ADDRESS in this case) and add the name to the catalog (see Figure 1.3).

The Paradox menu system works a bit differently than dBASE. In Paradox, you select an action, such as **View**, and then an object such as a specific table. Paradox always starts from the menu system. Paradox uses Lotus 1-2-3 style menus rather than drop-down menus like dBASE. While you work, you can get to the current menu by pressing **F10** (the menu key). To create a table, select Create from the menu and enter the table name (ADDRESS). The initial Paradox menu is shown in Figure 1.4. The column definition form is similar to dBASE, but instead of entering a separate type and width, the column width is part of the type definition (see Figure 1.5). After entering the definitions, hit **F2** to save the new table. Note that Paradox has longer column names than dBASE IV and allows spaces and lowercase letters. Lowercase is treated as uppercase (you couldn't define two columns called Address and ADDRESS in the same table)—it is simply available to make the names easier to read.

Now that some properties of columns have been displayed, it's time to look at the rows. Rows store the facts (columns) about a particular object or event. The order that the information appears in a relational database is inconsequen-

```
Layout   Organize   Append   Go To   Exit                    11:47:12 am
                                              Bytes remaining:    3911
 Num  Field Name  Field Type  Width  Dec  Index

  1   FIRST       Character     15          N
  2   LAST        Character     15          N
  3   ADDRESS     Character     25          N
  4   CITY        Character     15          N
  5   STATE       Character      2          N
  6   ZIP         Character      5          N
  7   PHONE       Character     12          N






Database D:\dbase\files\<NEW>    Field 7/7                      Num
         Enter the field name. Insert/Delete field:Ctrl-N/Ctrl-U
Field names begin with a letter and may contain letters, digits and underscores
```

**Figure 1.2   Definition for the ADDRESS table in dBASE.**

tial. You should not rely on a row's location for any of your database operations; i.e., the record number should not be used as an identifier and the *next* or *prior* record has no dependence on the current record. Rather, a row should be

```
Catalog   Tools   Exit                                 11:50:27 am
                        dBASE IV CONTROL CENTER

                   CATALOG: D:\DBASE\FILES\UNTITLED.CAT

   Data      Queries     Forms      Reports     Labels    Applications

 <create>   <create>   <create>   <create>   <create>   <create>
 ADDRESS







File:        ADDRESS.DBF
Description:

Help:F1  Use:↵  Data:F2  Design:Shift-F2  Quick Report:Shift-F9  Menus:F10
```

**Figure 1.3   ADDRESS has been added to the dBASE catalog.**

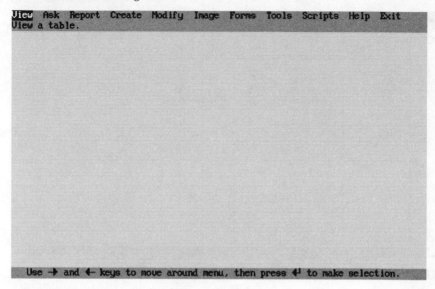

**Figure 1.4    The initial Paradox menu.**

identified by the values in its column(s).  One of dBASE's major shortcomings as a relational system is that it is highly dependent upon a row's number and position within the table. Paradox displays row numbers and allows some references to the numbers.  With both programs, you should avoid row number references as much as possible.

There are two approaches to handling row numbers, and both can cause confusion as data is added to, or deleted from, a table, or when a table is sorted. In Paradox, the row number may change as the table is modified in any fashion—even when data is appended to the end of a keyed table.  Thus, the position of a row is not a reliable identifier because it may change.

The dBASE approach is almost exactly opposite: The number is permanently tagged to a row unless an explicit **Insert** instruction rebuilds and renumbers the table.  When a dBASE table is used in a sorted view, its number no longer reflects the position within the current view.  Thus, the dBASE row number is a fairly reliable indicator of position.  However, that position may have no relevance. If you are looking at a table sorted by zip code and tell dBASE to move to the row numbered one higher, it won't move to the next zip code (except by chance), but will skip to some seemingly random location based on the order the rows were entered.  Certainly, as will be demonstrated, there are ways to work around this.  But the point is that row numbers have very little relevance in a relational system.

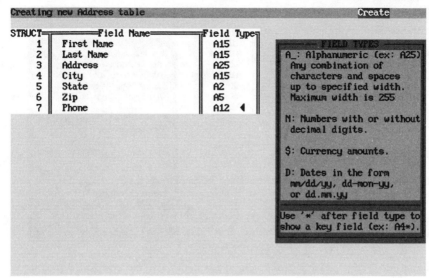

**Figure 1.5    Definition for the ADDRESS table in Paradox.**

Another requirement of a relation is that each row should be unique. If two or more rows have identical information (i.e., each and every column has the same value), there is no way to uniquely identify one. This becomes important when establishing links between two or more tables. Nevertheless, most databases allow duplicate values. At best, duplicates waste storage space, and at worst they can cause inaccurate results for queries.

Now, you may immediately think of some exceptions to these rules. What if the order of entry *is* important, as when making payments on a loan? Or what if, as in the case of dBASE, a duplicate value is distinguished by its position? In a truly relational system, such information would become part of the table definition (one of the columns). A row may be tagged with the date, time, or even an arbitrary sequence number if such information is important. To repeat, the only reliable and consistent way to identify a row is by the values in its columns.

Likewise, columns should be identified only by name. As you change the database (for example, adding new columns for additional information), you will not need to change the underlying programming to identify a column. Note: Because a column is identified by name, you may define the columns in any order you find convenient. And you may define a presentation or data entry order that differs from the definition order.

Paradox includes support for primary keys—a column or combination of columns that uniquely identify a row. The key columns must be the first

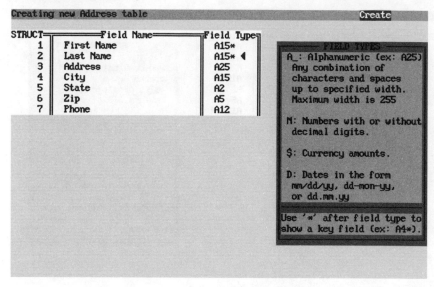

**Figure 1.6    Paradox keys defined on First Name and Last Name.**

columns in the table (i.e., the order of the key columns within the table definition is important). An asterisk is placed after the data type to define the keys. Thus, to form a key from first and last name, in the preceding example, the table definition would look like Figure 1.6.

Under this definition, Paradox would not allow duplicate rows. Indeed, it would not allow duplicate combinations of first and last names, even if the remaining columns had distinct values. The table becomes a relation. As a side effect, Paradox will always present the table in key order, which can be a nuisance at times. If Paradox required keys on all of its shared tables (those tables available to several users over a network), it would come much closer to a true relational database. Even so, it would still fall short of the mark in several other areas.

Although none of the packages require primary keys, you should try to design your applications as if they do, and take measures to avoid duplication. In Paradox, do this by defining key columns in shared tables. In dBASE, write routines to scan for duplicate values and take corrective measures such as prompting the user for new key values or deleting exact copies. When using an index, tell dBASE to hide duplicates; although they don't appear in the view, the data is still there and can create undesireable side effects.

Wherever possible, avoid multiple column primary keys by defining an arbitrary key column. For example, in the ADDRESS table define a client number. The numbering scheme and sequence don't matter as long as each

```
Catalog   Tools   Exit                                    2:57:09 pm
                        dBASE IV CONTROL CENTER
                   CATALOG:  D:\DBASE\FILES\UNTITLED.CAT

    Data        Queries       Forms       Reports      Labels     Applications

  <create>     <create>     <create>     <create>     <create>     <create>

  ADDRESS




File:         ADDRESS.DBF
Description:

Help:F1  Use:◄┘  Data:F2  Design:Shift-F2  Quick Report:Shift-F9  Menus:F10
```

**Figure 1.7    The ADDRESS entry in the dBASE catalog.**

entry is unique.  This has several advantages:  Clients can have the same name
(such as John Smith) without adding more columns to the key.  And you will
save storage space when working with foreign keys since the full name need
not appear in other tables.  There are times when multiple column keys are
necessary (as when defining one to many relations, a topic covered later), but
you should strive for short keys.

Additionally, avoid duplicating content across table columns.  The phone
number example from the beginning of this chapter demonstrates one such case.
Any time there is such duplication of information, normalize the tables (i.e.,
create multiple tables using a key reference to form a link).  If you are using
numbers to distinguish column names (such as Phone1 and Phone2), it is time
to consider normalization.

There are a few exceptions, however.  For example, you might call a two-line
address Add1 and Add2, but these are really quite distinct facts.  Usually, one
address line is a street address and the other a suite number or company name.
But, when in doubt, normalize.  Although it may seem inconvenient at first, in
the long run, normalization will make reporting, querying, and database maintenance much easier.

Following the example in the Introduction, let's add support for multiple
phone numbers.  To do this, take the phone number out of the ADDRESS table,
add a client number, and make a new PHONE table.  Thus, the relation is
normalized.  This should be a fairly simple process in an RDBMS.

The ADDRESS table appears under the data column in dBASE (see Figure 1.7). First, open ADDRESS by selecting it with the cursor, and hitting Enter. Then, choose Modify structure/order from the menu (see Figure 1.8). You will see the same table definition form used to create the table. Move to the first Field Name (column) and hit **Ctrl-N** to open a blank column. Type in the new column name and description (CLIENTNUM, Character 6, Index=Y). Now move to the PHONE column description and hit **Ctrl-U** to delete it. The new definition should resemble Figure 1.9. Call up the menu (**F10**) and select **Exit**, **Save Changes**. Finally, you will be asked if you want to confirm the changes; answer **Y**.

Now that the structural changes have been made, you can define a PHONE table. Simply select **Create** and fill in the column names and data types as shown in Figure 1.10. **Exit and Save Changes**, and enter PHONE as the new table name.

To start table modifications in Paradox, select **F10** (the Menu key), **Modify**, **Restructure** (Figures 1.11 and 1.12). When asked for a table name, hit Enter to see a list of available tables (Figure 1.13) or simply type **Address**. At the top of the column definition form, hit Ins to open a new column definition (see Figure 1.14) and enter **Client Number** and **A6***. The asterisk tells Paradox that a key is desired (no duplicate client numbers allowed). Now, move down to Phone, and hit Del to remove the definition. Finally, hit **F2** to save the new

**Figure 1.8    Changing a dBASE table definition.**

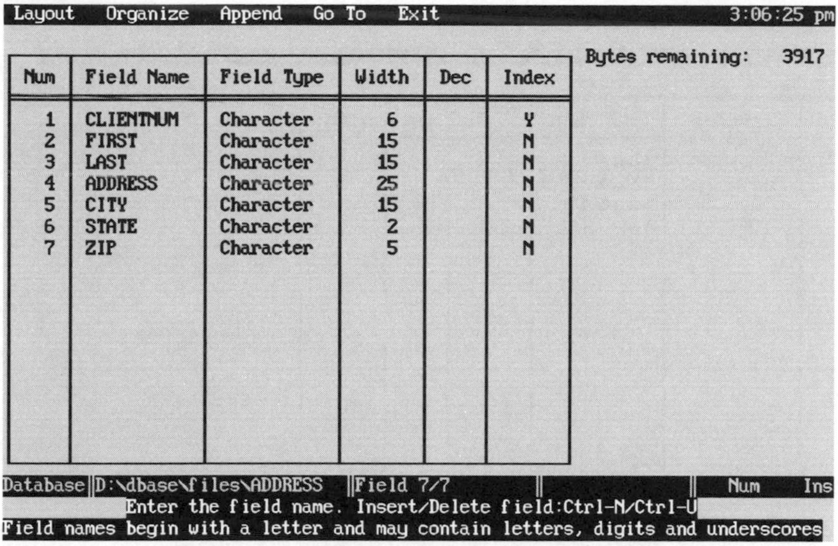

```
 Layout   Organize   Append   Go To   Exit                        3:06:25 pm
                                                        Bytes remaining:   3917
 Num │ Field Name │ Field Type │ Width │ Dec │ Index
  1  │ CLIENTNUM  │ Character  │   6   │     │   Y
  2  │ FIRST      │ Character  │  15   │     │   N
  3  │ LAST       │ Character  │  15   │     │   N
  4  │ ADDRESS    │ Character  │  25   │     │   N
  5  │ CITY       │ Character  │  15   │     │   N
  6  │ STATE      │ Character  │   2   │     │   N
  7  │ ZIP        │ Character  │   5   │     │   N

 Database │D:\dbase\files\ADDRESS   │Field 7/7                    │ Num   Ins
          Enter the field name. Insert/Delete field:Ctrl-N/Ctrl-U
 Field names begin with a letter and may contain letters, digits and underscores
```

**Figure 1.9    The revised ADDRESS definition in dBASE.**

definition. Paradox will ask for confirmation of any deleted fields, as shown in Figure 1.15.

Paradox will place the ADDRESS table in your workspace (Figure 1.16). You may either clear it from the workspace with the **F8** (Clear Image) key, or leave it and bring the menu back up with the **F10** key. Use **F10, Create, Phone** and define the phone number table (Figure 1.17). Note that both the Client Number and Phone columns are keyed. This prevents duplicates of Client Number and Phone combinations. If only Client Number had been keyed, each client could have only one phone number. Hit **F2** to save the new definition.

## Summary

Table definition and modification is a fairly simple process under dBASE and Paradox. But do not let the simplicity fool you! As you will soon discover, you should plan ahead to make your table structures match the final form as closely as possible. As you add new elements to the design, such as table dependencies and data validation, you will want to protect that investment of time—your best investment is a sound design.

```
Layout    Organize    Append    Go To    Exit                    3:09:55 pm

                                               Bytes remaining:    3958
  Num   Field Name    Field Type   Width   Dec   Index

   1    CLIENTNUM     Character       6            Y
   2    PHONE         Character      12            N
   3    EXT           Character       4            N
   4    NOTES         Character      20            N




Database D:\dbase\files\PHONE    Field 4/4                   Num
              Enter the field name. Insert/Delete field:Ctrl-N/Ctrl-U
Field names begin with a letter and may contain letters, digits and underscores
```

Figure 1.10    The PHONE table definition for dBASE.

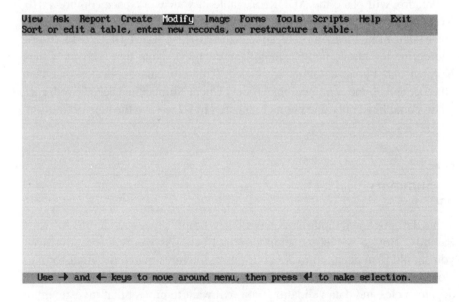

```
View  Ask  Report  Create  Modify  Image  Forms  Tools  Scripts  Help  Exit
Sort or edit a table, enter new records, or restructure a table.






                     Use → and ← keys to move around menu, then press ↵ to make selection.
```

Figure 1.11    The Paradox menu resembles Lotus 1-2-3.

**Figure 1.12    The Paradox submenu under Modify.**

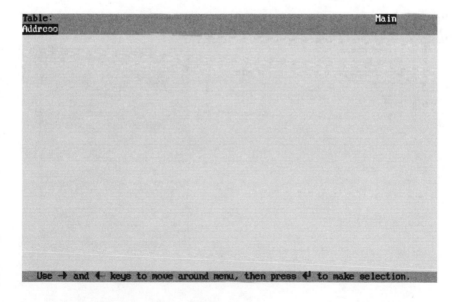

**Figure 1.13    Table selection under Paradox.**

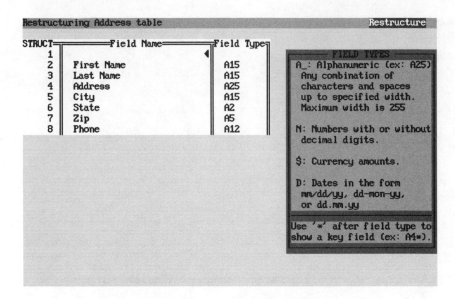

**Figure 1.14   Opening an initial field definition to create a new key.**

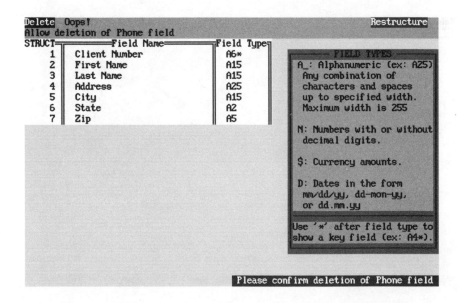

**Figure 1.15   The ADDRESS table is now keyed on Client Number Phone.**

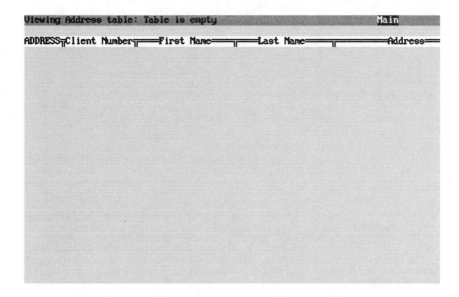

**Figure 1.16    The revised ADDRESS table appears on the workspace.**

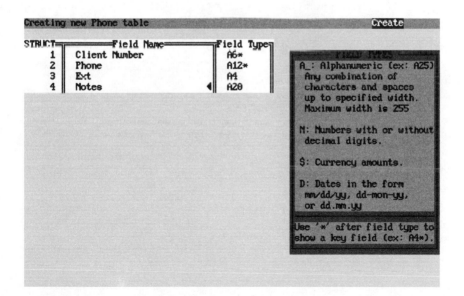

**Figure 1.17    The Paradox PHONE definition.**

# 2

# Data Entry and Validation

Now that a couple of tables have been created, it's time to add data. Many entry tasks require data validation in one form or another. In a relational database, these validation procedures are known as integrity constraints or rules. These internal rules keep the database in a consistent and accurate state. An RDBMS that truly supports integrity constraints provides absolutely no method for bypassing the constraints, of which Codd defines five types: domain, column, entity, referential, and user-defined.

Because neither of the packages discussed in this book supports domains, neither of them supports domain constraints either, which is rather unfortunate, since it would make many operations much simpler. For example, if a domain of telephone numbers could be defined, requiring that each number meet a format such as 123 456-7890, every time a phone number was placed in the table, the database would keep it in a consistent format. Furthermore, it would not be possible to enter telephone numbers in a different format, such as a European format, unless the new format was added to the rule.

Column constraints are similar to domain constraints, but are applied only to a single column in a single table, and they confer additional restrictions on the domain; i.e., the column constraints do not replace domain constraints, but work in conjuction with domain rules. An example of a column constraint is a table of customers in Minneapolis that limits the telephone column (in the telephone number domain) to 612 area codes. Because neither dBASE nor Paradox supports domains, the column constraints must also take on the characteristics of domain constraints. This means that whenever constraints are desired, they must be defined in every column of every table—not a very pleasant task.

The maintenance required without domains may not seem overwhelming at first. After all, once a format such as a telephone number has been defined, it's done and isn't likely to change. But consider items such as part numbers. These may appear in several tables (e.g., customer orders, vendor orders, inventory, suppliers). If you get a new supplier and need a longer stock number (the data type is considered part of the constraint) or a new format, you'll have a lot of redefinition ahead to do. A true RDBMS would apply the change to each affected table automatically.

Entity constraints are integral to the database system. They prevent the occurrence of duplicate primary keys or missing primary key values (nulls within the primary key). To allow missing primary key values is asking for disaster. Consider a table keyed on social security numbers (a very handy, unique number with which to identify people). If a missing (unknown) social security number is allowed within a table, how will it be possible to prevent data duplication? The person may already exist in the table with a known social security number, or perhaps several numbers are absent—what then is the method to tell them apart? The RDBMS specification eliminates such problems by forbidding null marks as part of the primary key.

Referential constraints are similar to entity constraints, but apply to foreign keys. Such constraints require a matching primary key for each foreign key. For example, the client numbers (foreign key) in the PHONE table exist in the ADDRESS table (assuming that the client number acts as the primary key for the ADDRESS table). This not only requires that a table with a foreign key rejects non-matching values (as shown in later examples), but also that a primary key cannot be deleted when referenced by a foreign key (a feature not supported in dBASE or Paradox).

User-defined constraints create inter-table dependencies with definable formulas; for example, requiring that the number of parts shipped in a table of orders not exceed the number of parts on hand in an inventory table. In a true relational database, these constraints would be stored as statements or equations in a table.

## Insertion, Deletion, and Update

Changes to data within the database are classified by three operations: insertion (adding new rows to the table), deletion (removing existing rows), and update (changing data in an existing row). A relational database should allow a single command to affect several rows.

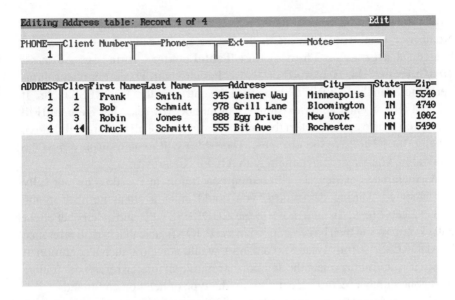

**Figure 2.1  ADDRESS and PHONE in Edit mode. ADDRESS is currently selected for editing.**

First, a look at raw-data entry (no fancy forms or views) and single-row entry—to save space figures for all of the intermediate steps will not be given. Since Paradox uses a row/column format by default, it will be used for our first example. Remember to prefix each menu command with **F10** (the menu key). Select **View, Phone**; and then **View, Address**. You will see two empty tables—a table name followed by column names. To add data to these tables, you may hit either **F9** (Edit) or **Alt-F9** (CoEdit). For this exercise, however, select Edit. This restricts other users from entering data while work is in progress and allows for more menu options. Blank rows open up on each table image.

Managing multiple tables with Paradox is nearly effortless. When several images are on the workspace, Paradox will display as many as it can fit on a single screen. The current image will be highlighted. Because in this exercise ADDRESS was selected last, it is the current image. At this point, simply type in the address data for each column and hit Enter to move to the next column. The complete ADDRESS table can be seen in Figure 2.1. The columns in this figure are shorter than the default so that it is possible to see most of the address entries. Normally, Paradox would scroll back and forth as data is entered.

You can move between the images on the current workspace with **F3** (Up Image) and **F4** (Down Image). Images that do not fit on the screen will scroll off, but remain active. In this example, **Up Image** will move up to the PHONE table. Before data is entered here, place an integrity constraint on the Client Number column: Hit **F10**, **ValCheck**, **Define**, move to the Client column, and hit the Enter key. Then select **TableLookup**, type in **Address**, **JustCurrentField**, **HelpAndFill**. Now, Paradox will check the client numbers entered in the PHONE table against the entries in the ADDRESS table. It will not let you enter a non-existent client number (by selecting **HelpAndFill** the option is also open to select the number from a list of all valid possibilities). Finally, hit **F2** to save the changes. The tables will remain displayed in the work area; you may remove them with **Alt-F8** (Clear All).

As mentioned earlier, the referential constraints in Paradox are not fully implemented. During data entry, you could enter a client number in the PHONE table (e.g., 5), then move to the ADDRESS table and delete that client entry. You would then have a client 5 in the PHONE table that had no reference in ADDRESS. A truly relational database would not allow such a condition to exist. It would either reject the deletion or remove all foreign references (delete the phone number record) depending on the type of deletion command.

The preceding steps were an example of a single-record operation. Although you could enter multiple records, the system *commits* each row as it is entered. The single-record orientation is more apparent in CoEdit mode than Edit mode. Edit mode is really something of a hybrid between multiple-record and single-record operations. Unlike CoEdit mode, Edit mode allows *rollback* to a previous state (the **Alt-U**, or undo operation in Paradox). But Edit mode limits table access to a single person. A relational database should allow several people to access a single table and still perform *transaction processing* (data entry with rollback and multiple-record commit).

Paradox implements multiuser transaction processing through **Modify**, **DataEntry**, *TableName*. This option brings up an empty table called ENTRY that has all of the characteristics of the base table. The ENTRY table for the PHONE table is shown in Figure 2.2. Here it is possible to enter, delete, and rollback entries to your heart's content without affecting the base table. Then, when you commit the transaction with **F2**, the entire ENTRY table is added to the base table. Workspace operations are restricted to the ENTRY table; even if you have placed other tables on the workspace, you cannot access them until DataEntry mode ends.

Data entry in dBASE is limited to single-record operation. In dBASE, select the **Address** table (in the data column) and then choose **Display data**. dBASE will display a default entry form (a vertical list of column names and input areas). At this point, enter the data as you would in any other computer entry screen (see Figure 2.3). Note that the cursor will automatically advance to the next field if the current field is filled (this can be a bit disconcerting to first-time

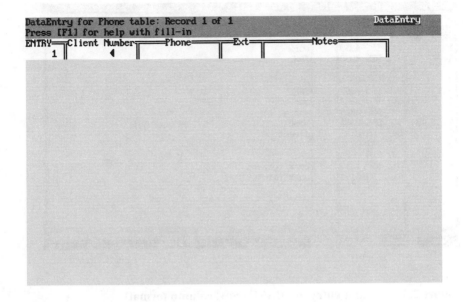

**Figure 2.2  Paradox ENTRY table for phone. This allows data entry without modifying existing entries.**

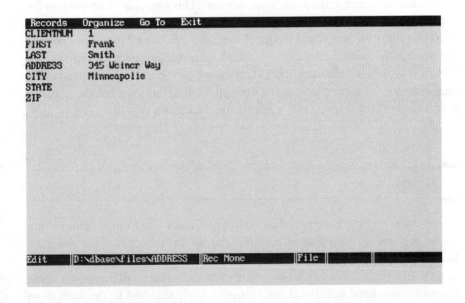

**Figure 2.3  dBASE data entry in a single-record form (the default).**

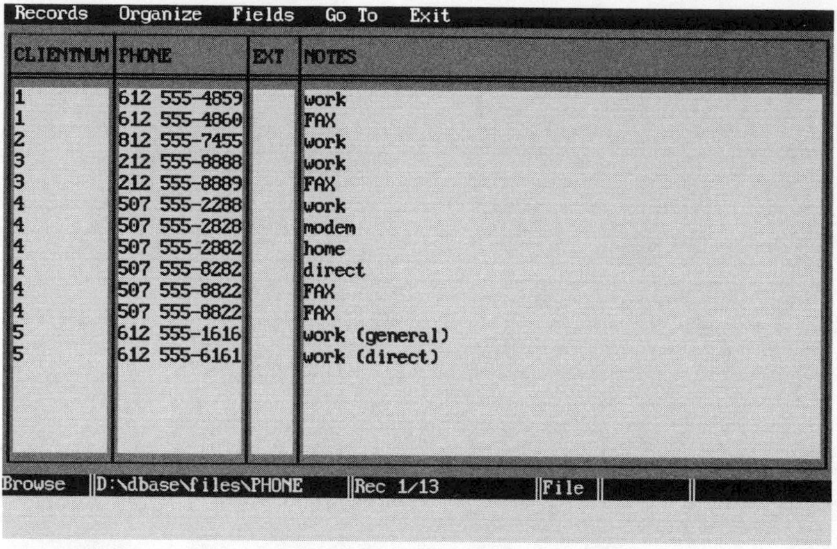

**Figure 2.4   Tabular entry in dBASE (row, column format).**

users). When you've finished entering new data, select **Exit** from the menu with **Alt-E**.

You are now back at the main menu screen. This time, take a shortcut to the data entry screen. Move to **Phone** and hit **F2**. This immediately moves you into Data Entry mode. While in Data Entry, you can use **F2** to toggle between the standard form and a tabular view, which resembles the Paradox default (see Figure 2.4). Unlike Paradox, dBASE does not provide for a value restriction on a column. You can place constraints on form definitions, but they are not enforced at the table level (as a true relational database should).

## Forms

So far, data entry has been presented in a spreadsheet-like format. This is very useful for seeing several rows and for getting an overall feel for the data. However, for most tables the entire row will not be seen; usually, data entry tasks will be limited to a single row. Furthermore, the data will frequently come from a standardized form, or at least mimic a fairly standard layout such as an order form. So, it should come as no surprise that both databases let you design custom forms for data entry (in fact, a default form for dBASE has already been

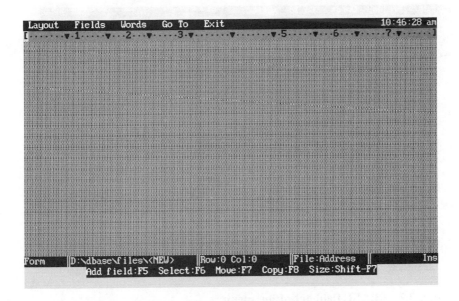

**Figure 2.5** The dBASE form definition screen.

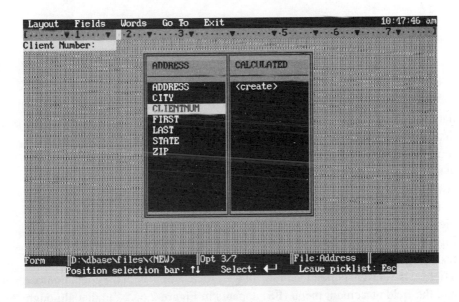

**Figure 2.6** Selecting a field for placement on the dBASE form (F5).

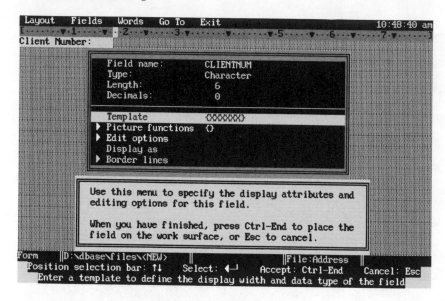

**Figure 2.7   dBASE field definition menu.**

shown). For example, address entry is much simpler in the following format (data entry areas are in square brackets):

```
Client Number:      [ClientNum]
Name:               [First] [Last]
Street Address:     [Address]
City, State, Zip:   [City] [State] [Zip]
```

While working with forms, data columns will be referred to as fields and data rows as records. Because this is not in a tabular format, it maintains the distinction between a data entry area (field) and location within the form (column or row). Also, forms allow for calculated fields, which do not appear at all in the base tables, and it would be inappropriate to refer to such fields as columns.

In the dBASE Forms column select **Create, Use different database file or view, ADDRESS.DBF.** You will be in a form definition screen resembling Figure 2.5. Use the cursor to move around on the form. To enter descriptive text, simply move the cursor to the desired location and type the text. To place a field at the current cursor location, hit **F5.** An example with the client number and the field placement menu (**F5**) appears in Figure 2.6. Note that although dBASE does not allow calculated columns in the table definition, calculated

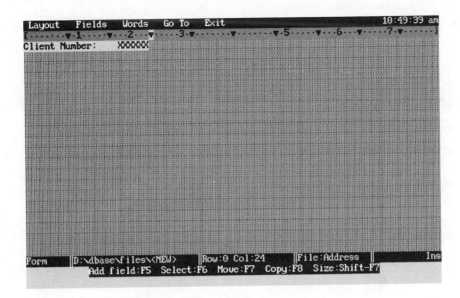

**Figure 2.8    Placing the Client Number field.**

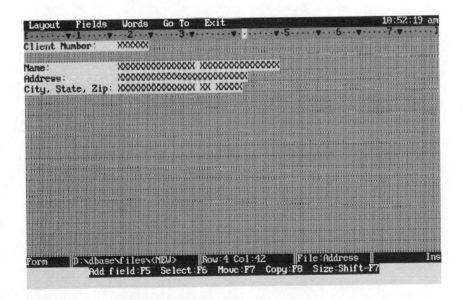

**Figure 2.9    The finished ADDRESS form.**

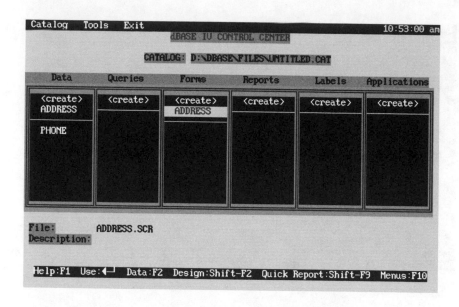

**Figure 2.10    The ADDRESS form in the dBASE catalog.**

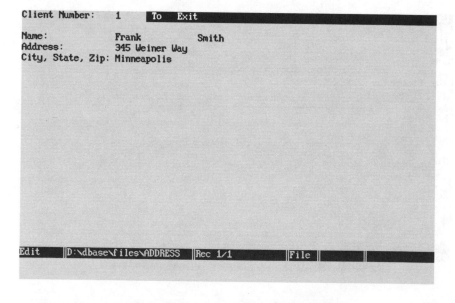

**Figure 2.11    Viewing ADDRESS data in the new form.**

Designing new F form for Address                    Form    1/1
< 1, 1>

**Figure 2.12    The Paradox form definition screen.**

fields may be placed in a form. Next, you will see a definition area resembling Figure 2.7.

The template defines the displayed width on the form (for very wide fields you might want to define a smaller template, which can be scrolled). The remaining choices allow integrity checks, a topic covered later. For now, the displayed width doesn't change, so simply hit **Ctrl-End** to place the field on the form (see Figure 2.8). A finished form is shown in Figure 2.9. Select **Exit, Save changes and exit** when you are done with the layout. Name the form (call it **Basic Address**) to return to the main menu.

You will see that ADDRESS has appeared under Forms (Figure 2.10). If you select **ADDRESS, Display Data**, you will see the existing data displayed in the new form (Figure 2.11) At this point, you may page or cursor through the data, change data, or enter new rows. To leave the form, select **Exit, Exit** from the menu. Note that, as designed here, the form partially covers the menu. Normally, you should place your first field a few lines down to leave the menus showing. If you do cover the menu, it will pop up over the form when you make a menu selection.

In Paradox, select **Form, Design, Address, F, Basic Form**. Paradox labels forms with the letter "F" (the default), or a number between 1 and 14. You may enter an optional description, **Basic Form**, in this case, which appears as the menu description when later selecting the form. A blank form is shown in Figure 2.12. As with dBASE, you may enter text at any position on the page.

**Figure 2.13   Selecting a field for placement from the list (Field, Place).**

Designing new F form for Address          Form    1/1
< 1,22>
Client Number: _____

**Figure 2.14   Placing the field on the form. The -s represents the space used by the field ("Client Number: " was simple text typed from the keyboard).**

```
Field to place at cursor:                               Form  Ins 1/1
Zip
Client Number:      _____

Name:                 _____  _____
Address:              _____
City, State, Zip:  _____  __
```

**Figure 2.15  The placed fields are removed from the Regular selection list.**

To place a field, select **F10**, **Field**, **Place**, **Regular**. Select the field from the list (see Figure 2.13).

Paradox will ask for the field location. If you have not already moved to the desired spot, use the cursors to position the field. Hit Enter to place it on the form. At this point, Paradox will assign the field its default width, which you may change by moving the cursor to a new endpoint. Again, hit Enter when the width is correct (Figure 2.14). Continue placing fields until the form is completed. Note that as regular fields are placed, Paradox removes them from the menu, making it easier to track usage (Figure 2.15). Paradox also allows display-only columns which always appear as a complete field list (**Field**, **Place**, **DisplayOnly**). And, like dBASE, Paradox defines calculated fields through the form (**Field**, **Place**, **Calculated**). When you're done with the layout, hit **F2** to save the form.

To use a Paradox form, you must first place the table in the workspace—in this case, **View**, **Address**. Then, either select the default form with the **F7** key, or use **F10**, **Image**, **Pickform**. The latter method will show all of the current table's defined forms and descriptions in a menu. Figure 2.16 shows the new form as applied to the Address table. Unlike dBASE, Paradox does not automatically enter Edit mode. If you want to alter data, you must select either Edit or CoEdit (**F9** or **Alt-F9**, respectively).

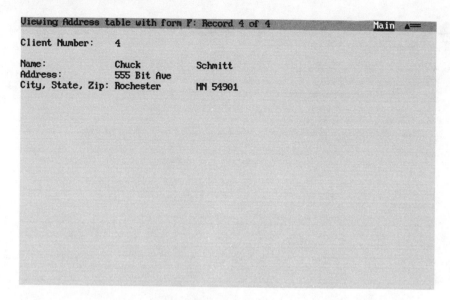

Figure 2.16   **Viewing ADDRESS with the form.**

## Constraints Revisited

This chapter began with a description of integrity constaints. It's now time to take a more practical look at how integrity constraints are implemented with Paradox and dBASE. Paradox manages contraints more rigorously than dBASE, though it is by no means complete. dBASE column constraints rely on form definitions: They are easy to bypass—simply define a different form or enter data without a form—and hence more difficult to manage. The constraints within each form are totally independent. With Paradox, any attempt to manually enter an unacceptable value will be rejected. It is still possible, however, to import or add unacceptable data from one file or table to another. This places an additional burden on your error-checking protocols when transferring data from one table to another.

Paradox enforces referential constraints during data entry and modification only (a client could be deleted from ADDRESS, but the matching PHONE entries would be retained). dBASE does not support foreign keys, and referential constraints are entirely non-existent.

dBASE has no primary key support (except through SQL, which limits dBASE operations) and Paradox allows nulls in the key; for example, the client number could be left off one of the entries in the ADDRESS table defined earlier; or, in dBASE (and non-keyed Paradox tables), two clients with the same number could be defined.

Some of the problems with constraints as implemented in both packages relates to the level at which they are defined. dBASE is very close to the top at the form level. Paradox enforces integrity at a lower level (table defintion), but not low enough to prevent some problems, such as appending data from one table to another. If you ever have a chance to work with other Borland products, you will see further evidence of this approach. For example, Borland has a Paradox Engine for accessing tables from C or Pascal—the engine completely bypasses constraints (you can't even read the rules to force a C or Pascal program to comply).

This strategy will change in the coming years. Borland will be moving the integrity constraints to a much lower level—close to the point at which the file is written to disk. Both dBASE and Paradox (as well as other applications using dBASE and Paradox files) will enforce constraints more thoroughly.

Let's see how to apply the limited constraints that are available through dBASE and Paradox—Paradox first since it is a bit more thorough on this point. Because the PHONE and ADDRESS tables are keyed, an entity constraint is already established: Duplicate keys are forbidden. So, how does Paradox enforce such a constraint? There are three possibilities, depending on the data entry method.

| Editing Address table: Record 8 of 8 | | | | | Edit |
|---|---|---|---|---|---|

| ADDRESS | Client Number | First Name | Last Name | Address | City |
|---|---|---|---|---|---|
| 1 | 1 | Frank | Smith | 345 Weiner Way | Minneapolis |
| 2 | 2 | Bob | Schmidt | 978 Grill Lane | Bloomington |
| 3 | 3 | Robin | Jones | 888 Egg Drive | New York |
| 4 | 4 | Chuck | Schmitt | 555 Bit Ave | Rochester |
| 5 | 4 | Violation | 1 | | |
| 6 | 4 | Violation | 2 | | |
| 7 | 4 | Violation | 3 | | |
| 8 | 4 | ◀ Violation | Last | Will stick | |

**Figure 2.17   Attempted entry of duplicate keys in Edit mode.**

```
Viewing Address table: Record 4 of 4                                    Main
ADDRESS┬Client Number┬First Name┬Last Name┬───Address───┬───City───
   1  ┃ 1            ┃ Frank    ┃ Smith   ┃ 345 Weiner Way ┃ Minneapolis
   2  ┃ 2            ┃ Bob      ┃ Schmidt ┃ 978 Grill Lane ┃ Bloomington
   3  ┃ 3            ┃ Robin    ┃ Jones   ┃ 888 Egg Drive  ┃ New York
   4  ┃ 4            ┃ Violation┃ Last    ┃ Will stick     ┃
```

**Figure 2.18    After hitting F2, all but the last duplicate keys are removed.**

```
Coediting Address table: Record 5 of 5                                CoEdit
Entering new record - not yet posted to table
ADDRESS┬Client Number┬First Name┬Last Name┬───Address───┬───City───
   1  ┃ 1            ┃ Frank    ┃ Smith   ┃ 345 Weiner Way ┃ Minneapolis
   2  ┃ 2            ┃ Bob      ┃ Schmidt ┃ 978 Grill Lane ┃ Bloomington
   3  ┃ 3            ┃ Robin    ┃ Jones   ┃ 888 Egg Drive  ┃ New York
   4  ┃ 4            ┃ Chuck    ┃ Schmitt ┃ 555 Bit Ave    ┃ Rochester
   5  ┃ 4            ┃ Violation┃ 1     ◀ ┃                ┃
```

**Figure 2.19    Attempting to enter duplicate keys in CoEdit mode.**

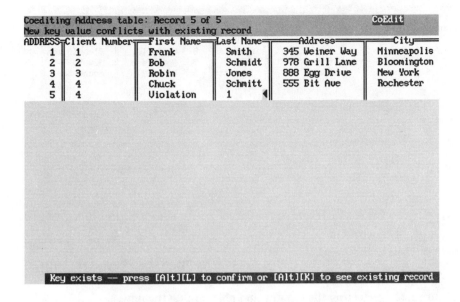

**Figure 2.20    When an attempt is made to move to another row, Paradox warns that there is a key violation.**

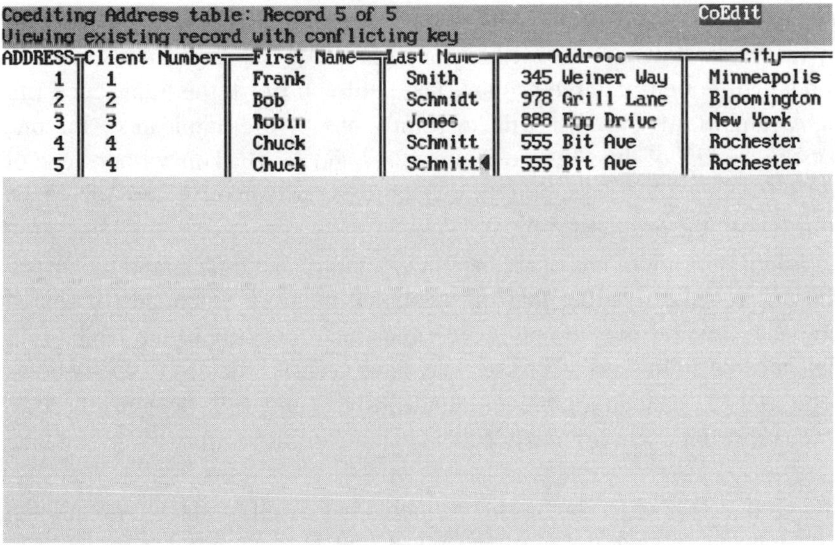

**Figure 2.21    Using Alt-K to select the other key.**

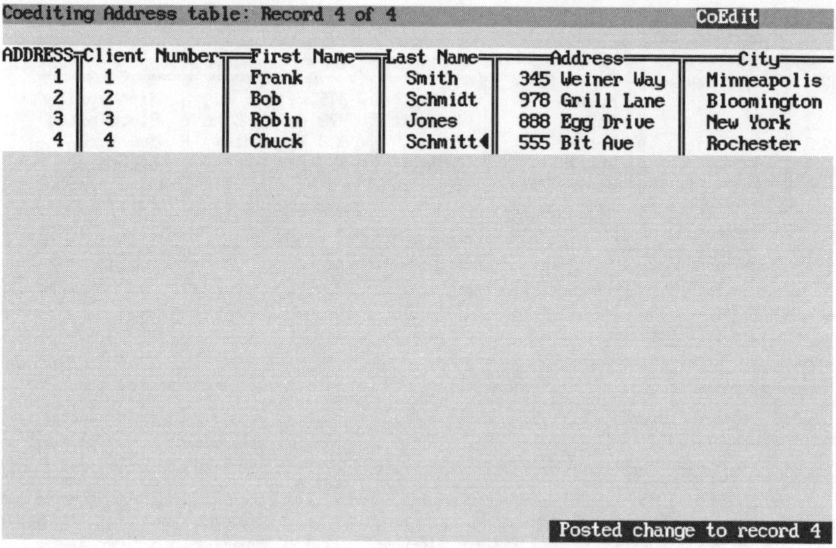

**Figure 2.22   Selecting the old key and abandoning the new.**

## Entity Constraints

Thus far, Edit (F9) or CoEdit (Alt F9) have been used to enter new data. Edit is by far the most dangerous method for adding data to a keyed table because Paradox will not enforce the primary key until you finish the transaction (hit **F2**). At that point, Paradox will keep only one of the duplicates—the one closest to the end of the file (see Figures 2.17 and 2.18). This violates one of Codd's features: A transaction should be rejected (i.e., **F2** should not be allowed) until the problem is fixed.

CoEdit is a bit more reasonable about violations. To understand the operational differences, consider that the relational model is intended for shared operations. Several people may need simultaneous access to the table. Edit locks the table so that no other user may have access, whereas CoEdit allows several users to change a table simultaneously. Thus, Edit does not need to enforce rules until you are ready to leave, but CoEdit requires an immediate fix.

In Figure 2.19 a violation has been entered in CoEdit mode, but no attempt has been made to leave the row. In Figure 2.20 an attempt has been made to move to another row. Paradox returns a message that a matching key already exists. At this point it is possible either to hit **Alt-L** to accept the new value (and destroy the old) or **Alt-K** to toggle between the two. Figure 2.21 shows

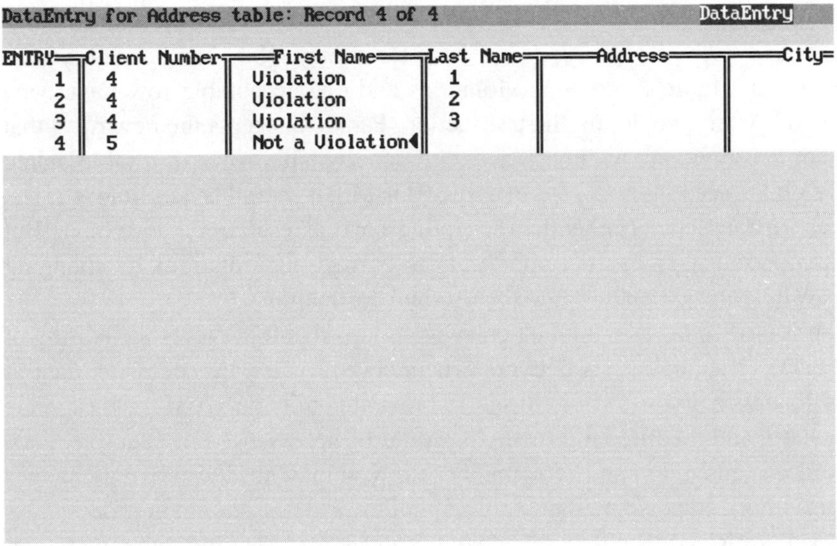

```
DataEntry for Address table: Record 4 of 4                    DataEntry
ENTRY┬Client Number┬───First Name════╦Last Name═══════Address══════════City═
    1 ║ 4           ║ Violation        ║ 1                                 ║
    2 ║ 4           ║ Violation        ║ 2                                 ║
    3 ║ 4           ║ Violation        ║ 3                                 ║
    4 ║ 5           ║ Not a Violation◄  ║                                  ║
```

**Figure 2.23    Attempting to enter duplicate keys in DataEntry mode.**

that **Alt-K** has been hit to see the existing value. It is possible to continue toggling between the new and old entries with **Alt-K** until a choice is made. In this case, the old row is maintained (see Figure 2.22). Optionally, the Client Number of the new row could have been changed to 5 if both rows were wanted.

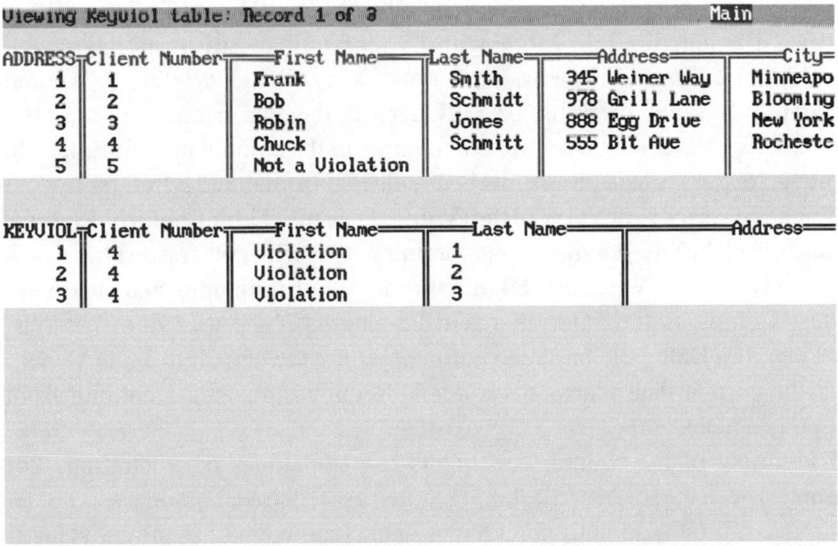

```
Viewing Keyviol table: Record 1 of 3                             Main
ADDRESS┬Client Number┬───First Name┬───Last Name═══════Address══════════City═
     1 ║ 1           ║ Frank        ║ Smith        ║ 345 Weiner Way ║ Minneapo
     2 ║ 2           ║ Bob          ║ Schmidt      ║ 978 Grill Lane ║ Blooming
     3 ║ 3           ║ Robin        ║ Jones        ║ 888 Egg Drive  ║ New York
     4 ║ 4           ║ Chuck        ║ Schmitt      ║ 555 Bit Ave    ║ Rochestc
     5 ║ 5           ║ Not a Violation ║           ║                ║

KEYVIOL┬Client Number┬───First Name┬───Last Name═══════════════Address══════
     1 ║ 4           ║ Violation    ║ 1                                 ║
     2 ║ 4           ║ Violation    ║ 2                                 ║
     3 ║ 4           ║ Violation    ║ 3                                 ║
```

**Figure 2.24    After hitting F2, the duplicate keys are placed in a table named KEYVIOL.**

A brief example of **Modify**, **DataEntry** for handling multiuser transactions was already shown. Now let's see how DataEntry mode handles entity constraints. In Figure 2.23, three violations and one acceptable row have been entered. After completing the transaction, Paradox accepts the new rows that do not cause violations, and places the unacceptable rows in a table called KEYVIOL (see Figure 2.24). In a true RDBMS, it should be possible to reject the entire transaction (rather than accepting a partial result as Paradox has). But at least Paradox gives the opportunity to correct the violations by changing KEYVIOL and appending it to the original destination.

The disadvantage of the data entry method is that it prevents the editing of old data. Of course, on a network where several users are accessing data, it may be desirable to restrict editing to prevent confusion. And thus, separate data entry and modification methods would be necessary. For example, once an order is entered in an invoicing system, you may need to prevent changes by unauthorized personnel who are unfamiliar with the shipment process. As defined, an RDBMS has three separate modes for changing data: insertion, deletion, and update. DataEntry is fairly faithful to the insertion mode.

## Column Constraints

Paradox column constraints are defined while in Edit Mode (CoEdit will not work). After entering Edit Mode with **F9** (or **Modify**, **Edit** from the menu), hit **F10** to view the Edit menu (see Figure 2.25). Paradox refers to column constraints as value checking, or **ValCheck** in the edit menu. To set a constraint, select **ValCheck**, **Define**. Then move to the column and hit Enter. In Figure 2.26, the Phone column has been selected from the PHONE table.

You may select **LowValue**, **HighValue**, **Default**, **TableLookup**, **Picture**, or **Required** in any combination—defining one will not erase others of a different type. **LowValue** and **HighValue** are simply minimum and maximum values. **Default** is the value that will be entered if the user does not type anything. If a Date field has been defined, setting the default to TODAY will enter the current date unless overridden. Required prevents a column from accepting a blank entry.

The timing of the column constraints can sometimes be frustrating. For example, if you cursor over a column marked as Required, Paradox will not let you move off the field until you enter a value (and will not require a value if you never move the cursor through it). Ideally, you could define when the constraint should take effect (either upon passing over the field, attempting to

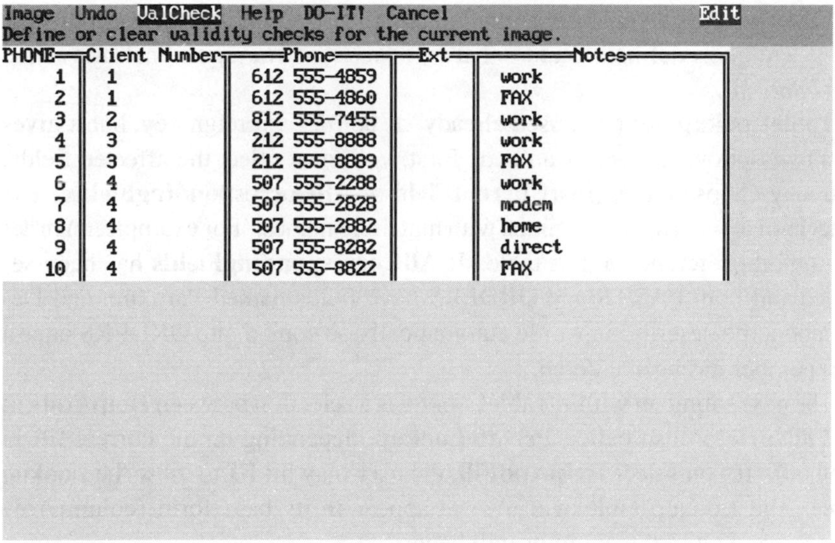

```
Image  Undo  ValCheck  Help  DO-IT!  Cancel                          Edit
Define or clear validity checks for the current image.
PHONE═╦Client Number╥══════Phone══════╦══Ext══╦═══════Notes═══════
   1  ║ 1             ║  612 555-4859   ║       ║ work
   2  ║ 1             ║  612 555-4860   ║       ║ FAX
   3  ║ 2             ║  812 555-7455   ║       ║ work
   4  ║ 3             ║  212 555-8888   ║       ║ work
   5  ║ 3             ║  212 555-8889   ║       ║ FAX
   6  ║ 4             ║  507 555-2288   ║       ║ work
   7  ║ 4             ║  507 555-2828   ║       ║ modem
   8  ║ 4             ║  507 555-2882   ║       ║ home
   9  ║ 4             ║  507 555-8282   ║       ║ direct
  10  ║ 4             ║  507 555-8822   ║       ║ FAX
```

**Figure 2.25    The Edit menu  ValCheck defines column constraints.**

move to another row, or ending the transaction). Likewise, a default value will appear only if the user moves over the column with the cursor.

Paradox is missing a *unique* constraint to prevent duplication within a column. While you may define a primary key to prevent duplications, a true

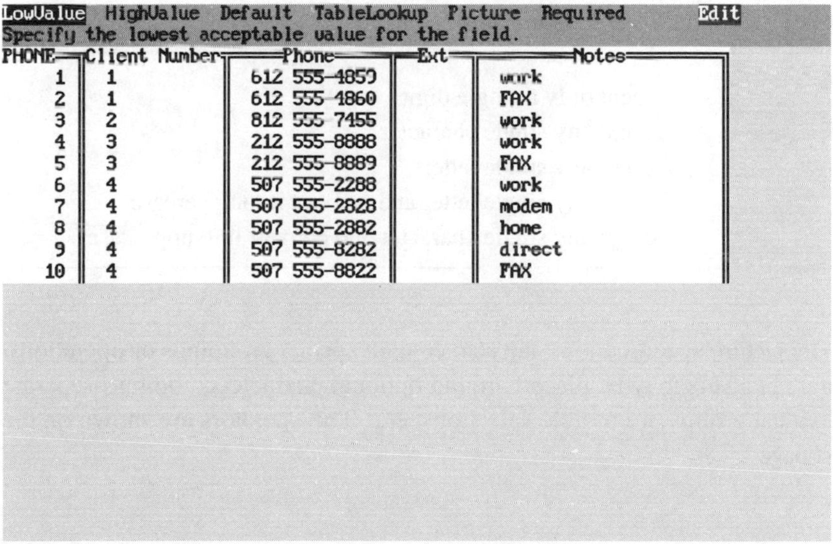

```
LowValue  HighValue  Default  TableLookup  Picture  Required     Edit
Specify the lowest acceptable value for the field.
PHONE═╦Client Number╥══════Phone══════╦══Ext══╦═══════Notes═══════
   1  ║ 1             ║  612 555-4859   ║       ║ work
   2  ║ 1             ║  612 555-4860   ║       ║ FAX
   3  ║ 2             ║  812 555-7455   ║       ║ work
   4  ║ 3             ║  212 555-8888   ║       ║ work
   5  ║ 3             ║  212 555-8889   ║       ║ FAX
   6  ║ 4             ║  507 555-2288   ║       ║ work
   7  ║ 4             ║  507 555-2828   ║       ║ modem
   8  ║ 4             ║  507 555-2882   ║       ║ home
   9  ║ 4             ║  507 555-8282   ║       ║ direct
  10  ║ 4             ║  507 555-8822   ║       ║ FAX
```

**Figure 2.26    The constraint options available after selecting a field.**

RDBMS should let you define additional unique columns or column combinations. Uniquely defined columns that are not used as a key are sometimes called *candidate keys*.

**TableLookup** has been used already. It defines a foreign key, but it gives us a few options not yet examined. First, you must select the affected fields; you may choose either **JustCurrentField** or **AllCorrespondingFields**. The latter choice will fill any columns with matching names. For example, an order form might reference a part table. If **AllCorrespondingFields** has been selected and both PARTS and ORDERS have fields named PartNum and Description, the description would automatically be copied into ORDERS once a part number has been entered.

The next submenu within TableLookup is a selection between **HelpAndFill** or **FillNoHelp** (also called **PrivateLookup**, depending on the current fill-in method). If you select **HelpAndFill**, the user may hit **F1** to view the Lookup table. The Lookup table will always appear in its base form (column/row format), and all of the columns will be visible.

**Picture** has been saved for last since it is a bit more complicated than the other options. **Picture** allows format specifications such as telephone numbers, social security numbers, and so forth. A picture may contain representative symbols, such as **#**, which specify numbers, uppercase letters, etc. The symbols are as follows:

| Symbol | Picture Definition |
|--------|--------------------|
| # | Accept only a single digit |
| @ | Accept any single character |
| ? | Accept any single letter |
| & | Accept any single letter and convert it to uppercase |
| ! | Accept any single character and convert it to uppercase |

The picture specification may also contain special groupings or operations. Square brackets may be placed around optional characters, commas separate individual groups of possible selections, etc. The operators are shown on the next page.

| Operator | Group Definition |
|---|---|
| [ ] | Optional selection |
| , | Group separator |
| * | Repeat the next character indefinitely |
| *n | Repeat the next character n times |
| ; | Take the next character literally |
| { } | Leave a decision pending until the final } |

Any other characters are interpreted literally as part of the format. Thus, a - will require a - in the final format. A social security number format would look like #########. The literal character is required to use one of the reserved symbols as a character: ;# would accept only # as a valid entry. Paradox reads the format specification from left to right and always works with the first possible match, and Paradox will automatically enter literal text whenever possible (in the social security number above, Paradox will automatically insert the - after each group of digits). But, because of the way our minds group items, this can cause some confusion. For example **Peter,Paul,Mary** would appear to allow either **Peter**, **Paul**, or **Mary** as a valid entry. But, if you try to enter **Paul**, Paradox will not comply. Paradox matches the **P** to Peter and immediately completes the entry with **Peter**. You can backspace to leave only **P**, and then complete it with **Paul**, but this is very awkward. Instead, you may create a special grouping: **P{eter,aul},Mary**. If you do not like automatic entry, you could use **P{e{t}{e}{r},a{u}{l}},M{a}{r}{y}**, but this adds too much complexity for most applications.

A typical example for address entries that demonstrates several picture features, is the Zip Code field. Many databases contain both U.S. and Canadian addresses. So, you could use a ten-character field with the following picture:

```
*5#[-*4#],&#& #&#
```

This allows a five-digit zip code with an optional nine-digit designation (e.g. 55417 or 55417-1734), or a Canadian postal code such as N2M 3B5.

Note that Paradox does not apply validity checks retroactively. Existing entries may violate a newly defined constraint (something that is not allowed under Codd's rules). Likewise, Paradox will not check rows transferred from one table to another, again in violation of Codd's rules. Such operations become dangerous by opening possibilities for integrity violations, but are necessary for proper management in a relational system. For example, if you need to define tighter constraints for particular tasks, you should create a new

**Figure 2.27   dBASE constraints available through Fields, Modify fields in the form definitions.**

table with the same structure (**Tools**, **Copy**, **Table**, *OldTableName*, *New-TableName*) and place tighter constraints on the new table. Then, after·entering the new data, simply add the contents of the new table to the old (**Tools**, **More**, **Add**, *NewTable*, *OldTable*, *NewEntries*). Such operations will be covered in more depth later. For now, simply be aware of this technique.

## dBASE Constraints

As mentioned, dBASE constraints are limited to the currently applied form. Like the Paradox table transfers, this can lead to invalid data within tables. Within the Form design area, the constraints are selected from **Fields**, **Modify field**. The resultant choices are shown in Figure 2.27. Most of the value-checking functions are located in **Edit options** (see Figure 2.28). If **Editing Allowed** is set to **No**, the field will behave like a Paradox DisplayOnly field—the user cannot modify that particular field. Several other options resemble the Paradox selections. Smallest value allowed and Largest value allowed are simply the minimum and maximum values; and you may select a default value.

Unlike Paradox, you may specify some simple conditional statements. For example, **Permit edit if** will allow editing only if the specified condition is true. If **State<>" "** is specified for the Zip field, then the cursor could not be moved into the Zip field unless data has been entered in the State field. Likewise,

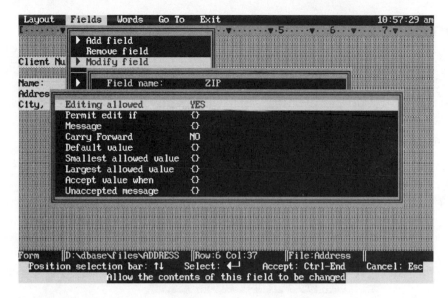

**Figure 2.28    Selections available under Edit Options.**

**Accept value when** will not let you leave the field until the specified condition has been met. Note that you cannot reference fields outside the current table. The message areas let you define messages which appear on the screen when a field is selected or a value is rejected.

The dBASE template is similar to the Paradox picture. It sets the acceptable input format. However, dBASE templates do not allow selection groups or optional characters. The template symbols are:

| Symbol | Description |
|---|---|
| 9 | Accept only a single digit |
| # | Accept a digit, space, decimal point, or sign |
| X | Accept any single character |
| A | Accept any single letter |
| N | Accept any single letter or digit (or "_") |
| ! | Accept any single character and convert it to uppercase |
| Y | Accept y or n (and convert lowercase to uppercase) |
| L | Accept T, F, Y, or N |

Any other character will be used as a literal (only that character will be accepted). If the template is applied to a numeric field, the **9** template will accept signs and a few other options are available:

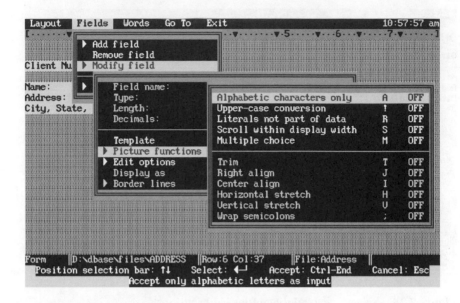

**Figure 2.29   dBASE constraint functions available for alphanumeric fields.**

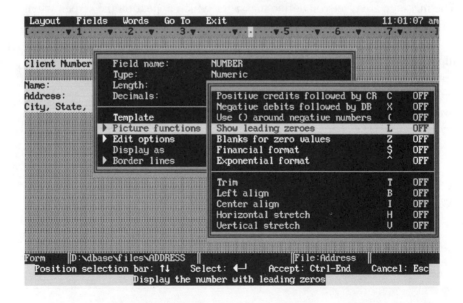

**Figure 2.30   dBASE constraint functions available for numeric fields.**

| Symbol | Description |
| --- | --- |
| . | Sets the position of the decimal point |
| , | Adds commas to numbers |
| * | Show leading 0's as an asterisk |
| $ | Show leading 0's as the currency symbol |

Picture functions place further global restrictions on the data. Perhaps the most useful function is **Literals not part of data**. If this is turned on, any literals defined in the template are not stored with the data. This can save storage space by eliminating formatting characters (such as the -s between social security and phone numbers). Figure 2.29 shows the functions available for alphanumeric fields. The numeric functions are shown in Figure 2.30.

General formatting (such as selection from groups and alignment operations) is set through the **Function** options:

| Option | Description |
| --- | --- |
| ! | Convert all lowercase to uppercase |
| ; | Forces a line wrap at ; in the text (for memo fields) |
| A | Accept only alphabetic characters |
| H | Applies word wrap margins to memo fields |
| I | Center alignment |
| J | Right alignment |
| M | Specify an option list for input (e.g., **Red,White,Blue**) |
| R | Remove literal characters from input |
| S$n$ | Creates a scrolling field $n$ characters wide |
| T | Remove leading and trailing blanks |
| V$n$ | Creates a vertical column $n$ characters wide |

## Null Marks

A few points about null marks have been discussed (Rule 4), but beyond the prohibition of null marks within a primary key, there are some other inconsistencies affecting their use. Codd maintains that a null mark should not be treated as a special value (for example, using an empty field as a null). Rather, a null should be a separate indicator that tells the database, "Ignore the data in this field." Paradox has limited support for nulls and dBASE does not support nulls at all.

In Paradox, if you do not enter a value in a numeric field, the entry will remain blank (null). Furthermore, you can test for the presence of a blank number with a function called **IsBlank** ( ) or within a query with the keyword **blank**. Paradox treats nulls as a *value*, and every data type has a null. In Paradox, an empty text field and a null field are considered the same, but a true RDBMS would make a distinction. For example, a person may not have a middle name, or the middle name may be unknown—both cases should be representable.

## Summary

This chapter presented the basics behind building a table. You now should be able to create a table and add data to it. And you have seen how forms are created and used. Integrity constraints have been discussed, along with their limited application to Paradox and dBASE. Thus far, however, only a few hints of the power that a multiple-file application affords have been demonstrated. Next, the relational operators that form the basis for our analytical tools will be presented.

# 3

# The Relational Operators

The only link between tables illustrated thus far is the Foreign Key (a link which dBASE doesn't really support). To really use the data, rather than just reference it for value confirmations, methods for comparing and/or combining data from several tables must exist. This is the purpose of the relational operators.

Codd defines 80 relational operators. Neither Paradox nor dBASE comes close to supporting all 80, and many which do not apply to these packages will not be covered in this book. Several of the 80 are fairly esoteric and are designed to support features that go well beyond the capabilities of dBASE and Paradox, such as optimizing retrieval for distributed data.

A relational operator is applied to one or two relations. The result of a relational operator is a new relation, to which other operators may be applied. These attributes are fundamental to a relational system. The intent is to allow a divide and conquer strategy. Let's say that after specifying the conditions, you discover that you have retrieved more data than you had intended. Rather than starting from scratch, you may pare down the data—generally a much faster process.

The most frequently used operators fall into three classes: **Project**, **Select**, and **Join**. **Project** returns designated columns from a single table. In essence, it simply removes columns that you may not be interested in seeing. Of course, to maintain its relational basis, it must remove any duplication that results from the trimming. For example, to learn which clients have placed orders, a simple **Project** could be run on an INVOICE table that would return a table with only a single column (the Client Number column). A client, by placing several orders, might appear in the INVOICE table several times, but the **Project** should return only one row for each client.

**Select** takes a different tack: It returns designated rows. Of course, in a truly relational database, row numbers have no meaning, so rows would not be selected by position. Instead, some search or filtering criteria would be designated that would return the desired rows. This implies a matching operation of some type; Codd uses the term *theta-select*. *Theta* refers to the comparison operator used to select the rows: There are ten comparison operators, hence ten forms of **theta-select**. The operation is performed on a column (e.g., find all occurrences of a particular client number). The ten forms are:

| *Operator* | *Function* |
|---|---|
| = | Select all rows that match a designated value |
| <> | Select all rows that do not match the designated value |
| < | Select all rows less than the designated value |
| <= | Select all rows less than or equal to the designated value |
| > | Select all rows greater than the designated value |
| >= | Select all rows greater than or equal to the designated value |
| G< | Select rows with the largest value less than the designated value |
| G<= | Select rows with the largest value less than or equal to the designated value |
| L> | Select rows with the smallest value greater than the designated value |
| L>= | Select rows with the smallest value greater than or equal to the designated value |

Paradox and dBASE support all of the Version 1 operators (all but the last four, which are additions to the relational model unique to Version 2). Although **theta-select** applies to a single column, we will frequently want to **Select** based on several columns. By the very nature of a relational database, we could build several intermediate results on single-column **Selects** and then combine them into a final result. But considering how frequently you may need multiple-column operations, this approach would be quite awkward, so a relational database should provide a *Boolean extension to theta-select*. Put simply, you should be able to combine requests; for example, find all invoices (rows from the INVOICE table) for orders placed yesterday

```
SELECT on Date=Today-1
```

**and** which had items placed on backorder

```
SELECT on Backorder Quantity=0
```

The third major class of operators falls under **Join**. **Join** combines two tables into a single result on the basis of a comparison operator. Thus, like **Select**, there are ten forms of *theta-join*. With **Select**, a constant (user-defined) value is used as the basis of comparison. With **Project**, you designate a column from each table to use as the basis for comparison. This operation was alluded to while building the PHONE and ADDRESS tables in the preceding chapter. The Client Number would normally be the basis for a **theta-join using =** (or **equi-join**) between ADDRESS and PHONE.

A standard **theta-join** returns all columns from both tables. Although there are ten different forms of **theta-join**, you will use the **equi-join** most frequently. In this case, there is redundancy in the table because the Client Number column from PHONE and the Client Number column from ADDRESS will contain identical values. Thus, a special operator called *natural join* performs an **equi-join**, but eliminates one of the redundant columns (e.g., only one copy of the Client Number would appear in the resulting **natural join** of the tables ADDRESS and PHONE).

There are three possible relationships between **join**ed tables: one-to-one, one-to-many, and many-to-many. In a one-to-one relationship, each row of one table matches exactly a single row in another table. The two tables share a primary key; for example, both tables might have a single-column key on a client number so that a person's first and last names could be stored in separate tables keyed on Number:

| Number | First |
| --- | --- |
| 1 | John |
| 2 | Jane |

| Number | Last |
| --- | --- |
| 1 | Smith |
| 1 | Doe |

A **natural equi-join** would produce

| Number | First | Last |
| --- | --- | --- |
| 1 | John | Smith |
| 2 | Jane | Doe |

In a one-to-many **join**, one row in the first table relates to several rows in the second table.  Typically, the join will be between a primary key in the first table and a *portion* of a primary key (or non-key columns) in the second.  This is the most common case, and frequently forms the basis of the many-to-many **join**.  Consider a table of phone numbers (keyed on Number and Phone) **joined** to the last **natural equi-join**.

| Number | Phone | Purpose |
| --- | --- | --- |
| 1 | 555-1234 | work |
| 1 | 555-4321 | home |
| 2 | 555-5678 | home |
| 2 | 555-8765 | work |
| 2 | 555-9876 | FAX |

| Number | First | Last | Phone | Purpose |
| --- | --- | --- | --- | --- |
| 1 | John | Smith | 555-1234 | work |
| 1 | John | Smith | 555-4321 | home |
| 2 | Jane | Doe | 555-5678 | home |
| 2 | Jane | Doe | 555-8765 | work |
| 2 | Jane | Doe | 555-9876 | FAX |

Although one of the tables usually is linked through a primary key, the only requirement is that one side have a unique identifier in the column(s) used to establish the one-to-many **join**.  A listing of people might use a client number as the primary key, for example, but it could also include a social security number.  Because the social security number is also unique, it can act as a unique identifier for the *one* side of a one-to-many **join**.

In a many-to-many **join**, several rows in one table match several rows in another.  Frequently, a many-to-many **join** is a compound statement requiring three tables, and is called *third normal form*.  It is built from two one-to-many relations, which share a common table on the *one* side of the relationship.  Third normal form is not a requirement for many-to-many **joins**, but it does simplify other aspects of the database design in many packages.

As an example of a many-to-many **join** that does not use third normal form, consider a table of addresses (keyed on Number and Address) **joined** to the table of phone numbers.

| Number | Address | B/S |
| --- | --- | --- |
| 1 | 123 Main | bill |
| 1 | 321 Main | ship |
| 2 | 888 Center | bill |

| Number | Address | B/S | Phone | Purpose |
| --- | --- | --- | --- | --- |
| 1 | 123 Main | bill | 555-1234 | work |
| 1 | 321 Main | ship | 555-1234 | work |
| 1 | 123 Main | bill | 555-4321 | home |
| 1 | 321 Main | ship | 555-4321 | home |
| 2 | 888 Center | bill | 555-5678 | home |
| 2 | 888 Center | bill | 555-8765 | work |
| 2 | 888 Center | bill | 555-9876 | FAX |

A relational database also supports a *Boolean extension to theta-join.* Like the comparable **Select** feature, this simply allows a comparison between multiple columns. Common applications for the **Boolean extension** are tables with multiple column keys (find a match between column 1 of the key **and** a match between column 2 of the key).

There are several relational operators that do not fall under the **Project, Select**, and **Join** classes, including set operators (**relational union, intersection, difference**, and **relational division**) and the manipulative operators (**relational assignment, insert, update**, and **delete**). **Update** and **delete** have a few variations that deal with foreign and primary key changes.

The set operators are similar to the set structures you learned in school. **Relational union** operates on two tables that have identical structures (i.e., the domain definitions match, although the column names may differ). It combines the rows from both tables into a single result and removes any duplicated primary keys. Thus, **relational union** is similar to addition. Likewise, **difference** acts like subtraction. To build the result table for **difference**, rows that exist in the second table are removed from the first. **Intersection** returns the rows that appear in both tables.

**Relational division** is a bit more complicated. In some respects, it resembles **difference**, just as division and subtraction have similarities in mathematics. Let's look at a mathematical example first: 7 / 3. This expression can be evaluated by subtracting three while counting the number of sets created. You can subtract 3 items from 7 twice, resulting in two sets of 3 with 1 item remaining.  Two groups of three items have been created—the group specific-ier is the divisor (3).

**Relational division** creates groupings, too.  With tables, however, the divi-sor is a set, rather than a number.  Consider a set of fruit baskets, labeled by number, with each item in the basket listed:

| Basket | Item |
|--------|------|
| 1 | Apples |
| 1 | Oranges |
| 1 | Grapes |
| 2 | Apples |
| 2 | Grapes |
| 2 | Pears |
| 3 | Oranges |
| 3 | Pears |
| 3 | Bananas |
| 4 | Oranges |
| 4 | Apples |
| 4 | Bananas |

Now, a set for the divisor must be designated—in this case, a set of fruit. The question is, "How many baskets contain apples and oranges?"  The divisor set thus includes apples and oranges.  Note that in **relational division**, the dividend includes a pair of columns and the divisor a single column.  The divisor looks like:

| Item |
|------|
| Apples |
| Oranges |

The result includes the baskets with apples and oranges:

| Basket |
|--------|
| 1 |
| 4 |

The remainder includes everything from the divisor that was not required to create the result (this includes fruits from baskets 1 and 4 that were not needed).

| Basket | Item |
| --- | --- |
| 1 | Grapes |
| 2 | Apples |
| 2 | Grapes |
| 2 | Pears |
| 3 | Oranges |
| 3 | Pears |
| 3 | Bananas |
| 4 | Bananas |

If nothing else, this example should dispel the myth that comparing apples and oranges is a fruitless undertaking.

Perhaps you've noticed that the set operators include items similar to addition, subtraction, and division, but not multiplication. According to Codd, a relational database should *not* support a relational product, because a relational product could create truly gigantic tables, overwhelming the storage capacity and performance of the host computer. A relational product would combine each record of the first table with every record of the second.

It's worth noting that using such a product would reverse the effects of **relational division**. First, combine Basket 1 with apples and oranges (from the divisor), then combine Basket 4 with apples and oranges. You now have:

| Basket | Item |
| --- | --- |
| 1 | Apples |
| 1 | Oranges |
| 4 | Apples |
| 4 | Oranges |

If you add this product to the remainder, you will have a table identical to the original dividend (the storage order may be different, but remember that order is meaningless to a relational database).

**Relational assignment** may be applied to any of the relational operators described thus far. **Relational assignment** simply saves a table under a different name, just as algebraic assignment saves a value under a new name (e.g.,

A=7). **Relational assignment** is the first of the manipulative operators—those operators that change the contents of the database.

**Insertion** adds new rows to a table. The source table(s) need not have identical structures. If the inserted data creates duplicate rows (identical in all columns), only the unique rows will be inserted and the database will report that duplicate rows were detected. If the **insertion** includes rows that duplicate existing primary keys (but not identical in the remaining columns), the database will report that duplicate primary keys were detected.

**Update** changes data in existing rows. It may not be possible to update every derived relation (view). If the **update** affects a foreign key, the database should reject any changes that do not have a corresponding primary key in the referenced table (referential integrity must be maintained). The problem is even more acute if the **update** attempts to change a primary key—there may be several foreign keys in other tables that rely on the changed primary key. Consider a change to a client number in a CLIENT (or ADDRESS) table. There may be an Invoice table that references the client: If the database changes the client number without also changing that client's invoices, the invoices will be "lost." The database should reject primary key changes that have such dependencies. In order to work around this restriction, the database should provide a variant of **update** called **primary key update**.

**Primary key update** changes the primary key of a table. Additionally, it finds all dependent foreign keys and changes them in order to maintain referential integrity. The database can find primary keys of unrelated tables, which use the same domain type, and change matching keys in these *sibling* tables, too (at the user's discretion, sibling tables may be excluded from the change). To continue the previous example, the primary key of the CLIENT table would be changed, as would matching references to the client in the Invoice table.

There is one more important **primary key update** scenario. Perhaps a client number is changed, but all of the invoices have been fulfilled. Rather than changing all of the foreign keys, you could select **primary key update with marking**. The database will then mark all of the matching foreign keys as missing (null) but applicable. In the "ideal" database, the foreign key value would be retained (you could still see the old client number), but the data would be marked as missing (note again the distinction between a null *value* and a null *mark*).

**Deletion** removes rows from the target relation. Like **update** and **insert**, the source relations need not have the same structure as the target. Some derived relations (views) may not allow **deletion**, and **deletion** is subject to the same referential restraints as **insert**. A relational database provides special **primary key deletion** and **primary key deletion with marking** to mark or delete dependent foreign keys.

The preceding operators cover the basic feature set of relational operators. There are even more in a category called advanced operators, several of which deal with distributed databases in which portions of the database may be kept on a local site and other portions at a remote site. Additionally, many of these operators work internal to the database; most users would not specifically request the operator. As an example of such an advanced operator, consider a **semi-theta join**.

A database of regional clients is kept in Los Angeles; it is a fairly short list and billing is processed out of New York City for sites in cities throughout the United States. The Invoice table in New York is gigantic. The Los Angeles and New York sites are connected by modems over a phone line. The Los Angeles office wants a **theta-join** between their clients and the matching invoices; the result is to be stored on the Los Angeles computer.

Rather than send the entire INVOICE database from New York to Los Angeles, the system in Los Angeles would **project** a list of clients (a simple column of client numbers). The client number list would be shipped to New York and **join**ed to the Invoice table. The result of this intermediate step is the **semi-theta join**, and the table created is much smaller than the entire INVOICE table (call it LA_INVOICE). LA_INVOICE would then be shipped back to Los Angeles. Finally, the database in Los Angeles would join LA_INVOICE with the client database to complete the process.

The more practical advanced operators for your work include the **outer equi-join**. The first example of an **equi-join** matched entries in a PHONE and ADDRESS column by referencing the Client Number. An issue left unresolved at the time was, "What happens if there is an entry without a match?" If no match is found in a standard **equi-join**, the unmatched row does not contribute to the result. But there may be cases in which it is necessary to see the unmatched entries. Consider a client who has given an address, but no phone number. If a full directory is desired (addresses and phone numbers), an **equi-join** would not generate a complete list, but the **outer equi-join** would, placing null marks where data is unknown. It's even possible to have a phone number without an address (assuming, for the moment, that the PHONE table is independently keyed and has no foreign-key reference to ADDRESS). Consider a simplified example:

**Address**

| Client Number | First |
|---|---|
| 1 | Frank |
| 2 | Robert |
| 4 | Chuck |

**Phone**

| Client Number | Phone Number |
|---|---|
| 1 | 612 555-4859 |
| 2 | 812 555-7455 |
| 3 | 212 555-8888 |

A full, or **symmetric outer-join** would generate the following table (Xs designate the null marks):

| Address-> Client Number | Phone-> Client Number | First | Phone Number |
|---|---|---|---|
| 1 | 1 | Frank | 612 555-4859 |
| 2 | 2 | Robert | 812 555-7455 |
| X | 3 | X | 212 555-8888 |
| 4 | X | Chuck | X |

There are also two partial **outer-join**s: the **left** and **right outer-join**. Left and right refer to the order in which the tables are designated (in this example, ADDRESS is first, so ADDRESS is the left side). The **left outer-join** draws unmatched data only from the table on the left:

| Address-> Client Number | Phone-> Client Number | First | Phone Number |
|---|---|---|---|
| 1 | 1 | Frank | 612 555-4859 |
| 2 | 2 | Robert | 812 555-7455 |
| 4 | X | Chuck | X |

Similarly, the **right outer-join** draws unmatched data only from the table on the right:

| Address-> Client Number | Phone-> Client Number | First | Phone Number |
|---|---|---|---|
| 1 | 1 | Frank | 612 555-4859 |
| 2 | 2 | Robert | 812 555-7455 |
| X | 3 | X | 212 555-8888 |

The **outer-join**s include some nearly redundant information. The first two columns in the examples are not quite the same, because there is some missing information. But looking at the results, the redundancy is obvious. The **natural outer-join**s will remove this perceived redundancy. The **symmetric outer natural join** follows:

| Client Number | First | Phone Number |
|---|---|---|
| 1 | Frank | 612 555-4859 |
| 2 | Robert | 812 555-7455 |
| 3 | X | 212 555-8888 |
| 4 | Chuck | X |

The results of the **left outer natural join** and **right outer natural join** should be obvious, so they are not presented here.

Codd defines a host of **outer T-joins** and **inner T-joins** that use the comparison operators (as in a **theta-join**). The **T-joins** maintain a one-to-one correspondance between the two tables, rather than the one-to-many correspondance of a standard **theta-join**. The mechanics of these operators are complicated and are not widely supported in many databases (and not at all supported by Paradox or dBASE). To learn more about **T-joins**, read Codd's definitions in *The Relational Model for Database Management: Version 2.*

## Summary

The relational operators are the heart and soul of a relational database. As you work with the operators, some, such as **project** and **select**, should be easy to learn. Others will be more difficult—particularly the more advanced **joins**. However, a few basic **selects**, **projects**, and **joins** should be sufficient for most of your work. If you learn the simple operators well, you should be able to conquer most of the problems you encounter. As you continue learning about operators in the next chapter, you should practice writing queries so that you become proficient with these methods.

# 4

# Queries

When relational operators are used to filter and combine data from tables, the process is called a *query*. In the previous chapter, the method for expressing the results of relational operations was not addressed. The results are tables, but how do they appear to the user? The database system generally stores them internally (either in memory or temporary files), and these internal operations allow many different operators to be combined into a single query. Thus, you might **join** two tables, **project** only a few of the columns, and **select** a few rows. You never need see all of the intermediate steps required. The database might even rearrange the intermediate steps for more efficient operation by using optimization methods. It is through the use of the **relational assignment** operator or a *view* that the result becomes usable.

As illustrated in the previous chapter, **relational assignment** creates a new table; in this case, the query results are stored as they existed when the query was run. A **view**, on the other hand, is evaluated in real time. As data in the base tables change, the entries in the view change. The results may also be viewed from the other end. If the data in the new table is changed, the base tables are unaffected; if the data in a **view** is changed, the data in the base tables changes.

By default, Paradox returns all query results in a table called ANSWER. In effect, it is as if Paradox always applies **relational assignment** to a query. dBASE uses **views** as its query method—covered in more detail in the next chapter. Most of Paradox's relational operators are available through the QBE (Query By Example) feature. As defined in the last chapter, the most common of the basic operators are **Select**, **Project**, and **Join**.

**Project** will be discussed first, since Paradox always requires that the projection be specified. Using the ADDRESS table created in Chapter 1, choose **Ask, Address** from the menu. Paradox will place a query form on the workspace. The query form, shown in Figure 4.1, resembles the table from which it's derived. To select columns for the projection, move to the column(s) you want in the result and hit **F6**. A check mark (square root sign) will appear in the selected column(s). In Figure 4.2, the State column has been selected. Hit **F2** to process the query—the result is shown in Figure 4.3.

Notice the result (the ANSWER table): The original relation (ADDRESS) had four rows, but ANSWER has only three. Also notice that two of the addresses are in Minnesota. Paradox has eliminated the duplicates to maintain a relation (as an RDBMS should). Unfortunately, Paradox will let you override this by using **Alt-F6** (called CheckPlus); such an operation is shown in Figure 4.4. Try to avoid CheckPlus—there are usually better means for obtaining information about duplicated column values (such as count calculations).

To **Select** with QBE, you must place conditional statements within one or more columns of the query form. In Paradox, **Select** must be used with **Project**; i.e., you must use **F6** to place check marks in the desired columns. Frequently, you will want a pure **Select** (all columns included in the result); as a shortcut, hit **F6** in the far left column of the query form (under the table name) to check every column.

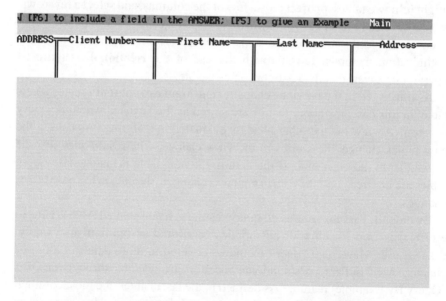

**Figure 4.1   The ADDRESS query form—note the resemblance to the base table.**

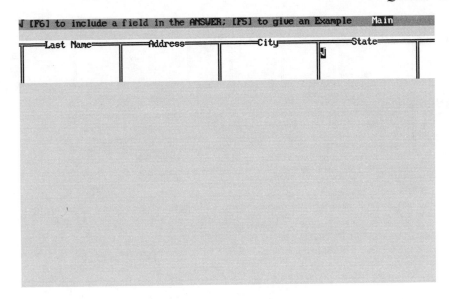

**Figure 4.2    Selecting a column with F6 (the check mark key).**

For the conditional portion, you may use any comparison operator (>, <, =, etc.) with a constant, variable, or link to another column value. These operators may be combined in various ways to widen or narrow the selected rows.

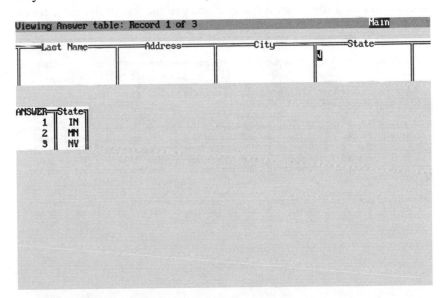

**Figure 4.3    The ANSWER is the projection of all states in the ADDRESS table.**

**Figure 4.4   Alt-F6 (check mark plus) includes duplicate rows in the ANSWER.**

Starting with a very simple example, select all clients from Minnesota. A portion of the query form and ANSWER appears in Figure 4.5. The expression should be read as if the column name appears to the left of the comparison

```
Viewing Answer table: Record 1 of 2                                    Main
ADDRESS┬Client Number┬First Name┬Last Name┬Address┬City┬State┬Zip┐
       √             √          √         √       √    √ =MN  √

ADDRESS┬Clie┬First Name┬Last Name┬────Address────┬City───────┬State┬Zip┐
   1   ║ 1  ║ Frank    ║ Smith   ║ 345 Weiner Way ║ Minneapolis ║ MN ║ 5540
   2   ║ 2  ║ Bob      ║ Schmidt ║ 978 Grill Lane ║ Bloomington ║ IN ║ 4740
   3   ║ 3  ║ Robin    ║ Jones   ║ 888 Egg Drive  ║ New York    ║ NY ║ 1002
   4   ║ 4  ║ Chuck    ║ Schmitt ║ 555 Bit Ave    ║ Rochester   ║ MN ║ 5590

ANSWER┬Clie┬First Name┬Last Name┬────Address────┬City───────┬State┬Zip┐
   1   ║ 1  ║ Frank    ║ Smith   ║ 345 Weiner Way ║ Minneapolis ║ MN ║ 5540
   2   ║ 4  ║ Chuck    ║ Schmitt ║ 555 Bit Ave    ║ Rochester   ║ MN ║ 5590
```

**Figure 4.5   A projection of all clients from the state of Minnesota.**

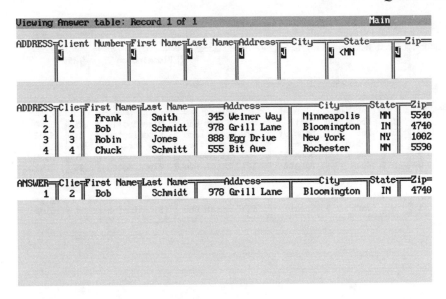

**Figure 4.6  Projection of all clients from states that appear before MN in an alphabetical list.**

operator; in this case, **[State]=MN**. Thus, **<MN** would select all states that appear before MN when listed alphabetically (see figure 4.6).

*Paradox Comparison Operators:*

| | |
|---|---|
| = | Equal |
| > | Greater than |
| < | Less than |
| >= | Greater than or equal to |
| <= | Less than or equal to |
| not | Not equal (may also be used with other operators) |

Note that Paradox does not support the greatest less than or least greater than operators.

If conditional statements are placed in several columns, the ANSWER must meet each specified condition. This is called a logical AND. To illustrate, add a new address: Jack Spratt, 1212 Steak Ave, Bloomington, MN 55420. The goal is to find all clients in Bloomington, AND further requires that Bloomington be located in Minnesota. There are now clients in both Bloomington, Indiana, and Bloomington, Minnesota, so the new select query must specify two columns as in Figure 4.7. Logical AND narrows the selection.

```
Viewing Answer table: Record 1 of 1                           Main

ADDRESS─Client Number─First Name─Last Name─Address─────City────────State══
        ▯             ▯           ▯          ▯      ▯ Bloomington  ▯ MN



ADDRESS─Clie─First Name─Last Name══════Address═══════City═══════State─Zip═
   1 │  1  │  Frank   │  Smith    │ 345 Weiner Way │ Minneapolis │ MN │ 5540
   2 │  2  │  Bob     │  Schmidt  │ 978 Grill Lane │ Bloomington │ IN │ 4740
   3 │  3  │  Robin   │  Jones    │ 888 Egg Drive  │ New York    │ NY │ 1002
   4 │  4  │  Chuck   │  Schmitt  │ 555 Bit Ave    │ Rochester   │ MN │ 5590
   5 │  5  │  Jack    │  Spratt   │ 1212 Steak Ave │ Bloomington │ MN │ 5542

ANSWER─Clie─First Name─Last Name══════Address═══════City═══════State─Zip═
   1 │  5  │  Jack    │  Spratt   │ 1212 Steak Ave │ Bloomington │ MN │ 5542
```

**Figure 4.7    Result of a logical AND: all clients from the city of Bloomington AND the state of Minnesota.**

To widen the selection, a logical OR must be used. The most general method is to add a row to the query form. The new row must have check marks in the same columns as the original row. In essence, two simultaneous queries are being built, and both must have the same projection. Suppose the goal is to find clients who are in either Minnesota or Indiana: Use a query resembling Figure 4.8. Note that = acts as the default comparison operator; it need not be specified. You can mix and match conditions between columns and rows (for example all clients in Minnesota OR a city named Bloomington in any state).

Frequently, the OR condition applies to a single column, as in the first OR example. Therefore, Paradox allows an explicit OR to separate conditions within a single column. The original OR query could be restated as shown in Figure 4.9.

**Join** adds multitable support to query processing. For example, to extract the phone numbers of the Minnesota clients, first establish the link between ADDRESS and PHONE. Paradox uses an example element for the link. Hitting **F5** while in a query form column begins an example definition. After hitting **F5**, type a name, which will appear in reverse video. Figure 4.10 shows an example named **CN** in the Client Number column of ADDRESS. The example name has no meaning, a number or any other alphanumeric combination could have been used. The characters are used only for matching other example elements in the query, and this is the key to their usage.

```
Viewing Answer table: Record 1 of 4                                    Main
```

| ADDRESS | Client Number | First Name | Last Name | Address | City | State | Zip |
|---------|--------------|------------|-----------|---------|------|-------|-----|
|         |              |            |           |         |      | MN    |     |
|         |              |            |           |         |      | IN    |     |

| ADDRESS | Clie | First Name | Last Name | Address | City | State | Zip |
|---------|------|------------|-----------|---------|------|-------|-----|
| 1 | 1 | Frank | Smith | 345 Weiner Way | Minneapolis | MN | 5540 |
| 2 | 2 | Bob | Schmidt | 978 Grill Lane | Bloomington | IN | 4740 |
| 3 | 3 | Robin | Jones | 888 Egg Drive | New York | NY | 1002 |
| 4 | 4 | Chuck | Schmitt | 555 Bit Ave | Rochester | MN | 5590 |
| 5 | 5 | Jack | Spratt | 1212 Steak Ave | Bloomington | MN | 5542 |

| ANSWER | Clie | First Name | Last Name | Address | City | State | Zip |
|--------|------|------------|-----------|---------|------|-------|-----|
| 1 | 1 | Frank | Smith | 345 Weiner Way | Minneapolis | MN | 5540 |
| 2 | 2 | Bob | Schmidt | 978 Grill Lane | Bloomington | IN | 4740 |
| 3 | 4 | Chuck | Schmitt | 555 Bit Ave | Rochester | MN | 5590 |
| 4 | 5 | Jack | Spratt | 1212 Steak Ave | Bloomington | MN | 5542 |

**Figure 4.8   Logical OR:  all clients from the state of Indiana OR the state of Minnesota.**

Now, select **Ask, Phone** to place a new query form for PHONE on the workspace. The ADDRESS query form will remain in place. By placing a **CN** example element in the Client Number column of the PHONE query form, the

```
Viewing Answer table: Record 1 of 4                                    Main
```

| ADDRESS | Client Number | First Name | Last Name | Address | City | State | Zip |
|---------|--------------|------------|-----------|---------|------|-------|-----|
|         |              |            |           |         |      | =MN or =IN |     |

| ADDRESS | Clie | First Name | Last Name | Address | City | State | Zip |
|---------|------|------------|-----------|---------|------|-------|-----|
| 1 | 1 | Frank | Smith | 345 Weiner Way | Minneapolis | MN | 5540 |
| 2 | 2 | Bob | Schmidt | 978 Grill Lane | Bloomington | IN | 4740 |
| 3 | 3 | Robin | Jones | 000 Egg Drive | New York | NY | 1002 |
| 4 | 4 | Chuck | Schmitt | 555 Bit Ave | Rochester | MN | 5590 |
| 5 | 5 | Jack | Spratt | 1212 Steak Ave | Bloomington | MN | 5542 |

| ANSWER | Clie | First Name | Last Name | Address | City | State | Zip |
|--------|------|------------|-----------|---------|------|-------|-----|
| 1 | 1 | Frank | Smith | 345 Weiner Way | Minneapolis | MN | 5540 |
| 2 | 2 | Bob | Schmidt | 978 Grill Lane | Bloomington | IN | 4740 |
| 3 | 4 | Chuck | Schmitt | 555 Bit Ave | Rochester | MN | 5590 |
| 4 | 5 | Jack | Spratt | 1212 Steak Ave | Bloomington | MN | 5542 |

**Figure 4.9   The logical OR as applied to a single field.**

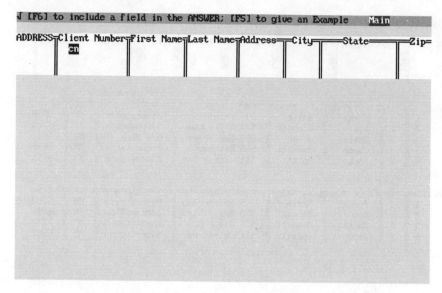

**Figure 4.10   Placing an example element with the F5 key.**

link between PHONE and ADDRESS is established since Paradox matches the two **CN** entries. Then check all columns in PHONE and place **MN** (as regular text) in the State column of ADDRESS. The query and result (the phone numbers of all Minnesota clients) are shown in Figure 4.11. Note that the column order in the ADDRESS query form has been altered so that all of the relevant columns are displayed (**Ctrl-R** rotates the column order). Combining a **Join** and **Project** so that only the phone numbers are displayed is a bit of cheating (but perfectly legitimate).

A more typical **Join** would show the name and address for each phone number by checking all of the ADDRESS columns. Only one of the Client Number fields needs to be checked—in general, keep the first appearance of the key (from ADDRESS in this case). Such a JOIN is illustrated in Figure 4.12. The columns have been narrowed with **Image, ColumnSize** to better show the complete query and ANSWER. Although the data appears truncated, it still exists in full.

If you attempt this query on your system, the ANSWER may be structured differently. Paradox has two methods for structuring an ANSWER. *TableOrder* keeps columns in the same order that they appear in the base tables; *ImageOrder* follows the rotated order that appears in the current query form (note that in Figure 4.12 [State] follows [First Name] in the query form, but follows [City] in ANSWER). This option is set through the Paradox Custom Configuration Program (see Appendix E).

| ANSWER | Client Number | Phone | Ext | Notes |
|---|---|---|---|---|
| 1 | 1 | 612 555-4859 | | work |
| 2 | 1 | 612 555-4860 | | FAX |
| 3 | 4 | 507 555-2288 | | work |
| 4 | 4 | 507 555-2828 | | modem |
| 5 | 4 | 507 555-2882 | | home |
| 6 | 4 | 507 555-8282 | | direct |
| 7 | 4 | 507 555-8822 | | FAX |

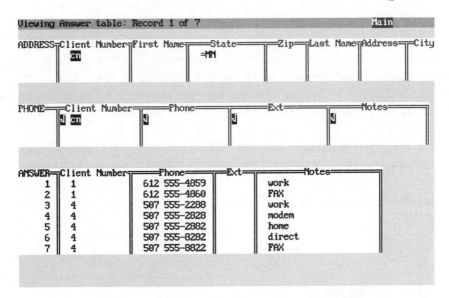

**Figure 4.11 Joining ADDRESS and PHONE through the example element CN to find phone numbers for Minnesota clients.**

The source of this potentially confusing result lies in a deviation from the RDBMS standard: The result of a query should be independent of the order in which it is expressed. In this case, if Paradox followed Codd's rules, the

| Clie | First | Last Na | Address | City | State | Zip | Phone | Ext | Notes |
|---|---|---|---|---|---|---|---|---|---|
| 1 | Fra | Smit | 345 We | Minn | MN | 55 | 612 555-4859 | | work |
| 1 | Fra | Smit | 345 We | Minn | MN | 55 | 612 555-4860 | | FAX |
| 4 | Chu | Schm | 555 Bi | Roch | MN | 55 | 507 555-2288 | | work |
| 4 | Chu | Schm | 555 Bi | Roch | MN | 55 | 507 555-2828 | | modem |
| 4 | Chu | Schm | 555 Bi | Roch | MN | 55 | 507 555-2882 | | home |
| 4 | Chu | Schm | 555 Bi | Roch | MN | 55 | 507 555-8282 | | direct |
| 4 | Chu | Schm | 555 Bi | Roch | MN | 55 | 507 555-8822 | | FAX |

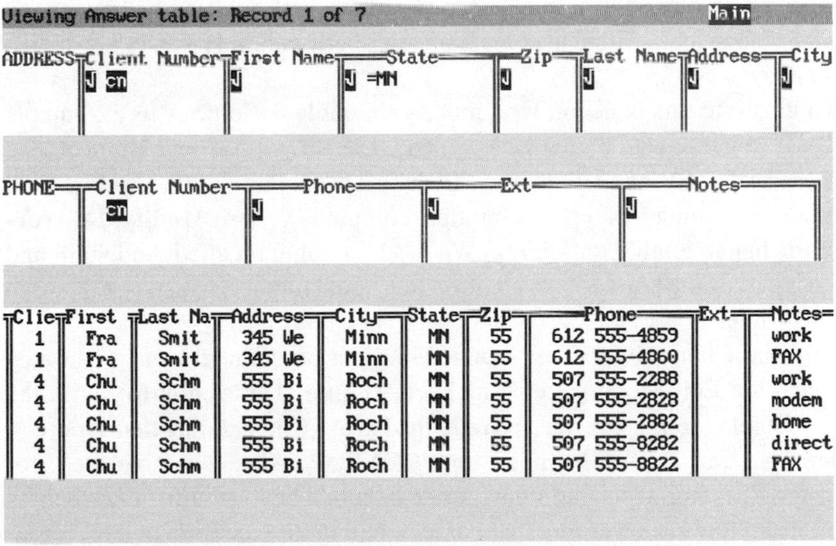

**Figure 4.12 A natural equi-join of ADDRESS and PHONE.**

columns would appear in alphabetical order (or an explicit order requested by the user); and if two columns shared the same name, the table name would be appended to the column name (Paradox will number them). Also, if the PHONE query form appeared above the ADDRESS query form, by Codd's definition the ANSWER should be identical. But if you try the same thing in Paradox, the columns from PHONE will appear before the columns from ADDRESS.

Because Paradox deviates from the RDBMS standard, you must be very careful when constructing queries (this is true for other database packages, too). If you are not consistent with query form placement (and field rotations, if **ImageOrder** is the default), you will have problems when you begin using the reporting features.

## More about Joins

In the last chapter, a simple example of a many-to-many **join** was given. As mentioned, for some database packages, third normal form is the preferred method for establishing a many-to-many relationship. Paradox is such a package. If the ADDRESS table were redesigned to support multiple client locations, relating ADDRESS to PHONE would require a many-to-many Join. In order to be able to use multitable forms (which will be discussed later) and foreign keys, a table with Client Number as a single column primary key is also necessary.

To illustrate this concept, let's modify the table definitions in the sample database. First, create a new table called CLIENT, with Client Number as a primary key (A6*) and Client as a 20-character column (A20). Address will need a new column to support a multiple column key. Use **Modify**, **Restructure** to change a table definition. We'll add a column called AddNum, and make it part of the key (A2* in addition to Client Number, which is A6*—see Figure 4.13).

Now the Client Number in ADDRESS must be defined as a foreign key (through the Edit Mode menu, **Valcheck**, **Define**, **TableLookup**). And the PHONE table foreign key must be redefined to use Client, rather than Address. When you first enter Edit mode for PHONE, Paradox will give the error message, "Lookup table can't have more than one key when fill-in or help is requested." This is a warning that Paradox will ignore the foreign key restriction until it is redefined or the condition is corrected by restructuring the Lookup table.

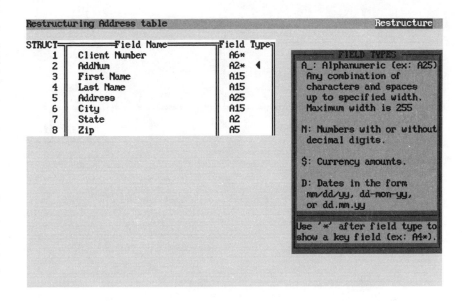

**Figure 4.13  Creating a multiple column key on ADDRESS (multiple addresses for each client).**

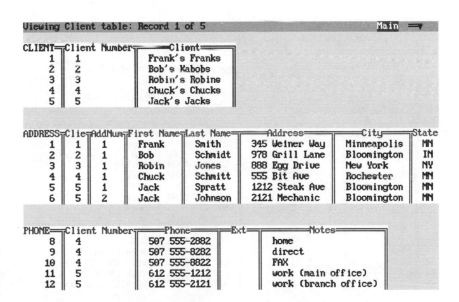

**Figure 4.14  The new base tables for the client database: CLIENT, ADDRESS, and PHONE.**

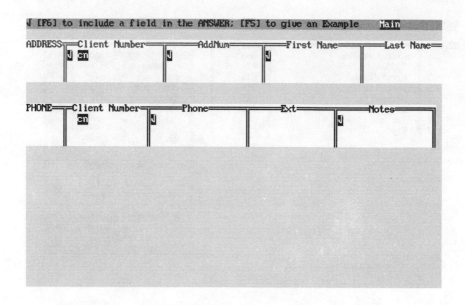

**Figure 4.15** **Using example elements to form a many-to-many join:  No special operators are needed, but the structure of the tables is important.**

| PHONE | Client Number | | Phone | | Ext | | Notes |
|-------|---------------|---|-------|---|-----|---|-------|
| | cn | | J | | | | J |

| ANSWER | Client Number | AddNum | First Name | Phone | Notes |
|--------|---------------|--------|------------|-------|-------|
| 1 | 1 | 1 | Frank | 612 555-4859 | work |
| 2 | 1 | 1 | Frank | 612 555-4860 | FAX |
| 3 | 2 | 1 | Bob | 812 555-7455 | work |
| 4 | 3 | 1 | Robin | 212 555-8888 | work |
| 5 | 3 | 1 | Robin | 212 555-8889 | FAX |
| 6 | 4 | 1 | Chuck | 507 555-2288 | work |
| 7 | 4 | 1 | Chuck | 507 555-2828 | modem |
| 8 | 4 | 1 | Chuck | 507 555-2882 | home |
| 9 | 4 | 1 | Chuck | 507 555-8282 | direct |
| 10 | 4 | 1 | Chuck | 507 555-8822 | FAX |
| 11 | 5 | 1 | Jack | 612 555-1212 | work (main office) |
| 12 | 5 | 1 | Jack | 612 555-2121 | work (branch office) |
| 13 | 5 | 2 | Jack | 612 555-1212 | work (main office) |
| 14 | 5 | 2 | Jack | 612 555-2121 | work (branch office) |

**Figure 4.16** **The result of the many-to-many join of ADDRESS and PHONE.**

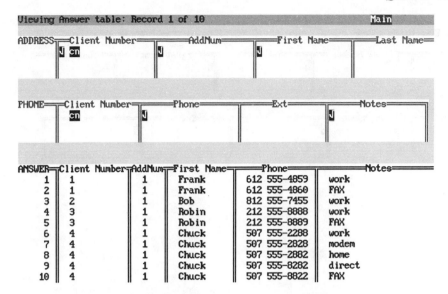

**Figure 4.17 Client 5 does not appear in ANSWER if data is not included in both ADDRESS and PHONE.**

The base tables for the new many-to-many **join** are shown in Figure 4.14. Client Number 5 (Jack's Jacks) now has two addresses and two phone numbers. Thus, PHONE and ADDRESS are the basis of the many-to-many relationship.

A many-to-many **join** appears the same as the examples of one-to-many **joins**, as shown in Figures 4.15 and 4.16. It is the underlying table definitions (ADDRESS and PHONE) that determine the end result. As you can see, for Client Number 5, each phone number is matched to each address.

Paradox uses an inner join by default. And in the examples presented thus far, inner and outer joins would give the same result. But consider two or more tables that are incomplete; perhaps there is a client address, but no phone number. An inner join would omit this client from the result, and an outer join would list the address and mark the phone numbers as "missing"—blank (null) columns in Paradox.

In Figure 4.17, Client 5's entries have been deleted from the PHONE table, and the query from Figure 4.15 has been re-executed. Client 5 no longer appears in the answer. To perform an outer join, you must place an ! after the example element; in this case, include all addresses, even if there is not a matching phone, so we place the ! after the example in the ADDRESS table. This is called a *left outer join*; it uses all of the rows from the first table (the one on the left when the query is stated from left to right). The query is shown in Figure 4.18 and the result in Figure 4.19.

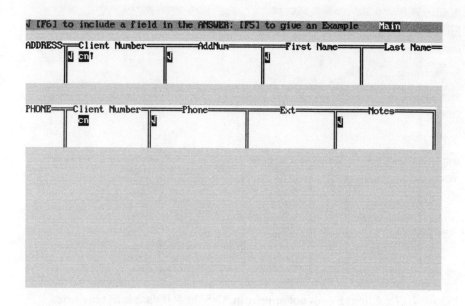

**Figure 4.18**  Using ! to create a left outer join between ADDRESS and PHONE.

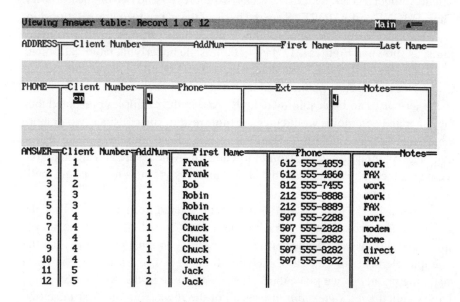

**Figure 4.19**  The result of the left outer join: Note the missing PHONE data for Client 5.

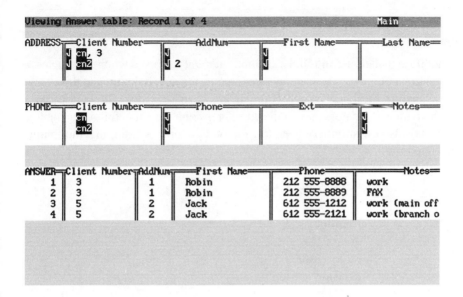

**Figure 4.20** **Using a logical OR between two tables. The example elements create a two row "link."**

A *right outer join* would require the ! in the PHONE query form, and would list all phone numbers including those without matching addresses. A *symmetric outer join* would require the ! in both query forms, and would list all occurrences from both tables. Note that the Client Number would appear for only those clients in the ADDRESS table unless checked in both forms.

When used for joining, example elements link tables as if their columns are side-by-side in one long table. Multiple rows may be used for OR queries, just as with single table queries. But you must place a distinct example element on each row and replicate the check marks in each query form (see Figure 4.20—note that the PHONE entries for Client 5 have been restored).

All of the **joins** used so far have been equi-joins; that is, the link is made through an exact (equal) match. Paradox may also be used for theta-joins. A theta-join is specified by placing the operator in *front* of the example element— they are used infrequently. Also, theta-joins can produce very large results since each row from one table can possibly match nearly every row in the other table. Theta-joins will not be covered in-depth, but you should be aware that they are possible.

## Example Elements and Calculations

In addition to their use in JOINs, example elements are used when creating new calculated columns. The calc operator creates the new column, and the example elements designate which columns are used. Paradox allows the basic mathematical operators in calculated expressions (see the following table). You may also use summary operators for totals, averages, counting, minimum, and maximum.

*Paradox Arithmetic Operators*

| | |
|---|---|
| + | Addition |
| - | Subtraction |
| * | Multiplication |
| / | Division |

*Paradox Summary Operators*

| | |
|---|---|
| sum | Total |
| min | Lowest value |
| max | Highest value |
| count | Count of items |
| average | Average |

Addition may be used to combine several text fields into a longer field. All of the summary operators will work with text, except sum and average. A special operator, AS, will rename the calculated column. By default, Paradox will name the column after the calculation (e.g., **Max of Client Number**, or **First + Last**).

As a simple example, let's create a list of the client numbers with a new column that combines the first and last names (see Figure 4.21). The calc expression may be placed in any convenient location. Calculated columns will be placed on the far right of the ANSWER in the order in which they appear in the forms. The new text column is the combined length of the original columns, plus any characters in the query. In this case, Name is 31 characters: 15 from First Name, 15 from Last Name, and 1 from the space.

Most of the operators require numeric data; **+**, **min**, **max**, and **count** accept alphanumeric. To demonstrate these, and other numeric-based features of Paradox, create a table called ORDERS (see Figure 4.22). Ordinarily, Invoice

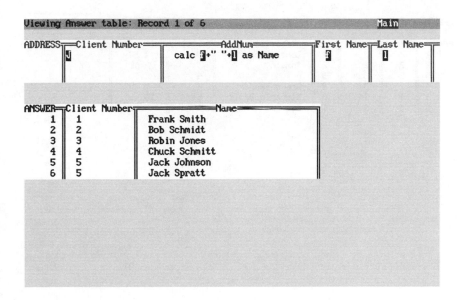

**Figure 4.21 Using a calculation query to combine results from two columns.**

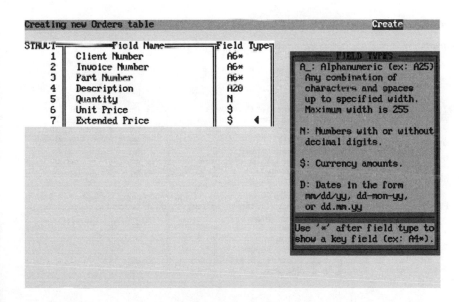

**Figure 4.22 The ORDERS table definition.**

```
Viewing Orders table: Record 6 of 6                              Main
ORDERS Client Invoice Part    Description   Quantity Unit Price Extended Pric
    1     2      2      1   Lamb Chops         9       1.50
    2     2      2      2   Tomato             7        .65
    3     2      3      3   Onion              4        .35
    4     2      3      4   Green Pepper       4        .35
    5     4      1      5   Electric Drill     5      10.00
    6     4      1      6   Bit Set            6       5.00
```

**Figure 4.23    Sample data in the ORDERS table.  The Extended Price has been kept empty.**

```
Viewing Changed table: Record 1 of 6                             Main
 Invoice Number Part Number Description Quantity Unit Price    Extended Price
                                           q         p         changeto q*p


ORDERS Client Invoice Part    Description   Quantity Unit Price Extended Pric
    1     2      2      1   Lamb Chops         9       1.50        13.50
    2     2      2      2   Tomato             7        .65         4.55
    3     2      3      3   Onion              4        .35         1.40
    4     2      3      4   Green Pepper       4        .35         1.40
    5     4      1      5   Electric Drill     5      10.00        50.00
    6     4      1      6   Bit Set            6       5.00        30.00

CHANGED Client Invoice Part   Description   Quantity Unit Price Extended Pric
    1     2      2      1   Lamb Chops         9       1.50
    2     2      2      2   Tomato             7        .65
    3     2      3      3   Onion              4        .35
    4     2      3      4   Green Pepper       4        .35
    5     4      1      5   Electric Drill     5      10.00
    6     4      1      6   Bit Set            6       5.00
```

**Figure 4.24    Using the changeto operator to calculate a value for Extended Price.  The old data is temporarily held in CHANGED.**

```
Viewing Answer table: Record 1 of 3                                    Main
```

| ORDERS | Client Number | Invoice Number | Extended Price | Part Number | Description |
|--------|---------------|----------------|----------------|-------------|-------------|
|        | √             | √              | calc sum       |             |             |

| ORDERS | Client | Invoice | Part | Description | Quantity | Unit Price | Extended Pric |
|--------|--------|---------|------|-------------|----------|------------|---------------|
| 1 | 2 | 2 | 1 | Lamb Chops | 9 | 1.50 | 13.50 |
| 2 | 2 | 2 | 2 | Tomato | 7 | .65 | 4.55 |
| 3 | 2 | 3 | 3 | Onion | 4 | .35 | 1.40 |
| 4 | 2 | 3 | 4 | Green Pepper | 4 | .35 | 1.40 |
| 5 | 4 | 1 | 5 | Electric Drill | 5 | 10.00 | 50.00 |
| 6 | 4 | 1 | 6 | Bit Set | 6 | 5.00 | 30.00 |

| ANSWER | Client Number | Invoice Number | Sum of Extended Price |
|--------|---------------|----------------|-----------------------|
| 1 | 2 | 2 | 18.05 |
| 2 | 2 | 3 | 2.80 |
| 3 | 4 | 1 | 80.00 |

**Figure 4.25    Grouping data by selection (F6) and calculating group totals with calc sum.**

Number and Part Number would be defined as foreign keys with corresponding tables. But to keep things simple, use a manual entry system (see Figure 4.23).

Notice that the ORDERS table has blank entries for the extended total. Rather than creating a new table each time an order is processed, the calculation can be stored in an existing table with the **Changeto** operator. As shown in Figure 4.24, a table called CHANGED is created. But this contains the old data; the new information is stored in the original table. The CHANGED table is a safety feature that lets you restore the original data if you make a mistake.

A combination of a standard query and summary calculation can be used to group summaries by field(s). For example, to extract the total of each Client/Invoice combination (or simply by Invoice Number), place a check mark in the appropriate field(s) and designate a sum, as shown in Figure 4.25.

## Relational Division and the Set Operators

Although Paradox does not have an explicit relational division operator, division can be applied through the Paradox Set operators. Consider the table of orders from Figure 4.25. To learn which clients ordered all items from a set, create a table of part numbers for vegetables (call the table VEGS) to act as the

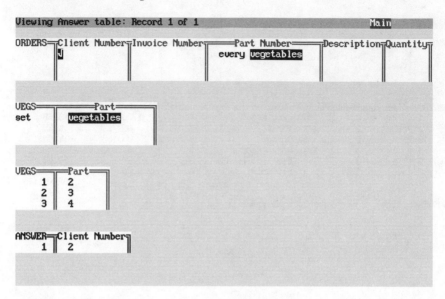

**Figure 4.26    Using set operators to find orders that included every vegetable.**

divisor. In this case, the set referred to is vegetables, so place the word **set** in the far left column of the VEGS query form. For division, *every* item in the set is to be referenced, so **every** becomes the set operator. The complete query (and result) is shown in Figure 4.26.

---

*The Paradox set operators are:*

---

no
every
only
exactly

---

They will not be covered in-depth since they go beyond the required operators for a relational database. Most of them have an obvious meaning: Find all clients who ordered **no** vegetables at all, find all clients who ordered **every** vegetable in the list, or find all clients who ordered **only** vegetables (nothing but vegetables). **Exactly** is the only term that is difficult to read as a standard phrase. It simply means both every and only. Thus, to have an order of **exactly** vegetables, you would have an order with some of every vegetable, but nothing else.

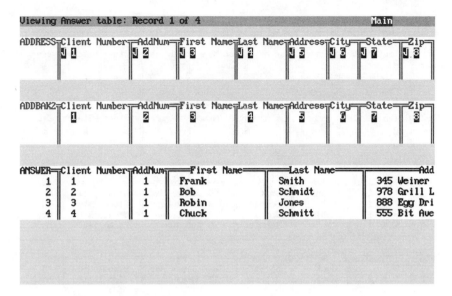

**Figure 4.27  Intersection matches all columns between two tables.  The ANSWER shows common rows.**

## Intersection, Union, and Difference

If two tables have identical rows, the result of an *intersection* will be the common rows.  Paradox does not have a single intersection operator, but you can get the same result by placing an example element in every field.  As changes have been made to the sample tables in the book, backups have been kept of the old data.  Intersection may be used to see which rows have remained unchanged, as shown in Figure 4.27.

Relational *difference* returns the rows that occur in the first table and not in the second.  Paradox does not have a difference operator, and constructing the equivalent requires two steps.  First, you must create a duplicate of the first table either by checking all of the fields in a query form or by copying the table with **Tools, Copy, Table**.  Then, use a delete query on the ANSWER to remove matching fields.  Using the ADDBAK2 as a set for comparison (to find the difference between ADDRESS and ADDBAK2), copy the ADDRESS table to ANSWER.  Then, use a delete query to remove ADDBAK2 rows from ANSWER.  The delete query (and final state of ANSWER) is shown in Figure 4.28.  Note that the figure shows a workspace that has been modified.  After processing the query, Paradox will remove the ANSWER query form and show

```
Viewing Answer table: Record 1 of 2                              Main

ANSWER=Client Number=AddNum=First Name=Last Name==Address==City==State==Zip
delete      1              2     3             4          5        6      7     8



ADDBAK2=Client Number=AddNum=First Name=Last Name==Address==City==State==Zip
            1              2     3             4          5        6      7     8



ADDBAK2=Clie=AddNum=First Name=Last Name========Address========City=====State
    1    1    1      Frank      Smith     345 Weiner Way   Minneapolis    MN
    2    2    1      Bob        Schmidt   978 Grill Lane   Bloomington    IN
    3    3    1      Robin      Jones     888 Egg Drive    New York       NY
    4    4    1      Chuck      Schmitt   555 Bit Ave      Rochester      MN


ANSWER=Clie=AddNum=First Name=Last Name========Address========City=====State
    1    5    1      Jack       Spratt    1212 Steak Ave   Bloomington    MN
    2    5    2      Jack       Johnson   2121 Mechanic    Bloomington    MN
```

**Figure 4.28   Relational difference:  Copy the first table to ANSWER; then delete the matching data in the second table from ANSWER.**

```
√ [F6] to include a field in the ANSWER; [F5] to give an Example   Main

ANSWER=========Client Number=========AddNum=========First Name======Last N
insert         1                     2              3               4



ADDBAK2=======Client Number=========AddNum=========First Name======Last Name=
              1                     2              3               4



ADDBAK2=Clie=AddNum=First Name=Last Name========Address========City=====State
    1    1    1      Frank      Smith     345 Weiner Way   Minneapolis    MN
    2    2    1      Bob        Schmidt   978 Grill Lane   Bloomington    IN
    3    3    1      Robin      Jones     888 Egg Drive    New York       NY
    4    4    1      Chuck      Schmitt   555 Bit Ave      Rochester      MN


ANSWER=Clie=AddNum=First Name=Last Name========Address========City=====State
    1    2    1      Robert     Schmidt   978 Grill Lane   Bloomington    IN
    2    5    1      Jack       Spratt    1212 Steak Ave   Bloomington    MN
    3    5    2      Jack       Johnson   2121 Mechanic    Bloomington    MN
```

**Figure 4.29   The first step of relational union:  Use an insert query to combine data from two tables.**

```
Viewing Answer table: Record 1 of 7                                    Main
ANSWER  Clie AddNum First Name Last Name      Address         City      State
   1     2     1    Robert     Schmidt    978 Grill Lane   Bloomington   IN
   2     5     1    Jack       Spratt     1212 Steak Ave   Bloomington   MN
   3     5     2    Jack       Johnson    2121 Mechanic    Bloomington   MN
   4     1     1    Frank      Smith      345 Weiner Way   Minneapolis   MN
   5     2     1    Bob        Schmidt    978 Grill Lane   Bloomington   IN
   6     3     1    Robin      Jones      888 Egg Drive    New York      NY
   7     4     1    Chuck      Schmitt    555 Bit Ave      Rochester     MN
```

**Figure 4.30    The final result of a union.**

the deleted rows—the former has been restored and the latter removed from the figure. When **difference** is used with an earlier version of the same table, it is possible find the changes and additions that have been made.

Relational *union* combines two tables, eliminating duplicate entries. Like relational **difference, union** requires several separate steps. The first step is the same: Create a copy of one table to ANSWER. Then, use an insert query to add the contents of the second table to the ANSWER. Figure 4.29 shows the query form and tables before processing the query. The union is between the set difference from the previous query (plus a "changed" row for Client 2) and ADDBAK2. Finally, query ANSWER (checking all columns) to remove duplicates. Figure 4.30 shows the final result of the **union**. This is almost the same as the original ADDRESS table. However, the modified data (Client 2) appears in both forms, old and new.

There are, however, simpler methods for achieving the same results, namely using **Tools, More, Add** and **Tools, More, Subtract**, but these bypass queries altogether. For now, concentrate on queries to better understand the next concept—views.

## Modifying and Saving Queries

Paradox leaves a query on the workspace until removed, unless the query includes a temporary table such as ANSWER. This is very useful when you make a minor mistake. By moving back to the query forms (using **F3** or **F4**), you can make changes and process the query again (**F2**). Of course, you'll lose the query if you leave Paradox or clear the workspace and define another query.

But if you design a fantastically complicated query with multiple joins and several conditions, and it is a query you will be using many times as you work with the database, retyping the query would be slow and error prone. What you need is a method for saving and restoring the query. Paradox provides this function through the menu **Scripts**, **Querysave**. You can give the query (script) a name of up to eight characters.

The query is restored to the workspace by selecting **Scripts**, **Play** and the name of the query (script). The query either may be executed (**F2**) or modified. Note that modifications will not affect the saved copy of the query—you must save it again if you want to store the changes. Paradox scripts are similar to macros—they are written in a programming language called PAL (Paradox Application Language), which goes far beyond saving and restoring queries, but that is a topic to be covered later.

# 5

# Views

Paradox queries take a snapshot of database tables as they exist at a certain time. The result is a new table that requires additional storage (disk) space. When dealing with large data sets on a multiuser system, a more interactive view of the data may be desired. Consider a network with several computers sharing a single database. If you retrieve an address through a query and another user later changes an address in the original table, the new address will not appear in the result table. In a view, however, the data will be updated.

Queries are like pictures of underlying data. Views, on the other hand, are like windows into the base tables themselves; they are a special interpretation of a query. In the "ideal" database, a query could be used either to create a table or a view.

dBASE QBE is very similar to Paradox—however, dBASE uses views as the primary expression of queries; Paradox uses **relational assignment**. Additionally, dBASE does not have a relational assignment operator (you must manually tell dBASE to copy the view to a file or use the SQL functions). On the other hand, Paradox does not have a true view feature, so most of our discussion of views will focus on dBASE.

A view should behave like a table. It should be possible to query a view or include a view in another view. The only limitation (by Codd's definitions) is that some views may not allow updates, insertions, and/or deletions. In some situations (particularly unions and many-to-many joins) it may be impossible for the RDBMS to determine which base table or which single row should be modified.

Let's look at a quick example in which a view should not allow updates: a many-to-many view of addresses and phone numbers. For each client's address, every phone number will also be listed:

| Client | Address | Phone |
|---|---|---|
| 5 | 1212 Steak Ave | 612 555-1616 |
| 5 | 1212 Steak Ave | 612 555-6161 |
| 5 | 2121 Mechanic Ave | 612 555-1616 |
| 5 | 2121 Mechanic Ave | 612 555-6161 |

If the phone number in the first row is changed, it will also change the phone number in the third row. Likewise, deleting any single row of this view would cause a second row to be deleted. These are not desirable side effects, and the database should disallow such operations. However, there are several view definitions that do not suffer such problems.

While most people can look at a view definition and decide which views are updateable and which are not, there are a few cases in which a computer program cannot make such a determination. Nevertheless, there are many cases where the computer *can* make the decision. The issue is complex enough that many database systems (including dBASE) prohibit changes to all views that address multiple base tables. As an additional restriction, dBASE does not allow a view within a query, making a divide and conquer approach awkward. Furthermore, dBASE does not remove duplicate values from the result unless specifically requested. Despite their limitations with respect to Codd's ideals, dBASE views remain a useful tool for presenting information.

dBASE views are created through the **Queries** menu and dBASE uses a Query by Example feature that is very similar to Paradox QBE. Query forms are placed on the workspace with **Layout, Add file to query** (**Alt-L,A**). Fields are selected with the **F5** key; as they are selected, the column format of the view is displayed across the bottom of the screen. Columns are added to the result in the order in which they are selected, so the resulting view definition may have a drastically different physical ordering than the underlying base tables. This can be a useful feature for organizing information—a relational database should allow the user to select column presentation order. Codd requires columns to be ordered alphabetically by name unless otherwise requested by the user (neither Paradox nor dBASE uses alphabetical column ordering for column results).

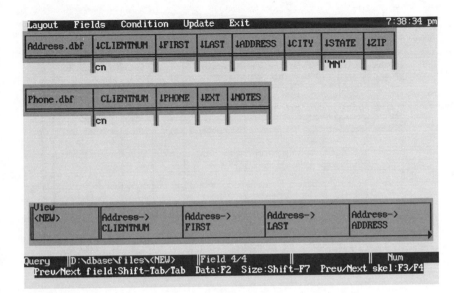

**Figure 5.1 A many-to-many join between ADDRESS and PHONE. Compare to Figure 4.12.**

dBASE examples do not require a special selection or definition method (in contrast to the Paradox **F5** key). As long as the text within the column is not prefixed by an operator, it will be used as an example element. To designate text as a selection criterion, rather than interpreting it as an example element, the text is placed in quotation marks, which act as a text operator. Most of these operations were covered in the preceding chapter (and Paradox QBE is very similar to dBASE), so the first example here is a moderately complex join. In fact, Figure 5.1 uses the same one-to-many join used in Paradox (Figure 4.12). The result is shown in Figure 5.2.

In dBASE, like Paradox, the **F3** and **F4** keys move between query forms on the query design screen, and **F2** will process the query without destroying the current design. Unlike Paradox, the query result and query design are presented in different work areas. When viewing the result, **Shift-F2** returns to the query design area. The query may be saved from either **Layout, Save this query** (to continue modifying the query) or **Exit, Save changes and exit** (to return to the dBASE main menu).

dBASE comparison operators are generally the same as Paradox. However, where Paradox uses **Not**, dBASE uses either **<>** or **#**.

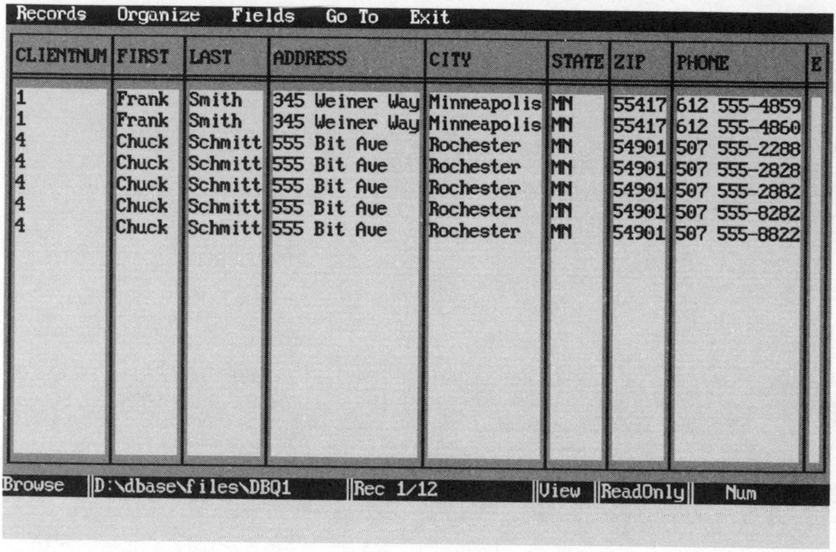

```
 Records   Organize   Fields   Go To   Exit

CLIENTNUM FIRST LAST    ADDRESS        CITY         STATE ZIP   PHONE            E
1         Frank Smith   345 Weiner Way Minneapolis  MN    55417 612 555-4859
1         Frank Smith   345 Weiner Way Minneapolis  MN    55417 612 555-4860
4         Chuck Schmitt 555 Bit Ave    Rochester    MN    54901 507 555-2288
4         Chuck Schmitt 555 Bit Ave    Rochester    MN    54901 507 555-2828
4         Chuck Schmitt 555 Bit Ave    Rochester    MN    54901 507 555-2882
4         Chuck Schmitt 555 Bit Ave    Rochester    MN    54901 507 555-8282
4         Chuck Schmitt 555 Bit Ave    Rochester    MN    54901 507 555-8822

Browse   D:\dbase\files\DBQ1      Rec 1/12         View  ReadOnly     Num
```

**Figure 5.2    The result of the many-to-many join between ADDRESS and PHONE.**

*dBASE Comparison Operators:*

| | |
|---|---|
| = | Equal |
| > | Greater than |
| < | Less than |
| >= | Greater than or equal to |
| <= | Less than or equal to |
| <> | Not equal |
| # | Not equal |

Conditionals (**and**s and **or**s) are specified as in Paradox; conditions are on the same lines or different lines. dBASE does not allow an **or** between conditions in the same field, but this does not limit its functionality—such constructions are simply a convenience in Paradox. dBASE allows summary calculations, and, like its example elements, a prefix such as **calc** is not required. The keyword is simply typed under the appropriate field:

---

*dBASE Summary Operators*

---

| | |
|---|---|
| SUM | Total |
| MIN | Lowest value |
| MAX | Highest value |
| CNT | Count of items |
| AVG | Average |

---

**COUNT** and **AVERAGE** may be spelled in full.

A dBASE view query may include calculated columns. **Fields, Create calculated field** will add a new image to the query called **Calc'd Flds.** When you select a calculated field with **F5**, dBASE will ask for a column name. Figure 5.3 displays a view that replaces the extended price with a calculated field derived from the quantity and unit price. A portion of the resulting view is shown in Figure 5.4; if the data is changed, the new EPRICE will be calculated on the fly. dBASE arithmetic operators are generally the same as Paradox. However, dBASE includes exponentiation.

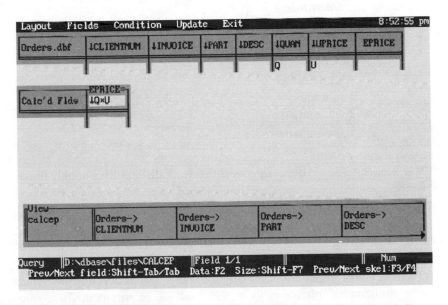

**Figure 5.3    Including a calculated column in the query (use F5 to define the column).**

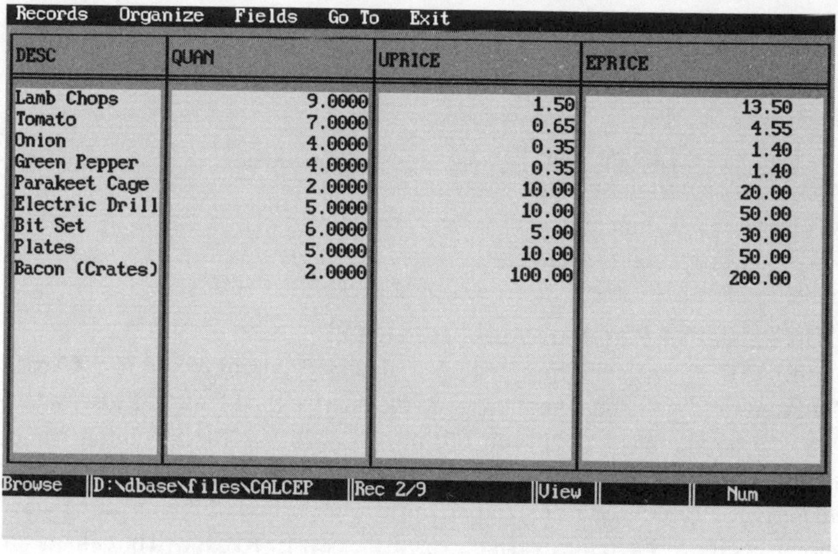

Figure 5.4   **A portion of the view using the query from Figure 5.3.**

*dBASE Arithmetic Operators*

| | |
|---|---|
| + | Addition |
| - | Subtraction |
| * | Multiplication |
| / | Division |
| ** | Exponentiation |
| ^ | Exponentiation |

There are a few special query operators that work differently, but only those that were mentioned for Paradox will be discussed here.  For example, to create outer joins with Paradox, an **!** was placed after the example element (in dBASE, the **every** operator is placed in *front* of the example element).  As with Paradox, most of these operators are placed in the far left-hand column (the two corresponding operators used with Paradox are **insert** and **delete**).

Perhaps the most important of the dBASE query operators is **unique**.  This operator eliminates duplicate rows in the result—a requirement for a true relational system, but a feature that most vendors ignore.  It is also extremely limited; **unique** will not work if the combined field lengths exceed 100 bytes.

As a simple example, consider a version of the ADDRESS table called DUPEADD (see Figure 5.5).  Note that the first and last rows duplicate the

| Records | Organize | Fields | Go To | Exit | | |
|---------|----------|--------|-------|------|---|---|

| CLIENTNUM | ADDNUM | FIRST | LAST | ADDRESS | CIT |
|-----------|--------|-------|------|---------|-----|
| 1 | 1 | Frank | Smith | 345 Weiner Way | Min |
| 2 | 1 | Bob | Schmidt | 978 Grill Lane | Blo |
| 3 | 1 | Robin | Jones | 888 Egg Drive | New |
| 4 | 1 | Chuck | Schmitt | 555 Bit Ave | Roc |
| 5 | 1 | Jack | Spratt | 1212 Steak Ave | Blo |
| 5 | 2 | Jack | Johnson | 2121 Mechanic Ave | Blo |
| 1 | 1 | John | Doe | 345 Whiner Way | Min |

| Browse | D:\dbase\files\DUPEADD | Rec 7/7 | File | Num |
|--------|------------------------|---------|------|-----|

Figure 5.5   A dBASE table with duplicate rows (DUPEADD).

| Records | Organize | Fields | Go To | Exit | |
|---------|----------|--------|-------|------|---|

| CUSTID | PART | QUAN | PRICE |
|--------|------|------|-------|
| 1 | 1 | 3 | 2.00 |
| 1 | 2 | 4 | 1.00 |
| 2 | 3 | 4 | 5.00 |
| 2 | 4 | 4 | 5.00 |
| 1 | 1 | 3 | 2.00 |

| Browse | D:\dbase\files\DUPEORD | Rec 1/5 | File | Num |
|--------|------------------------|---------|------|-----|

Figure 5.6   A dBASE table with duplicate rows (DUPEORD).

"key," ClientNum=1 AddNum=1. While the problem is obvious in this small table, in a very large database it is possible that someone might inadvertently duplicate a key value or accidentally add a duplicate entry instead of updating an existing entry. This is one common cause of duplicate entries.

Now consider a second table called DUPEORD (see Figure 5.6). This illustrates a common structural technique that creates duplicate entries. In this case, orders are processed in arrival sequence without identifying marks such as date or invoice number. The table is simply a list of the customer number, part number, quantity, and price. This example violates two rules of relational database design: The storage order affects the meaning (Rule 8), and the rows are not unique, and thus cannot be identified by value (Rule 2).

If DUPEADD and DUPEORD are **joined**, how should the database handle the duplicate information? Does the duplicate ADDRESS entry represent two separate clients or a single client whose data changed? For now, assume the latter. Does the duplicate ORDER entry represent a mistake, or was it a new order? Again, assume the latter. The result of a standard **join** links each duplicate address to every matching order (see Figure 5.7). This wasn't what was wanted: What appears as three orders for Client 1 in the order entry table, appears as six in the result.

Some of the duplication can be eliminated by using the unique query shown in Figure 5.8. Note that only the first address listing is used in these queries to clarify the result. But the result, Figure 5.9, is still not what was wanted. The duplication has been removed, but the system is still crossing orders between the two ClientNum=1 entries. This is not a problem with the dBASE query method, per se. Rather, it is a problem with allowing duplicate entries in a table (Paradox exhibits similar problems when tables are not keyed).

## dBASE Manipulative Queries

Manipulative queries in dBASE do not behave as a view, and their operation is very similar to the corresponding Paradox queries. But one primary difference between the two lies in their handling of row deletions. The manipulative operator to remove dBASE rows is **mark**; however, the rows are not automatically deleted from the table. Rather, they are marked for deletion, and removed later when the file is packed. If the file has not been packed, it is possible to reverse the operation with the **unmark** function.

From the main dBASE assist menu, select **Tools, Deleted, On** to display only those rows that have not been marked for deletion. When set to **Off**,

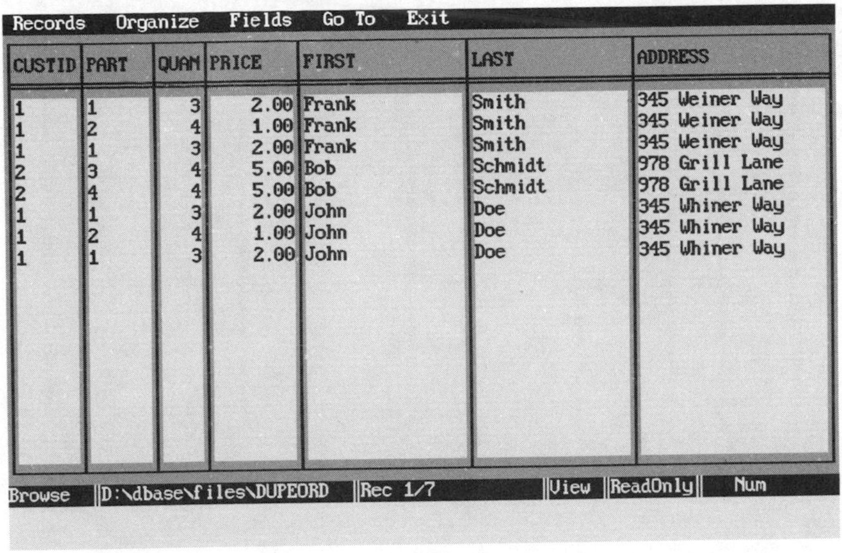

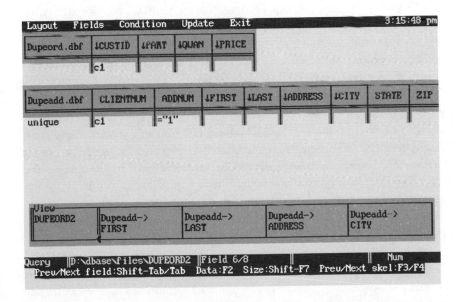

**Figure 5.7** The resulting view when duplicate rows are included in DUPEADD.

**Figure 5.8** Using the Unique operator to ignore duplicate data in the DUPEADD table.

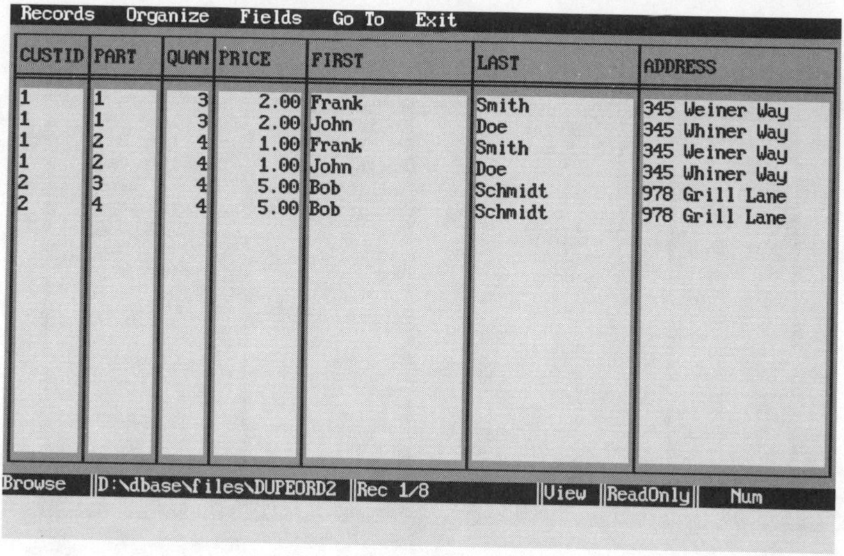

| CUSTID | PART | QUAN | PRICE | FIRST | LAST | ADDRESS |
|--------|------|------|-------|-------|------|---------|
| 1 | 1 | 3 | 2.00 | Frank | Smith | 345 Weiner Way |
| 1 | 1 | 3 | 2.00 | John | Doe | 345 Whiner Way |
| 1 | 2 | 4 | 1.00 | Frank | Smith | 345 Weiner Way |
| 1 | 2 | 4 | 1.00 | John | Doe | 345 Whiner Way |
| 2 | 3 | 4 | 5.00 | Bob | Schmidt | 978 Grill Lane |
| 2 | 4 | 4 | 5.00 | Bob | Schmidt | 978 Grill Lane |

Browse    D:\dbase\files\DUPEORD2    Rec 1/8    View    ReadOnly    Num

**Figure 5.9    The resulting view when the Unique operator is specified.**

marked rows will appear in the table, but a **Del** indicator will be turned on when the cursor is on the marked row. To permanently remove the marked rows, select **Organize, Erase marked records** from a **browse, modify structure** screen (in a network environment, this must be done from the **modify structure screen**). The **mark/unmark** feature may be used much like an undo feature in other programs—it gives you a chance to reverse an operation before "saving" the result.

The dBASE **append** is the equivalent of a Paradox **insert**. The query in Figure 5.10 inserts ClientNum, AddNum, First, and Last entries from the ADDRESS table into the DUPEADD table. The example elements designate the columns to use. Conditional statements could also be added to select specific rows. Note that dBASE labels the table that will be changed as the *Target*. To execute a manipulative query (**mark, unmark,** or **append**), select **Update, Perform the update** from the query menu.

With manipulative queries, data can be combined from several sources to affect the final action. Consider a remote warehouse that requires order information to process shipments. Rather than sending the entire INVOICE and ORDER information, you may want to extract only the required information and send a simple table. The query in Figure 5.11 combines address and order data from two tables into a single SHIPOUT table that could be sent to a remote location (city, state, and zip code have been excluded here for simplicity). Note the conditional statement under ADDRESS, AddNum: It draws only the first address for a client (you wouldn't want to ship the same order to multiple locations). The result appears in Figure 5.12.

## Multiple Table Operation

When altering data in the base tables, dBASE places very severe restrictions on operations involving several tables. Some examples of updating a table using several sources have already been shown. But updating several tables at once presents another problem. By Codd's definitions, such actions should be possible through views. However, a view composed of several tables is not updateable in dBASE. If only single-table views are updateable, is there any reason to use a view rather than simply editing the base table? The answer is, yes, there are some advantages to using single-table views. First, you can restrict access to selected rows within the table. Second, you can alter the presentation order. For example, suppose your company has several sales representatives who cover specific regions. In dBASE, you are able to create a view of ADDRESS that displays only selected states. A sample query is shown in Figure 5.13 and the resultant view is shown in Figure 5.14. It was precisely for applications such as this (limiting the scope or presenting data in

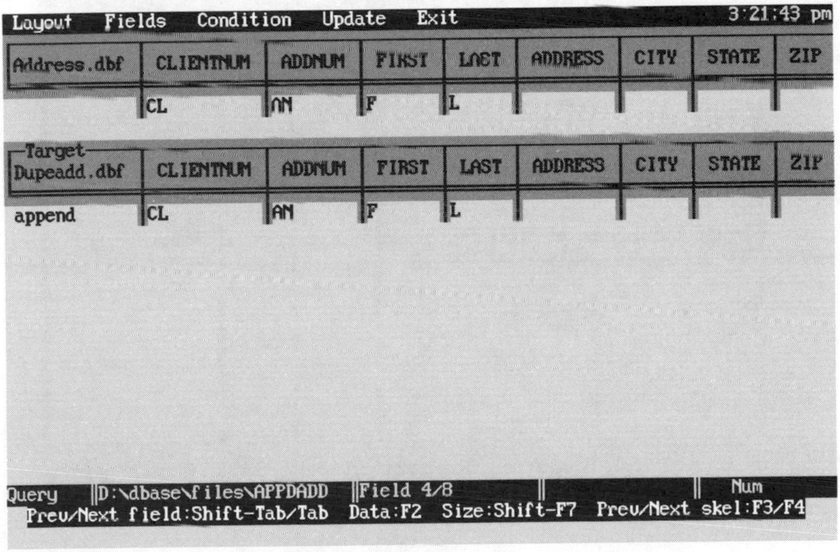

**Figure 5.10   A dBASE append query (used for row insertion).**

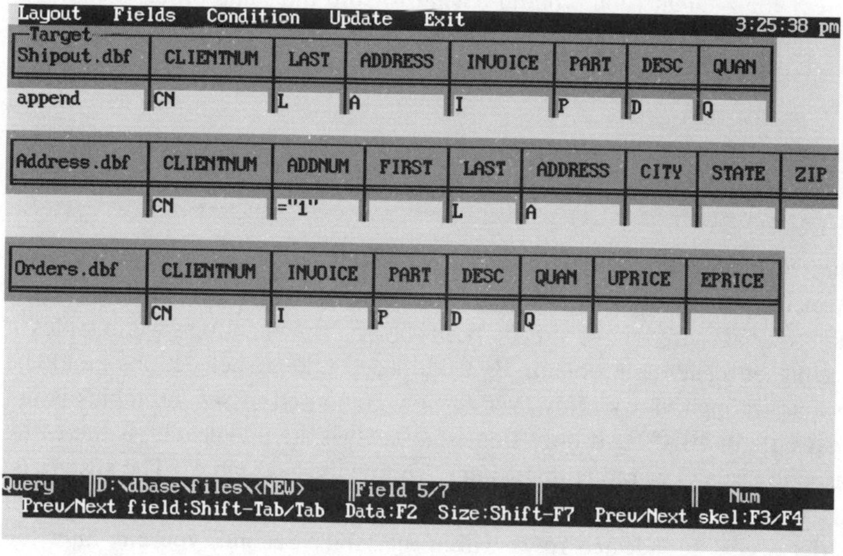

**Figure 5.11**  Using the append operator to combine data from two tables into a single destination.

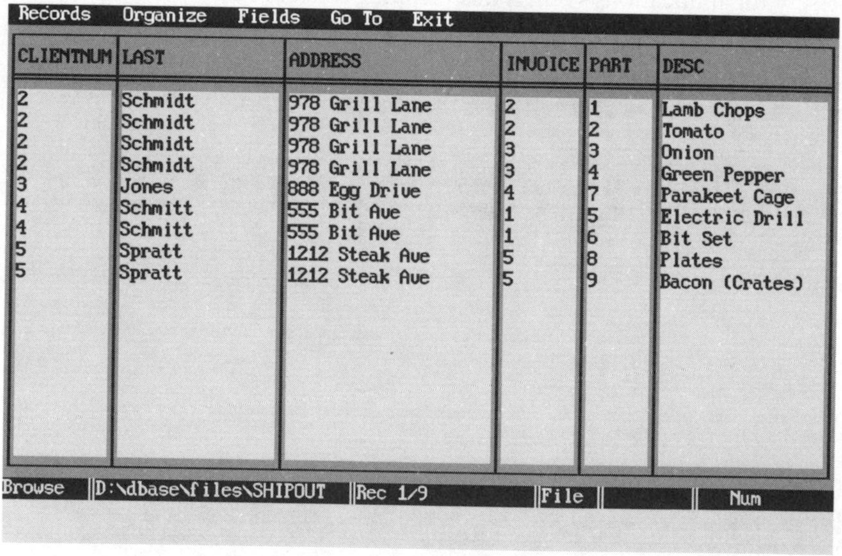

**Figure 5.12**  The result of an append query from two tables.

a specific order), that Codd allowed views to be updateable and rely on presentation order.

A dBASE view is sorted by placing either Asc# or Dsc# in the query image column—these create an ascending or descending sort, respectively. The number allows sorting on multiple columns, e.g., Asc1, Asc2, etc. If the column is not indexed, the resulting view will not be updateable (indexed columns are prefixed with a #). For the view to make use of indexes, you must turn on the feature through **Fields, Include indexes**.

If you have not yet created an index, you must return to the main menu, select the database file to index, and modify its structure. For a single field index, the index may be set through the structure form (see Figure 5.15); multiple fields indexes may be set through the **Organize, Create new index**, as shown in Figure 5.16. Figure 5.17 shows the view definition from Figure 5.13 with modifications that sort the view on the indexed columns Last and First. The result is shown in Figure 5.18.

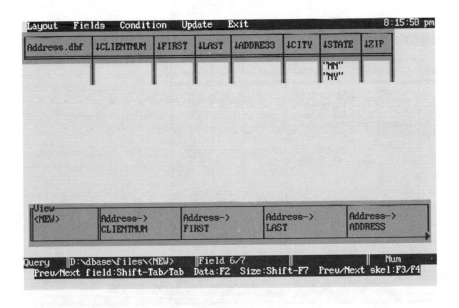

**Figure 5.13    Restricting a dBASE view to the specified states:   Minnesota OR New York.**

```
Records   Organize   Fields   Go To   Exit
```

| CLIENTNUM | FIRST | LAST | ADDRESS | CITY | STATE | ZIP |
|-----------|-------|------|---------|------|-------|-----|
| 1 | Frank | Smith | 345 Weiner Way | Minneapolis | MN | 55401 |
| 3 | Robin | Jones | 888 Egg Drive | New York | NY | 10021 |
| 4 | Chuck | Schmitt | 555 Bit Ave | Rochester | MN | 55901 |

```
Browse   D:\dbase\files\DBQ2      Rec 3/4          View          Num
```

**Figure 5.14**   A view restricted to Minnesota and New York.   The data in the base table may be edited using the view.

```
Layout   Organize   Append   Go To   Exit                    8:40:31 pm
```

Bytes remaining:   3917

| Num | Field Name | Field Type | Width | Dec | Index |
|-----|------------|------------|-------|-----|-------|
| 1 | CLIENTNUM | Character | 6 | | Y |
| 2 | FIRST | Character | 15 | | Y |
| 3 | LAST | Character | 15 | | Y |
| 4 | ADDRESS | Character | 25 | | N |
| 5 | CITY | Character | 15 | | N |
| 6 | STATE | Character | 2 | | N |
| 7 | ZIP | Character | 5 | | N |

```
Database  D:\dbase\files\ADDRESS    Field 3/7                      Num
          Enter the field name.  Insert/Delete field:Ctrl-N/Ctrl-U
Field names begin with a letter and may contain letters, digits and underscores
```

**Figure 5.15**   Changing the database structure to include an index on LAST.

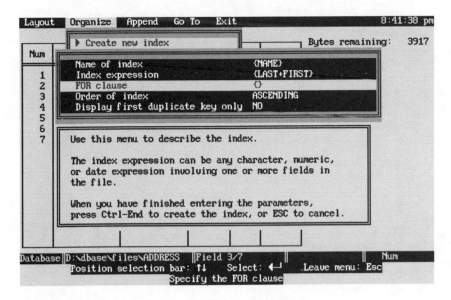

**Figure 5.16 Using the menu to create a multiple column index.**

## Paradox Multitable Forms

Paradox does not support views, although it does have linked multitable forms, which have a few minor similarities to views. The multitable form is severely limited in that it is not based on a query. On the other hand, it builds links between tables in such a way that the result is *always* updateable.

The Paradox multitable form more strongly resembles a hierarchical database rather than a relational database. In a hierarchical database there are two types of tables: parents and children. The child files "inherit" attributes from the parents. A common example would be an invoice: The parent record would contain the summary information about the order (name, address, invoice number, date, etc); the child records would include the order details such as part number, quantity, price, and description. Each detail record inherits the summary information such as invoice number and date.

A multitable form is built upon a base table called the *master* (which resembles the parent file of a hierarchical database). The tables linked to the master are called *detail tables*, and resemble child tables. The detail tables must be keyed and have at least one column in common with the master—the common columns establish the basis for the link. In a hierarchical database, the key information would be unnecessary and the data would be linked by record number.

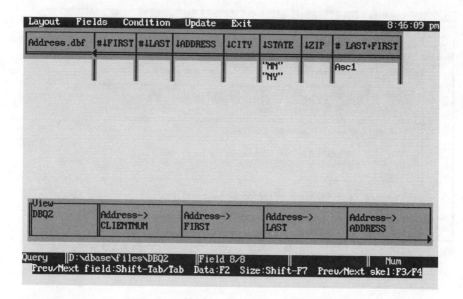

**Figure 5.17   The view definition required to sort the result on LAST+ FIRST.**

| Records | Organize | Fields | Go To | Exit | | | |
|---|---|---|---|---|---|---|---|
| CLIENTNUM | FIRST | LAST | ADDRESS | CITY | STATE | ZIP | |
| 5 | Jack | Johnson | 2121 Mechanic Ave | Bloomington | MN | 55420 | |
| 3 | Robin | Jones | 888 Egg Drive | New York | NY | 10021 | |
| 4 | Chuck | Schmitt | 555 Bit Ave | Rochester | MN | 55901 | |
| 1 | Frank | Smith | 345 Weiner Way | Minneapolis | MN | 55401 | |
| 5 | Jack | Spratt | 1212 Steak Ave | Bloomington | MN | 55420 | |

Browse     D:\dbase\files\DBQ2     Rec 6/6     View     Num

**Figure 5.18   A view sorted on LAST+FIRST.**

If multitable forms were based on a query (implemented as a **view**), any arbitrary link could be established. But, because multitable forms are established based on primary keys, multitable forms take careful planning. Additionally, multitable reports (which are covered later) have different design restrictions, so coordinating report and form designs can be difficult.

If the master and detail form share exactly the same key (a one-to-one relationship), the form design is very straightforward. One-to-many relationships (such as several items ordered by a single client) are much more common and more complex. In these cases, the detail tables *must* have multiple column keys (if you are following relational principles, this will have been done already).

The trick to using multitable forms lies in the detail tables. Each detail table that will be imbedded in the master must have a special form used for the link. The fields placed on the detail form must *not* include the common column(s); Paradox will copy the value in the common column from the master to the detail automatically. On the other hand, any portion of the detail key that does not appear in the master *must* appear on the detail form. The detail form is limited to one page, and it will use as much space in the master as the smallest rectangle that will display all of the text and data.

As an example, let's create a new table called INVOICE, which will have links to ORDERS and ADDRESS. The critical information in the invoice will be the invoice number, date, address number, and items order. All of these items except the date can be found in tables defined previously; thus, date will be the only unique column. Links to the address through the client and address numbers, and the orders through the invoice number, are necessary. The INVOICE table definition is shown in Figure 5.19; the detail form for the ADDRESS is shown in Figure 5.20. Note that neither the client number nor the address number appears in the detail form—the relationship is one-to-one.

The address has multiple column keys, so a **TableLookup**, **HelpAndFill** cannot be used to find the correct address. Instead, a one-to-many link can be used by adding the address number to the detail form. Then the address number field in the INVOICE table would remain unlinked, but still contain valuable data. In fact, there is a second advantage to this approach: Both a billing address and shipping address can be added to the form. Note that Paradox will not allow multiple detail forms from a single table; otherwise, a very elegant system would have been possible, which would actually display all of the relevant information. The revised INVOICE structure and ADDRESS detail form are shown in Figures 5.21 and 5.22.

The order information requires a little different twist. The addresses will display one at a time, a typical situation on an order form. But, because it is

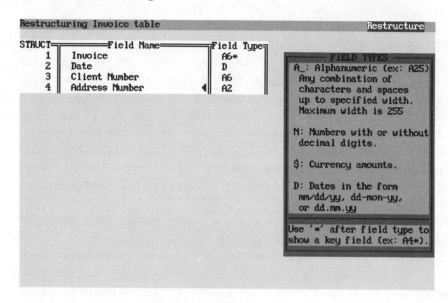

**Figure 5.19    The INVOICE table definition.**

preferable to see as many ordered items as possible, Paradox has a multirecord form. First, place the basic information on the form, as shown in Figure 5.23. For the extended price, a calculated field has been created: **Field**, **Place**,

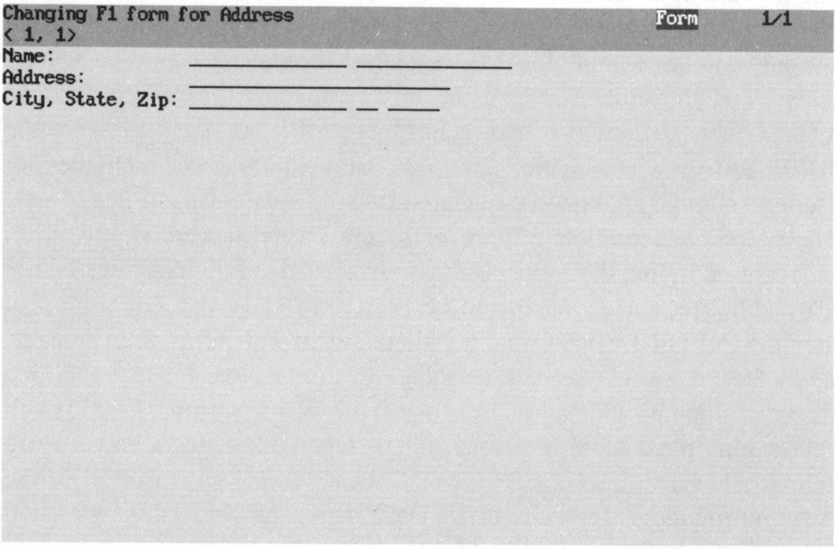

**Figure 5.20    The detail form for ADDRESS—the linked fields (Client Number and Address Number) must not be included on the form.**

**Calculated**, **[Quantity]** \* **[Unit Price]**. Although the table has a column for extended price, this must be calculated manually. By placing a calculated field, the results are visible immediately.

Now, copy the rows part way down the form with **Multi**, **Records**, **Define**. Move the cursor to the first character of the first field (Part Number) and hit Enter. Then move to the last character of the last field (the calculated Extended Price) and hit Enter again. Finally, move the cursor down the form to copy the rows and hit Enter when done. In Figure 5.24, four copies have been created for a total of five rows. If there are too many rows, they will not fit on the master form (the detail form can be adjusted further after it is in place on the master).

Once the detail forms have been created, defining the master is simple: Create a form for the INVOICE table; then place the basic fields (Invoice Number, Date, Client Number, Billing Address, and Shipping Address). Below this, or in any other convenient spot, place the address list with **Multi**, **Tables**, **Place**, **Linked**, **Address**, **2**, **Client Number** (note that the master table, INVOICE, is keyed on Invoice Number, but can be linked to Client Number). For clarity, place a border around imbedded tables with **Border**, **Place**, **Single-line** or **Double-line**.

Finally, place the items ordered with **Multi**, **Tables**, **Place**, **Linked**, **Orders**, **F**, **Client Number**, **Invoice**. The final design is shown in Figure 5.25. Figure

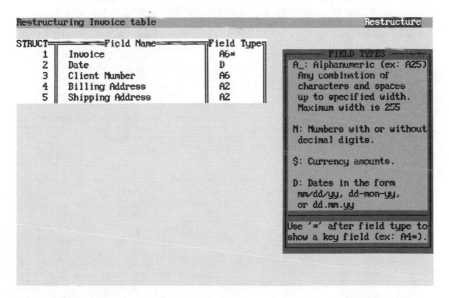

**Figure 5.21   The revised INVOICE definition for including both ship-ping and billing addresses.**

```
Changing F2 form for Address                              Form     1/1
< 3, 3>
Addr     Name:                    _____ _____
Number   Address:                 _____
  __     City, State, Zip:        _____ __ _____
```

**Figure 5.22   The ADDRESS detail form has been revised to include an Address Number.**

```
Designing new F form for Orders                          Form  Ins 1/1
< 1,61>
Part # Quan  Description          Unit Price   Extended Price
_____ ____  _____    _____   _____
```

**Figure 5.23   The base definition for a multirecord form using ORDERS.**

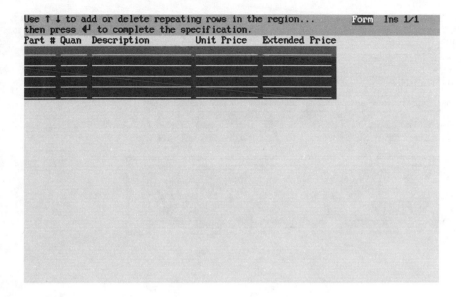

**Figure 5.24    Using the Multirecord option to expand the number of rows displayed on the form.**

5.26 shows a sample order. Cursor movement is limited to one table (master or detail), but you can move between tables with **F3** (image up) and **F4** (image down). Although only one address is displayed, **PgUp** and **PgDn** will display the other addresses when the cursor is in the imbedded ADDRESS table. In fact, in Edit or CoEdit mode, addresses may be added, deleted, or modified. Likewise, within the ORDERS portion, if more than five lines are entered, the region will scroll among the parts ordered on the current invoice.

While using multitable forms, you are actually working with only one table at a time (hence the **F3** and **F4** to move between imbedded tables). In a view, the master columns (Date and Address) would appear in several separate rows (once for each linked detail row). Although Paradox cannot create true views, it is useful to compare the hierarchical form structure to the relational view structure. One possible view configuration would look like:

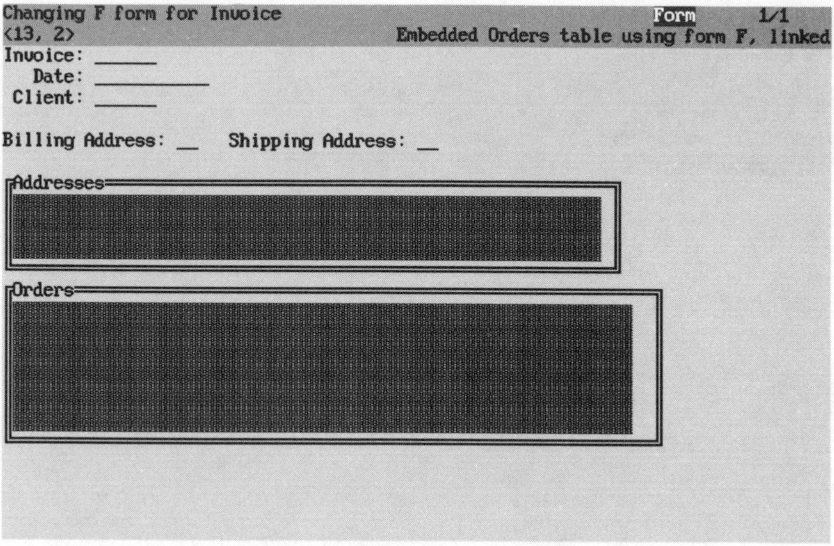

**Figure 5.25   A completed multitable form definition with links to AD-DRESS and the multirecord ORDERS form.**

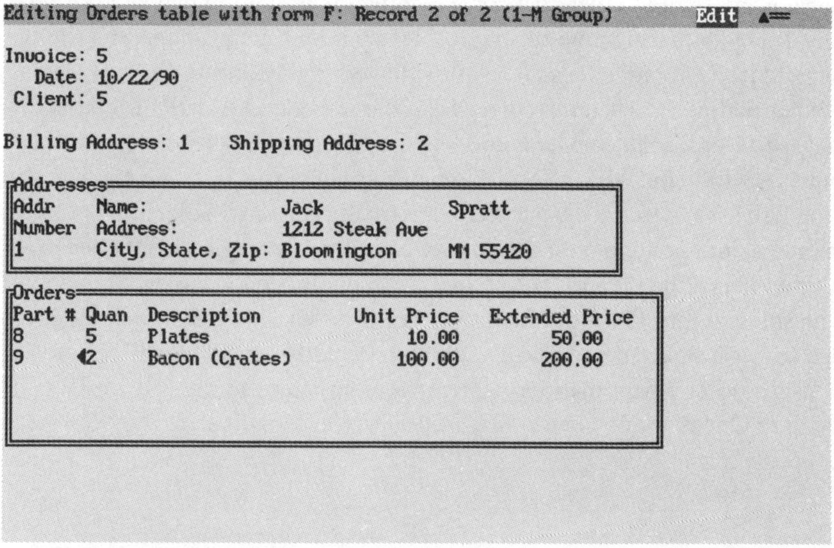

**Figure 5.26   Viewing an invoice using the multitable form. Note the multirecord entries in ORDERS.**

| Invoice | Client | Bill | Ship | Bill Last | Ship Last | Part | Quan | Price |
|---|---|---|---|---|---|---|---|---|
| 1 | 4 | 1 | 1 | Schmitt | Schmitt | 5 | 5 | 010.00 |
| 1 | 4 | 1 | 1 | Schmitt | Schmitt | 6 | 6 | 005.00 |
| 2 | 2 | 1 | 1 | Schmidt | Schmidt | 1 | 9 | 001.50 |
| 2 | 2 | 1 | 1 | Schmidt | Schmidt | 2 | 7 | 000.65 |
| 3 | 2 | 1 | 1 | Schmidt | Schmidt | 3 | 4 | 000.35 |
| 3 | 2 | 1 | 1 | Schmidt | Schmidt | 4 | 4 | 000.35 |
| 4 | 3 | 1 | 1 | Jones | Jones | 7 | 2 | 010.00 |
| 5 | 5 | 1 | 2 | Spratt | Johnson | 8 | 5 | 010.00 |
| 5 | 5 | 1 | 2 | Spratt | Johnson | 9 | 2 | 100.00 |

Changes to the address information would be prohibited because a change to a single value (e.g., the Billing address number) would change the values in other linked rows. Such an operation would create ambiguity: Did you intend to change only the row you edited (split the billing), or every associated row (change the bill for the entire invoice)? In a multitable form, you can see only one Bill and Ship entry and changes to that single entry are unambiguous.

In the preceding Paradox multitable form, the relationship between ADDRESS and ORDERS is many-to-many (a detail left out of the corresponding view example). A multitable form cannot establish a true many-to-many relationship without using third normal form (in this case, Invoice is the link between the two one-to-many relations). This feature prevents the row insertion and deletion problems associated with many-to-many relationships: Paradox can determine which base table is affected because you are still modifying a single base table rather than a conglomerate. In a true many-to-many view, each possible combination would form a unique row, and deleting a row becomes ambiguous. For example, if INVOICE had been a view expressed with a many-to-many relation between INVOICE, ADDRESS, and ORDERS, the entries for invoice 5 would appear as:

| Invoice | Last | Quan | Description |
|---|---|---|---|
| 5 | Spratt | 5 | plates |
| 5 | Spratt | 2 | Bacon (Crates) |
| 5 | Johnson | 5 | plates |
| 5 | Johnson | 2 | Bacon (Crates) |

Deletion would present a problem. There are two rows with orders for plates: the first name and plate combination (Spratt) and the second name and plate combination (Johnson). The database would have no way of knowing whether the order for plates or one of the names should be deleted. And, even if the database could make the determination, it would have the very disconcerting side effect of deleting two rows when only one was selected for deletion.

The Paradox multitable form, a hybrid hierarchical/relational approach, solves update problems. But it is not an ideal solution. Since multitable forms are not views, they cannot be queried. Likewise, the form cannot be used as the basis for a report. Further, multitable forms cannot be imbedded within other multitable forms (Paradox does not allow nested forms). All of these options would be possible with views (a view behaves like a table, except during update operations).

## Summary

The last two chapters have covered queries and the structure of query results: new tables and views. Most of the examples, thus far, have maintained a large degree of structural independence. But results are often more meaningful (or useful) when some type of physical structure is imposed. For this reason, Codd allows sorting within views. This chapter has hinted at some of the possibilities available through sorting, and ignored some of the related details that affect sorting and query performance. Now, it is time to take a more detailed look at these issues.

# 6

# Sorting

In the discussion on queries and views, two topics of great interest to database users were mentioned: sorting and indexing. These are the two methods a database uses to order data. While the underlying order of the data (where it is physically placed within a file) should not be important to a database user, the presentation order and access speed, which can be affected by file structure and user requirements, should.

An index is used internally by a database to improve access times. In the "ideal" relational database, the index is a performance feature only, and no other feature relies on an index (see Rule 8 in Chapter 1). If a database requires an index for certain operations, the index should be generated automatically. The index may use one of several different techniques— but, whichever method it uses, the index has an ordering effect on the data. By storing a list of (internal) record numbers in a special search order, the database can more rapidly find a given value.

One typical indexing method is called a *binary tree*. You can take a randomly ordered list, such as the one in Table 6.1, and find the name in the "middle" of the alphabetized list (Emily). All names that come before Emily create a list (the left side), and the names after Emily create another list (the right side). If you follow this process, writing the names to the left and right, you can build a tree diagram like the one shown in Figure 6.1. Alternatively, you can create a list with two columns, recording the ID numbers of the left names in the left column, and of the right names in the right column, as shown in Table 6.2 (in this example, there is one extra row—the first row points to the top of the tree). This list acts as an index.

If you were searching for Wes in the list of names, you would compare all nine names to your target value before finding the match. But if you use the index, you start at Emily and find that you need a larger value. So you take the right node (6) to Nancy. You still need a larger value, so you take the right node again (3) to Sue. Finally, you take another right node (9) to Wes. The search has been reduced from nine comparisons to four. The larger the list becomes, the more dramatic the performance improvement.

**Table 6.1—Names**

| ID | Name |
| --- | --- |
| 1 | Brad |
| 2 | Adam |
| 3 | Sue |
| 4 | Joshua |
| 5 | Emily |
| 6 | Nancy |
| 7 | David |
| 8 | Cheryl |
| 9 | Wes |

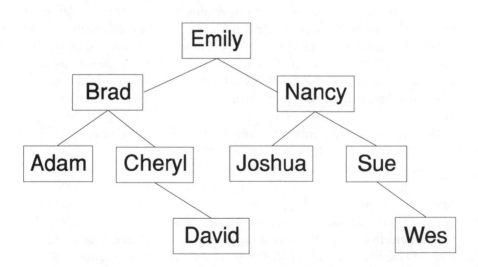

**Figure 6.1   A binary tree. Lower values (alphabetically) are placed to the left, and higher values are placed to the right.**

**Table 6.2—Index of Names**

| ID | Left | Right |
|----|------|-------|
| 0  | 5    | 5     |
| 1  | 2    | 8     |
| 2  | —    | —     |
| 3  | —    | 9     |
| 4  | —    | —     |
| 5  | 1    | 6     |
| 6  | 4    | 3     |
| 7  | —    | —     |
| 8  | —    | 7     |
| 9  | —    | —     |

While an index can dramatically improve performance when data is read, it must be regenerated each time the file is changed. In most database applications, far more tasks require reading data than writing data. Therefore, the additional delays after writing the file are frequently an acceptable trade-off for improved read times. And many database systems will delay the index regeneration until it is necessary. After editing, the data will mark the index as "out of date" and on the next read attempt, the database will regenerate the index or prompt the user for a regeneration.

Although the example shows indexing applied to random searches, similar techniques may be applied to sorting. As outlined above, you could not move *up* through the tree to find the "previous" or "next" name. Let's say you find Joshua, and then want the previous name on the list (Emily). There is no pointer back to Nancy, then Emily that could be used for this purpose. However, the storage method or search algorithms may be changed to implement such backtracking. Such an index would be useful for sorting.

While the presence of an index is noticeable to a user only as a performance improvement, sorting has a dramatic impact upon the user's interaction with the data. The user sees the records of a sorted table in an ordered fashion. In theory, a **view** allows an ordered list because it is not a physical representation of the data—any number of views may simulateously access the data in whatever order best fits the needs of the end user. On the other hand, a sorted table should not be used as a base relation—the performance penalty would be significant. If you were to use sorted base tables, the user would experience a severe performance penalty with every new resorting. Furthermore, multiple users could not choose distinct sort orders simultaneously.

The best example of a definable presentation order in the two packages being examined is a sorted view under dBASE. With dBASE, you can define several different sorted views into the same table. As we have seen, a dBASE file must be indexed on columns that contribute to the sort order. For example, the two views shown in Figures 6.2 and 6.3 display the same table (ADDRESS) in alphabetical order by name and zip code order, respectively. Note that the indexes are turned on with **Fields, Include indexes** so that the resulting views will be modifiable. The advantage of this approach is most apparent on a network where two or more users may be changing the same data. One user may view the data in zip code order, while the other views it in alphabetical order.

This type of operation simply is not possible in Paradox. Keyed Paradox tables are always stored in key order. To change the sort order, you must sort the data into a new, unkeyed table. This table may still be used with the relational operators, but note that it is no longer a true relation because it has no key. Of course, changes to this new, sorted table are not reflected in the original base table, as they would be in a view.

Billing applications frequently require many different sorting methods for the day-to-day operation of a business. While entering and reviewing orders for the day, you would probably order the view by Invoice number (or perhaps by sales representative with a secondary sort by invoice number). For applica-

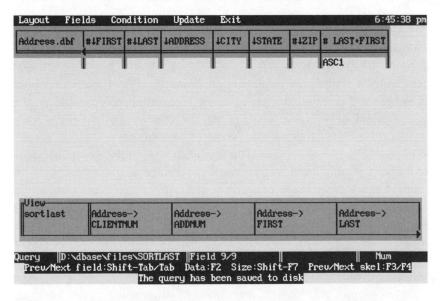

**Figure 6.2   dBASE view definition with an ascending sort by name (the sorted column does not appear in the view).**

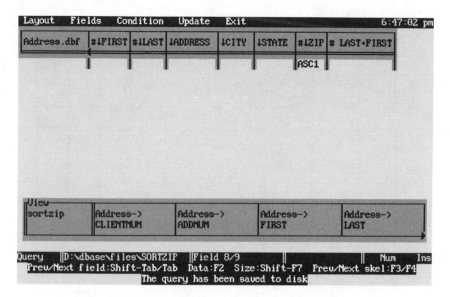

**Figure 6.3   dBASE view definition with an ascending sort by zip code.**

tions such as this, the sorted view can be an important tool in database development.

To return to the example of multiple network views, if Sue is working on a directory listing for client contacts, she can use a view sorted alphabetically by name. Meanwhile, someone else may be working on a mass mailing and looking at the addresses in zip code order. Both can make corrections (or additions) to the data simultaneously, while retaining the sort order that works best for each application. Examples of these two sort orders (defined by the previous view examples) are shown in Figures 6.4 and 6.5. Note the record numbers shown on the status line: dBASE still relies on the absolute position within the file when referring to the row (if the view were read-only, i.e., the indexes were not included, the record numbers would refer to the position within the view).

Certainly, you can avoid problems by ignoring the row numbers. When viewing the data on screen, you may not even notice the numbers. And when you start programming, you can use instructions like **Skip** (which moves relative to the current row order), rather than **Goto** (which moves to an absolute row number). However, there is one further aspect of physical ordering that is difficult to work around.

When creating an index with the **Organize**, **Create new index** selection under the table creation (or structure modification) menu, one of the choices is **Display first duplicate key only**. This choice, called **Unique** when writing

```
 Records   Organize   Fields   Go To   Exit

CLIENTNUM ADDNUM FIRST   LAST     ADDRESS          CITY         STATE ZIP

5         2      Jack    Johnson  2121 Mechanic Ave Bloomington  MN    55420
3         1      Robin   Jones    888 Egg Drive     New York     NY    10021
2         1      Bob     Schmidt  978 Grill Lane    Bloomington  IN    47401
4         1      Chuck   Schmitt  555 Bit Ave       Rochester    MN    54901
1         1      Frank   Smith    345 Weiner Way    Minneapolis  MN    55417
5         1      Jack    Spratt   1212 Steak Ave    Bloomington  MN    55420
6         1      Zachary Zed      8612 Zoo Lane     Zilch Gulch  ME    00112




Browse    D:\dbase\files\SORTLAST  Rec 6/7          View          Num    Ins
```

**Figure 6.4    Result of a dBASE view sorted by name.**

programs or working with the dot prompt, displays only one unique value from
the indexed column(s). It is similar to a primary key. However, it is not a
primary key. dBASE retains the data and hides the duplicates. It selects the

```
 Records   Organize   Fields   Go To   Exit

CLIENTNUM ADDNUM FIRST   LAST     ADDRESS          CITY         STATE ZIP

6         1      Zachary Zed      8612 Zoo Lane     Zilch Gulch  ME    00112
3         1      Robin   Jones    888 Egg Drive     New York     NY    10021
2         1      Bob     Schmidt  978 Grill Lane    Bloomington  IN    47401
4         1      Chuck   Schmitt  555 Bit Ave       Rochester    MN    54901
1         1      Frank   Smith    345 Weiner Way    Minneapolis  MN    55417
5         1      Jack    Spratt   1212 Steak Ave    Bloomington  MN    55420
5         2      Jack    Johnson  2121 Mechanic Ave Bloomington  MN    55420




Browse    D:\dbase\files\SORTZIP   Rec 7/7          View          Num    Ins
```

**Figure 6.5    Result of a dBASE view sorted by zip code.**

row to display by using the physical ordering in the file: the first occurrence of a duplicate value is the only one that displays.

In Figure 6.6 the Zip index has been changed to a unique index. Notice that Client 5 now displays only one entry (for a total of six rows) when the view used is defined on zip code order. If the view sorted by name is used, all seven rows appear. By Codd's definitions, an index should affect only the performance of a database, not its behavior.

Paradox keeps its indexes and sorting functions separate, although the sort will occur faster if the primary sort field is indexed. But Paradox cannot display different sort orders simultaneously. Borland sells a product called Paradox Engine that can access a table in sorted order by any single column. But there are other problems, such as the Engine's bypass of integrity checking. Additionally, you must have C or Pascal programming experience to use the Engine.

If a Paradox table has a primary key, it will *always* appear in primary key order. Tables that are not keyed may be sorted into any order with **Modify**, **Sort**, *TableName*, **Same**. Paradox presents a screen for specifying the sort order. Figure 6.7 shows a screen filled out for sorting alphabetically by last and first names. The sorted table is shown in Figure 6.8. Note that a query is used to create an ANSWER table (which is never keyed) in order to sort the results.

| Records | Organize | Fields | Go To | Exit | | | |
|---|---|---|---|---|---|---|---|
| CLIENTNUM | ADDNUM | FIRST | LAST | ADDRESS | CITY | STATE | ZIP |
| 6 | 1 | Zachary | Zed | 8612 Zoo Lane | Zilch Gulch | ME | 00112 |
| 3 | 1 | Robin | Jones | 888 Egg Drive | New York | NY | 10021 |
| 2 | 1 | Bob | Schmidt | 978 Grill Lane | Bloomington | IN | 17401 |
| 4 | 1 | Chuck | Schmitt | 555 Bit Ave | Rochester | MN | 54901 |
| 1 | 1 | Frank | Smith | 345 Weiner Way | Minneapolis | MN | 55417 |
| 5 | 1 | Jack | Spratt | 1212 Steak Ave | Bloomington | MN | 55420 |

Browse | D:\dbase\files\SORTZIP | Rec 7/7 | View | Num | Ins

**Figure 6.6 Result of a unique Index on Zip (only six of the seven rows now appear).**

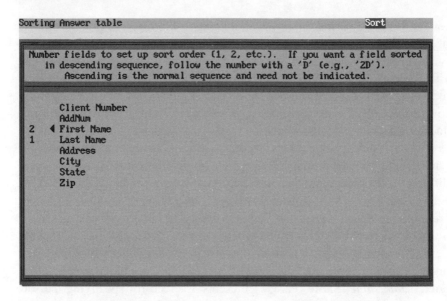

```
Sorting Answer table                                              Sort

 Number fields to set up sort order (1, 2, etc.).  If you want a field sorted
 in descending sequence, follow the number with a 'D' (e.g., '2D').
 Ascending is the normal sequence and need not be indicated.


        Client Number
        AddNum
   2  ◀ First Name
   1    Last Name
        Address
        City
        State
        Zip
```

**Figure 6.7   Paradox definition for an ascending sort by name.**

If a table is keyed, you may directly sort the table to another table with
**Modify, Sort,** *TableName, NewTableName.*  If the table is not keyed, you may
optionally sort to a different table with  **Modify**, **Sort**, *TableName*, **New**,

```
Viewing Answer table: Record 1 of 6                              Main

ANSWER══Clie═AddNum══First Name═Last Name══════Address══════════City══════State
     1    5    2     Jack       Johnson      2121 Mechanic    Bloomington   MN
     2    3    1     Robin      Jones        888 Egg Drive    New York      NY
     3    2    1     Bob        Schmidt      978 Grill Lane   Bloomington   IN
     4    4    1     Chuck      Schmitt      555 Bit Ave      Rochester     MN
     5    1    1     Frank      Smith        345 Weiner Way   Minneapolis   MN
     6    5    1     Jack       Spratt       1212 Steak Ave   Bloomington   MN
```

**Figure 6.8   Answer table sorted by name.**

*NewTableName*.  Of course, if the original table changes, the newly created sorted tables will not reflect the changes (they are not views).

Paradox always creates an index on the primary key(s).  However, this index is "under the covers;" i.e., you cannot delete the index from within Paradox and thus remove the primary key.  Paradox also supports indexes on any individual column.  Unfortunately, Paradox cannot create an index across several columns.  But Paradox will automatically apply indexes to any operations that will benefit from such an application.  A Paradox index is part of the object (table) definition; as such, the use of an index is not dependent upon language-specific features.  The separation of database management features from language-specific features is an important part of the relational database definition.

Paradox has two methods for creating indexes.  The first is to place a query on the workspace, and select **Tools**, **QuerySpeed**.  Paradox will analyze the query and generate indexes on columns that Paradox (in its less than infinite wisdom) thinks will improve performance.  However, this analysis misses some obvious optimizations.  When you begin to understand what operations will be enhanced by an index, you may want to generate indexes manually.

To force the generation of a specific index, you can use the **Index** command from within a program.  But it is too early in the book to cover programming, and there is a shortcut.  The **Alt-F10** key brings up a special debugging menu, intended for programming (see Figure 6.9).  For now, pay attention to only the **Miniscript** command.  This lets you enter a single command line.  Entering **Index** *TableName* **On** *ColumnName*, e.g., **Index "Address" On "Zip"**, will create an index.  If a table has a primary key, you may use **Index Maintained** in place of **Index**.  This generates an incrementally updated index.  Paradox completely regenerates a standard index whenever the base table has been changed and you later request an operation that uses the index.  On the other hand, **Maintained** indexes are only partially regenerated; the index is built in such a way that only a few changes are necessary to bring it up to date.

The columns that will make best use of indexes, and the type of index that works best are influenced by several factors: table size, data diversity, and frequency of updates, among others.  The more diverse the data values in a column, the more an index will help.  For example, if all of the addresses are in the same city, a zip code index may not help much.  But if there are many cities, a zip code index may improve performance dramatically.  Of course, both of these scenarios assume that a query or locate command will be looking for a specific zip code or range of zip codes.

Generally, the more rows a table has, the more an index will help (assuming sufficient data diversity).  A table with tens of thousands of rows may require several seconds to locate a particular value when no index is present.  With an

```
Play  RepeatPlay  BeginRecord  Debug  Value  MiniScript
Play a single line script.
```

| ADDRESS | Clie | AddNum | First Name | Last Name | Address | City | State |
|---|---|---|---|---|---|---|---|
| 1 | 1 | 1 | Frank | Smith | 345 Weiner Way | Minneapolis | MN |
| 2 | 2 | 1 | Bob | Schmidt | 978 Grill Lane | Bloomington | IN |
| 3 | 3 | 1 | Robin | Jones | 888 Egg Drive | New York | NY |
| 4 | 4 | 1 | Chuck | Schmitt | 555 Bit Ave | Rochester | MN |
| 5 | 5 | 1 | Jack | Spratt | 1212 Steak Ave | Bloomington | MN |
| 6 | 5 | 2 | Jack | Johnson | 2121 Mechanic | Bloomington | MN |

| ANSWER | Clie | AddNum | First Name | Last Name | Address | City | State |
|---|---|---|---|---|---|---|---|
| 1 | 5 | 2 | Jack | Johnson | 2121 Mechanic | Bloomington | MN |
| 2 | 3 | 1 | Robin | Jones | 888 Egg Drive | New York | NY |
| 3 | 2 | 1 | Bob | Schmidt | 978 Grill Lane | Bloomington | IN |
| 4 | 4 | 1 | Chuck | Schmitt | 555 Bit Ave | Rochester | MN |
| 5 | 1 | 1 | Frank | Smith | 345 Weiner Way | Minneapolis | MN |
| 6 | 5 | 1 | Jack | Spratt | 1212 Steak Ave | Bloomington | MN |

**Figure 6.9    The Paradox debugging menu (Alt-F10).**

index, the locate may finish in the blink of an eye. However, table modifications may slow down, or locates may become much slower, depending on the type of index used and how frequently the table is changed.

Once an index has been created, Paradox automatically regenerates the index sometime after the data has changed (e.g., editing a table, adding rows, deleting rows, etc.). Naturally, this regeneration takes time. If a table is changed and queried frequently, the time required for index regenerations may actually hurt performance. Paradox implements two different strategies for updating indexes, and this also affects the performance.

A standard index is generated only when the index is requested (e.g., a query or search on zip code) *and* the data has changed since the last index update. If a table goes through several cycles of changes without using the index, the index will not regenerate. Likewise, if the table later goes through several query cycles without changes to the data, the index will regenerate only after the first query. Often, the first person to use a query after a table has changed will notice the delay. Thereafter, the query will respond at a faster pace.

An incrementally updated index (**Index Maintained**) will update with every change made to a table. Rather than regenerating the entire index, it will make selective changes to the index that reflect the changes to the table. This can make editing a table noticeably slower (although it's not usually a dramatic difference), but queries and locates will not experience regeneration delays. It is best to use incrementally updated indexes first, then switch to standard indexes if such a switch seems warranted. You can force Paradox to use incremental indexes as the default through the Custom Configuration Program (see Appendix E).

When choosing an index type, the editing mode you will use most frequently can also be a factor. In regular Edit (**F9**) mode, the index will not be updated until the changes are processed (**F2**), no matter which index type you choose. Once changes have been made, **Ctrl-Z** will no longer use the index to locate a specific value in the column. However, if you use CoEdit (**Alt-F9**) mode *and* the index is incrementally maintained, the index will be updated as changes are made. For example, if you are correcting misspelled names in a long mailing list and have a maintained index on last names, you can rapidly find the old names by using **Ctrl-Z** in CoEdit mode (see Figure 6.10). **Ctrl-Z** would work in Edit mode, but after the first change it would be *much* slower.

No matter what order is used for storing or viewing data, both Paradox and dBASE can print reports in any arbitrary order that you wish. Although report printing is not a feature governed by the rules for RDBMS (which specifies how data is stored, located, modified, and presented to other programs), reports are certainly an important function in using a database.

Value: Schmitt — CoEdit
Enter value or pattern to search for.

| ADDRESS | Clie | AddNum | First Name | Last Name | Address | City | State |
|---|---|---|---|---|---|---|---|
| 1 | 1 | 1 | Frank | Smith | 345 Weiner Way | Minneapolis | MN |
| 2 | 2 | 1 | Bob | Schmidt | 978 Grill Lane | Bloomington | IN |
| 3 | 3 | 1 | Robin | Jones | 888 Egg Drive | New York | NY |
| 4 | 4 | 1 | Chuck | Schmitt | 555 Bit Ave | Rochester | MN |
| 5 | 5 | 1 | Jack | Spratt | 1212 Steak Ave | Bloomington | MN |
| 6 | 5 | 2 | Jack | Johnson | 2121 Mechanic | Bloomington | MN |

| ANSWER | Clie | AddNum | First Name | Last Name | Address | City | State |
|---|---|---|---|---|---|---|---|
| 1 | 5 | 2 | Jack | Johnson | 2121 Mechanic | Bloomington | MN |
| 2 | 3 | 1 | Robin | Jones | 800 Egg Drive | New York | NY |
| 3 | 2 | 1 | Bob | Schmidt | 978 Grill Lane | Bloomington | IN |
| 4 | 4 | 1 | Chuck | Schmitt | 555 Bit Ave | Rochester | MN |
| 5 | 1 | 1 | Frank | Smith | 345 Weiner Way | Minneapolis | MN |
| 6 | 5 | 1 | Jack | Spratt | 1212 Steak Ave | Bloomington | MN |

**Figure 6.10    Using Ctrl-Z to search for a name in the Last Name column.**

# 7

# Printing Data

Utilities that store and retrieve large amounts of data on your personal computer provide a wonderful way to organize many aspects of your business: accounting, billing, client contact, and more. But you also need utilities to get hard copies of the information. The information you can see on a single computer screen simply cannot compare with several sheets of paper strewn across a desktop (or even in nice piles, if you're more organized). And paper is frequently a more convenient and flexible data exchange format.

So, once you've entered or viewed your data through forms and found something interesting with queries, you'll need to print it out with reports. Like forms, reports are generally associated with a single table, and they add a few features for handling data groups and summaries. Again, because of the ambiguities between rows and columns in a table as opposed to rows and columns on the page, when referring to reports the record/field terminology will be used for tables.

Generally, reports are not considered part of a database management system. But because Paradox implements some of its modeling features through the reports, you should note some of the important structural differences between the multitable forms and reports. The reports forms are accessed through **Reports**, **Design**, *Tablename*, *Reportlabel*, *Report Description*, **Tabular|Free-form**. Similar to forms, the report label may be either the letter "R" or a number (1–14). If you enter the optional report description, it will be included in the report header (although it may be removed or changed once you are in the report design screen). The report style may be either tabular or free form; although tabular is the default, free form can emulate tabular, and it is usually preferable (the differences will be discussed later).

The basics of designing a free-form report are similar to designing forms. And, like the multitable form options, you may define multitable reports, which have a structure resembling a hierarchical database. However, multitable reports are based on the most detailed table of the link, rather than the most general table used by multitable forms. This structure creates problems for many-to-many relationships: Without a basis on the "one" side of the relationship, you cannot use third normal form. Rather, you must build a many-to-many query and use the ANSWER as the detail basis for the report (see "Using Reports on Several Tables" later in the chapter). Details about formatting the report are outlined in Appendix A. For now, we will cover the basics so that you may plan your table structure according to the available features.

Using the invoicing example from the last chapter, you could select the Orders table as the basis: **Reports**, **Design**, **Orders**, **1**, **Invoice**, **Free-form**. Paradox sets up a default report as shown in Figure 7.1. Two differences (compared to forms) that you should note immediately are the lines that say "form" and "page." These are called the form band and page band.

Report bands, such as form and page, divide the report into sections, and all items should be placed between these bands. The line before the page band will print only at the beginning of the report; in fact, you should probably remove the line with **Ctrl-Y** because it will cause the first page to start printing one line lower than the following pages.

```
Designing report R for Orders table                          Report     1/1
Report Header
....+...10....+...20....+...30....+...40....+...50....+...60....+...70....+...8*

 ─▼page───────────────────────────────────────────────────────────────────────



 mm/dd/yy                            Invoice                            Page 99

 ─▼form───────────────────────────────────────────────────────────────────────

 Client Number: AAAAA
 Invoice Number: AAAAA
 Part Number: AAAAA
 Description: AAAAAAAAAAAAAAAAAAAA
 Quantity: 999999
 Unit Price: (999,999,999.99)
 Extended Price: (999,999,999.99)

 ─▲form───────────────────────────────────────────────────────────────────────
```

**Figure 7.1    Paradox default free-form report layout.**

The form band is the section that is repeated for every single row in the table. As it stands now, for each record, the report will print a blank line, followed by a line for each field, followed by another blank line. Thus, the field contents will be printed on separate lines with two blank lines in between each row (one at the end of a record and another at the beginning of the next record).

The areas between the form and page bands (at the top and bottom of the screen) will print at the top and bottom of each page. This establishes the top and bottom margin, as well as any page labels. The default report places the current date, report title, and page number at the top of each page. A report may have nested group bands between the page and form bands; the groups sort and summarize the data on specific field values or ranges. Group bands make the report behave something like a sorted View. Each report may have a different sort order; the report sorting does not affect the order of the base tables.

The ORDERS table does not have enough information to print a complete invoice. The most important items missing from the table (and hence the report) are the billing and shipping addresses. This creates the first major stumbling block: Billing and shipping addresses are necessary. The billing and shipping address codes are located in the INVOICE table, but the actual addresses are stored in the ADDRESS table. As with forms, reports cannot use nested links. There is no address number link in the ORDER table, so the link cannot be made. While this relation worked when designing the multitable form, the different conceptual model for reports has "broken" the design.

To work around the problem, you must create an intermediate table with a more direct relation to details of ORDER. Figure 7.2 shows a query and ANSWER that provide the necessary structure. However, multitable reports require indexed summary tables (and ANSWER is never indexed). You can create an intermediate table (INVREP) that is always indexed, and add the results from ANSWER into the intermediate table (details about creating this table and report definition appear in Appendix A). If Paradox supported true view definitions, you would not need these intermediate tables and report definition would be greatly simplified.

Figure 7.3 shows a completed report definition for an invoice. Note the group on Invoice number that sorts the printout by Invoice number. The area between "group" and "form" prints summary information for each order (address data at the top and totals at the bottom). A sample of the resulting pages appears in Figure 7.4.

```
Viewing Answer table: Record 1 of 5                                    Main
INVOICE┬═Invoice══╤═Date══╤══Client Number══╤═Billing Address══╤═Shipping Address═
       ║ⓥ         ║ⓥ      ║ⓥ cn             ║ cnb              ║ cns
```

```
ADDRESS┬Client┬AddNum┬═First Name══╤══Last Name══╤══Address══╤══City══╤══Stat
       ║ cn   ║ cnb  ║ⓥ as First B ║ⓥ as Last B  ║ⓥ as Add B ║ⓥ as City B ║ⓥ as S
       ║ cn   ║ cns  ║ⓥ as First S ║ⓥ as Last S  ║ⓥ as Add S ║ⓥ as City S ║ⓥ as S
```

```
ANSWER┬═Invoice═╤════Date════╤═Clie╤First B══╤══Last B═══╤════════Add B═══════╤══Cit
   1  ║ 1       ║ 10/22/90   ║ 4   ║ Chuck   ║ Schmitt   ║ 555 Bit Ave        ║ Rochest
   2  ║ 2       ║ 10/22/90   ║ 2   ║ Bob     ║ Schmidt   ║ 978 Grill Lane     ║ Bloomin
   3  ║ 3       ║ 10/22/90   ║ 2   ║ Bob     ║ Schmidt   ║ 978 Grill Lane     ║ Bloomin
   4  ║ 4       ║ 10/22/90   ║ 3   ║ Robin   ║ Jones     ║ 888 Egg Drive      ║ New Yor
   5  ║ 5       ║ 10/22/90   ║ 5   ║ Jack    ║ Spratt    ║ 1212 Steak Ave     ║ Bloomin
```

Figure 7.2   Query to produce invoice summary information.

```
Changing report R for Orders table                         Report      1/1
Group Header for Invoice Number           [Invrep->first b]+" "+[Invrep->last b]
....+...10....+...20....+...30....+...40....+...50....+...60....+...70....+...8*
                                  Invoice
─────▼group Invoice Number──────────────────────────────────────────────────
Invoice Number: AAAAA

    Order date: mm/dd/yy

Bill to:                                  Ship to:
AAAAAAAAAAAAAAAAAAAAAAAAAAAAAAAA          AAAAAAAAAAAAAAAAAAAAAAAAAAAAAAAA
AAAAAAAAAAAAAAAAAAAAAAAAAA                AAAAAAAAAAAAAAAAAAAAAAAAAA
AAAAAAAAAAAAAAAAAAAAAAAAAA                AAAAAAAAAAAAAAAAAAAAAAAAAA

                                     Unit
Part    Description           Quan   Price      Total
─────▼form─────────────────────────────────────────────────────────────────
AAAAA AAAAAAAAAAAAAAAAAAAA 999999 (999.99) (9,999.99)
─────▲form─────────────────────────────────────────────────────────────────
                                          ──────────
                                          (9,999.99)

PAGEBREAK
─────▲group Invoice Number──────────────────────────────────────────────────
```

Figure 7.3   Final invoice report design.

```
                              Invoice

     Invoice Number: 4

          Order date: 10/22/90

     Bill to:                    Ship to:
     Robin Jones                 Robin Jones
     888 Egg Drive               888 Egg Drive
     New York, NY 10021          New York, NY 10021

                                      Unit
     Part    Description       Quan   Price     Total
     ---------------------------------------------------
     7       Parakeet Cage       2    10.00     20.00
                                                ---------
                                                20.00




                              Invoice

     Invoice Number: 5

          Order date: 10/22/90

     Bill to:                    Ship to:
     Jack Spratt                 Jack Johnson
     1212 Steak Ave              7121 Mechanic Ave
     Bloomington, MN 55420       Bloomington, MN 55420

                                      Unit
     Part    Description       Quan   Price     Total
     -----   ----------------------------------------
     8       Plates              5    10.00      50.00
     9       Bacon (Crates)      2   100.00     200.00
                                                ---------
                                                250.00
```

**Figure 7.4    The last two pages of the Paradox Invoice printout.**

## Using Reports on Several Tables

As noted earlier, reports do not really fall under the scope of database management. Rather, they are often considered a language-specific feature. However, Paradox treats a report as part of the object (table) definition; each report is connected to a specific table. This is often confusing to novice Paradox users who want to create a report that can be used with several tables. For example, the PHONE table may have a report that prints a phone directory. But perhaps a phone directory for a single city or state is the general goal; not an entire directory. In such a case, create a query to select the desired rows. But the resulting ANSWER table will have no report definitions.

As long as the ANSWER table matches the structure of an existing table (in this case, the PHONE table), you can copy the report definition with **Tools, Copy, Report, DifferentTable,** *Source Table, Source Report Number, Destination Table, Destination Report Number.* In many cases, the resulting ANSWER does not resemble any existing table. If the structure of the ANSWER is one that you will be using repeatedly, you can create a template table (for example **Tools, Copy, Table, Answer, Template,** followed by **Tools, More, Empty, Template**), and then design a report for the template. Then, every time you need a report for a similarly structured ANSWER, you can copy the report definition from the template to the ANSWER table.

If there are several reports to copy, or you want to include other items such as forms in the copy, you may use **Tools, Copy, JustFamily,** *Source Table, Destination Table.* The **JustFamily** copy will copy all reports, forms, integrity constraints, and settings from one table to another. As a general rule, use the **JustFamily** copy rather than **Reports** or **Forms** because it is so much more convenient (fewer steps). However, there are cases where **JustFamily** should be avoided. For example, if the destination table has existing reports that might be overwritten, you may want to specify the particular report to copy, and possibly give it a different report number in the destination table.

## dBASE

The View feature of dBASE makes reports simpler than Paradox (although, as already seen, views are severely limited for use with forms). You can simply create a view with all of the required links, and then design a report for that view. For the examples, new dBASE tables were created to match ORDERS and INVOICE from the Paradox examples. Note that the query requires two links to ADDRESS, one for the billing address and the second for the shipping address. You create the separate links by placing two copies of the ADDRESS query image on the query form, as shown in Figure 7.5. Note that dBASE prompts for a unique name for the second use of a field. The remainder of the query is shown in Figure 7.6.

Remember that, unlike a Paradox multitable form or report, the view is visible as a single table. Each invoice is now more than a single row and repeats

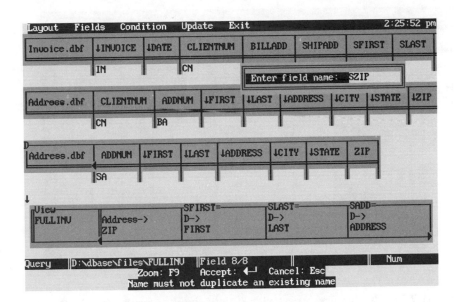

**Figure 7.5  Multiple Address links established for the Invoice report view.**

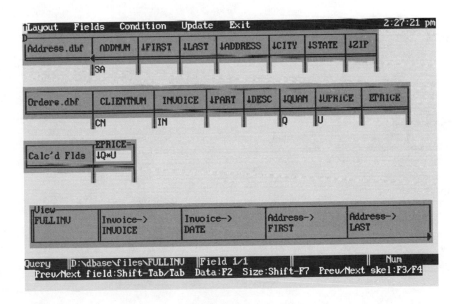

**Figure 7.6  The complete view definition linking Invoice, Address, and Orders.**

```
  Records   Organize   Fields   Go To   Exit

 INVOICE DATE      FIRST LAST    ADDRESS        CITY        STATE ZIP    SFIRST S
 2       10/22/90 Bob   Schmidt 978 Grill Lane Bloomington IN    47401  Bob    S
 2       10/22/90 Bob   Schmidt 978 Grill Lane Bloomington IN    47401  Bob    S
 3       10/22/90 Bob   Schmidt 978 Grill Lane Bloomington IN    47401  Bob    S
 3       10/22/90 Bob   Schmidt 978 Grill Lane Bloomington IN    47401  Bob    S
 4       10/22/90 Robin Jones   888 Egg Drive  New York    NY    10021  Robin  J
 1       10/22/90 Chuck Schmitt 555 Bit Ave    Rochester   MN    54901  Chuck  S
 1       10/22/90 Chuck Schmitt 555 Bit Ave    Rochester   MN    54901  Chuck  S
 5       10/22/90 Jack  Spratt  1212 Steak Ave Bloomington MN    55420  Jack   J
 5       10/22/90 Jack  Spratt  1212 Steak Ave Bloomington MN    55420  Jack   J




 Browse   D:\dbase\files\FULLINV   Rec 1/9        View  ReadOnly    Num
```

Figure 7.7   The Invoice report view—note the data replication in the
first few columns. While this replication would make data modification
difficult, it is normal for reporting.

```
 Layout   Fields   Bands   Words   Go To   Print   Exit          7:29:09 pm
 [.....▼.1....▼..2...▼...3.▼......▼..▼.....▼.5....▼..6...▼....7.▼.....
                      INVOICE
 Report    Intro  Band
 Group  1  Intro  Band
 Invoice: XXXXXX
    Date: MM/DD/YY

 Bill to:                        Ship to:
 XXXXXXXXXXXXXXXXXXXXXXXXXXXX     XXXXXXXXXXXXXXXXXXXXXXXX
 XXXXXXXXXXXXXXXXXXXXXXXX         XXXXXXXXXXXXXXXXXXXXXXXX
 XXXXXXXXXXXXXXXXXXXXXXXX         XXXXXXXXXXXXXXXXXXXXXXXX

 Part # Quan Description           Price     Price

 Detail          Band
 XXXXXX 9999 XXXXXXXXXXXXXXXXXXXX 9,999.99 99,999.99
 Group  1  Summary Band

                                            99,999.99
 Report    D:\dbase\files\INVREP   Line:1 Col:42   View:FULLINV   Num    Ins
           Add field:F5  Select:F6  Move:F7  Copy:F8  Size:Shift-F7
```

Figure 7.8   The dBASE report definition based on the Invoice View.

all of the one-to-one information (such as shipping and billing addresses). Although there are several replicated columns within the view, this data replication does not use disk space. The result of the view is shown in Figure 7.7. As with Paradox reports, you may select grouping operations to summarize the repeated data. But with dBASE you have the advantage that links are not required—any relationship that can be defined in a View may be exploited in the report. The report definition, shown in Figure 7.8 is nearly identical in layout to the Paradox definition.

## Summary

Reports are usually considered a programming extension to the database. Although most modern database tools include a report generator similar to those used by dBASE and Paradox, it usually generates programming code that is used to print a report. In fact, this is the approach used by dBASE: When you finish designing a report, you will see messages indicating that dBASE is compiling it. A tool such as a report or form generator will not always give you the flexibility you need for input and output. Furthermore, it may not give you enough power for effective integration of your database tasks. Once you have mastered reports, forms, and design, you should add at least some programming skills to your repertoire.

# 8

# Programs

When reading about database systems, you may find references to two different languages. There is a relational language used by the database (Codd calls this RL), and the programming, or *host language* (the topic of this chapter). The relational language is the query language; for dBASE and Paradox, this is Query by Example. dBASE and Paradox also provide limited support for SQL (Structured Query Language), another relational language used by many different database systems.

Writing such programs in a general-purpose host language requires a proficiency in the language used. dBASE and Paradox take another approach: building a language into the database system. This can help overcome some of the deficiencies of the database itself (deficiencies in terms of the features advocated by Codd). And, since programming is part of the database package, it has tools that can help you write programs.

The introduction to queries showed that both dBASE and Paradox lack an explicit relational assignment operator. With a host programming language, you can record the steps necessary to copy or rename the result query. This program then has the effect of a relational assignment operator. If structured properly, it can become a general-purpose *subroutine* that can be called from other programs. In effect, you can create your own relational operators to replace features that are missing in the basic set.

But programming involves much more than replacing missing relational components. Even in a "perfect" system, programming would play an important role. The features of a database management system are complete enough to build a working application. You can create tables, add or change the data in tables, find specific information, and design forms and reports. But as you are probably beginning to realize, although a database simplifies data management, there are still many steps that you must use to create the final (or recurring) reports that you will need from the system. Many of these steps are repetitive: add orders; at the end of the day, find new orders; print the new orders. "Surely," you think, "there must be some shortcuts." And there are: You can write programs.

Programs, a sequence of instructions that performs repetitive tasks, are not a part of Codd's definition of a database system. In fact, the database itself is a file manager and programming tasks are assigned to general-purpose host languages such as COBOL, FORTRAN, PL/I, C, Pascal, and BASIC. Such an approach works best with a tight integration of the database and operating system, as if DOS itself ran the database as a natural extension of opening, writing, and closing files. Such functionality is more common in the world of minicomputers and mainframes than in PCs. But, OS/2 is making progress in this area with database servers.

Programming plays an important role in any database system, and to design database systems effectively, it is crucial that you understand programming basics (even if you will not be writing most of the programs yourself). Paradox calls programs *scripts*; and if you use Lotus 1-2-3, you may be familiar with the term *macros*. dBASE makes a distinction between programs (which are named) and macros (which are assigned to a function key). Paradox requires names for all scripts, although special procedures may be assigned to particular key combinations. dBASE and Paradox take very different approaches with their programming features. The heart of dBASE lies at the "dot prompt," whereas Paradox is built around its menu system.

Nevertheless, there are certain programming concepts that apply to most languages, whether they are application specific (as is the case with Paradox and dBASE), or more general purpose (such as C, BASIC, and Pascal). Once you have learned a programming language, each additional language becomes easier to learn. Most of the popular programming languages are procedural; they have a starting point and execute steps sequentially. Frequently, each line in a program listing consists of a single step (or a few related steps such as item selections from a menu).

Each language supports comparison operations (to compare two items) and logical operations (to combine comparisons). Similar operations were illustrated in database queries. But, rather than selecting rows from tables, a comparison statement within a program becomes the basis of a decision, which can alter the execution order of the program steps. For example, if an invoice has been paid, you could tell the program to skip a section of the program that calculates finance charges on delinquent accounts.

When a programming language is application specific, the design of the application flavors the programming language. For example, dBASE was originally a command-based system. It presented a dot (akin to the C> prompt of DOS) at which you typed special sentences called commands (commands are words, such as **Copy** that tell a system to perform an operation). The side effects show through: Sometimes dBASE displays the individual commands in a box when using the menus (for example, try a **re-index**), and several commands and options are not available through the menu system.

Likewise the side effects of the Paradox menu system affect its programming language. Where dBASE uses simple commands for all of its tasks, Paradox emulates the menu system within its language. For example, menu commands are placed in curly braces:

```
{Tools} {Copy} {Table} {Address} {Answer}
```

Paradox does have direct commands for the more common operations: **Copy "Address" "Answer"**, or **Rename "Address" "Answer"** (commands that you can substitute for relational assignment). But, if you turn on the system trace, you will still see Paradox step through the menu as if the entire command sequence had been entered.

At the simplest level, you may simply start recording a script (or macro), save it, and then later recall it to repeat the sequence. In dBASE, you start macro recording from the opening screen with **Tools, Macros, BeginRecording,** *FunctionKey*. Perform the sequence of commands you wish to record and then hit **Shift-F10, E** to end the recording. You should save the macro with **Tools, Macros, Save library,** *LibraryName*. Now you can replay the macro with **Alt-***FunctionKey*. If you want to record a macro from within another area of dBASE (such as the form design screen) you may use **Shift-F10, Begin recording**. To use the macros in another session, you must load the macro library with **Tools, Macros, Load library,** *LibraryName*.

Paradox can also record keystrokes. To begin recording, hit either **Alt-F3** or select **Scripts, BeginRecord,** *ScriptName* from the menu. Enter the sequence to record, and hit **Alt-F3** (or **Scripts, EndRecord**) when you are done. If you use the **Alt-F3** method for recording, the script will be given the name *Instant*. You may later change this name with **Tools, Rename, Script, Instant,** *NewName*. To recall the script, use **Scripts, Play,** *ScriptName*. Unlike dBASE, assigning the script to a function key is not straightforward (though it is possible).

With both dBASE and Paradox, the key sequences will be recorded *exactly* as you type them. If you use cursor controls, your cursor movements will be recorded; if you type letters or spell out filenames, the letters and names will be recorded. But remember that database operations should not rely on position, so it is imperative that you not use cursor movement whenever possible. Cursor movement can keep a sequence from operating properly when the environment changes. For example, if a list of files changes (and it almost certainly will) the cursor may no longer move to the correct file. Or, if a later version of the program changes the menus, the cursor motion sequence may no longer select the correct menu choices.

As a simple example, consider a Paradox script that pulls up a query form for ADDRESS, checks all the fields, unchecks the first field, and then processes the query. The final recorded script is:

```
{Ask} {Address} Check Right Check Do_It!
```

Note that only menu commands appear in brackets. Key names are spelled without any extraneous punctuation (thus, Right is the right cursor arrow). Paradox assigns special names to the function keys. In this example, *Check* for **F6**, and *Do_It!* for **F2**. It's difficult to move around in a query form without using the cursor, hence this shortcoming in the script. If the table structure were to change, the first field (the one that is unchecked) might be different. For this reason, it's generally preferable to use **Scripts**, **QuerySave**. However, as you'll see later, there are even better methods for programming queries.

Paradox scripts are stored as simple text files. If you prefer, you can load them into your favorite editor or word processing program to change them. Or you can use the Paradox Editor with **Scripts**, **Editor**, **Edit**, *ScriptName*. dBASE, on the other hand, records macros in a more compact, coded form. They may be edited with **Tools**, **Macros**, **Modify**, *FunctionKey*. dBASE programs (detailed below) are stored as standard ASCII files and may be edited with your favorite program.

Consider a simple dBASE macro that opens the view FULLINV and then prints the associated report INVREP (opening the view isn't strictly necessary in dBASE). The macro recorded:

```
{rightarrow}fullinv{Enter}
u{rightarrow}{rightarrow}invrep{Enter}
pv
```

dBASE uses curly braces around the special key names (such as the cursors and Enter key). File and menu choices are simply recorded as plain text. The cursor keys are required when moving around the control panel (for example, right to the Query column, then right twice more to the Report column). After selecting FULLINV, the letter "u" selects **Use view**. And, after selecting the INVREP report, "pv" selects **Print Report**, **View report on screen**.

In both the Paradox and dBASE recorded sequences, cursor codes create potential problems. When recording keyboard activity, it is almost impossible to work without some use of the cursor. But the insertion of cursor control sequences is not the only problem with recorded macros. During the recording process, the programs will save every keystroke, whether or not it is correct. While you can usually back out of a wrong menu choice or improper action, the whole sequence is recorded for posterity. This can hinder performance, sometimes severely (e.g., processing a view or query, realizing it's not quite correct, and then processing again). Of course, you can always use the editor to remove extraneous commands, but when you have recorded a long sequence, it can be difficult to comprehend.

There is yet another disadvantage to recording a command sequence: It is difficult to conditionally alter the execution sequence. What if the next step depends on the result of the previous step? For example, if you process a query and there are no results, you might want to try a different query or simply halt the process rather than print an empty page.

Scripts and macros can be a useful tool for recording short sequences and learning some basics behind the programming process. This is particularly true of Paradox where the script recording process creates a program. In dBASE, macros and programs share few similarities. In either case, a program can call the recorded sequence. But Paradox is unique in that a recorded script may be changed into a true program.

The Paradox Application Language (PAL) is a good starting point for programming examples because the Paradox menu system is so tightly intc grated with recorded scripts. Although Paradox has an automatic application generator (which is more useful than automatic recording), it is difficult to get the fine level of control that is sometimes necessary in programming an application. While it is possible to modify the generated code, you must figure out how the code works. In the long run, it is often easier to write your own application so you have a "feel" for the way the system works.

You can write PAL scripts two ways: Call the editor from Paradox, or use your own word processor or editor outside of Paradox. With the latter approach, you must save the file without any formatting codes (your word processing program may call this ASCII, text-only, or non-document mode). When the script is saved, it must have a file extension of .SC (as in FOOBAR.SC). The PAL editor is started by selecting **Scripts**, **Editor**, **Write**, *ScriptName* (for a new script), or **Scripts**, **Editor**, **Edit**, *ScriptName* (to change an existing script).

You can customize Paradox to call your own word processor from the **Scripts**, **Editor** menu (see Appendix E). Use this approach if you will be writing many scripts. The PAL Editor simply does not provide enough features for extensive use. For example, you cannot copy or move blocks of text, or search and replace text. In fact, beyond basic insertion (by typing) and deletion of text, all you can do is merge an entire file into the current file. There is but one advantage to the PAL Editor: When you are running a script and it stops because of an error, it will take you to the line that caused the error. If you use your own editor, you may lose this capability, although there are several on the market that do support this feature.

A short section of code that makes a copy of a table should give you an idea how program development works. It will also demonstrate several of the concepts behind programming: commands, variables, procedures, functions, input, output, loops, and conditions.

As shown previously, Paradox uses curly braces to enclose menu selections. Thus, {Ask} {Address} works like selecting **Ask**, **Address** from the menu. You may prefix menu commands with the word **Menu**:

```
Menu {Ask} {Address}
```

The **Menu** command acts like the **F10** key. However, if Paradox is not already displaying the menu, the first command in braces will automatically generate an **F10**. In some respects, this makes the **Menu** command optional. In general don't include it in scripts,;however, there are times when it helps to include it. The **Menu** command will always take Paradox to the base menu. If you happen to miss a selection, this will keep Paradox from getting "stuck" on a command.

For example, some menus ask for **Cancel** or **Replace** if a file is about to be overwritten. **{Tools} {Copy} {Table} {Foo} {Bar}** will work, as long as the table BAR does not exist. But, if BAR does exist, Paradox expects **{Cancel}** or **{Replace}** as the next selection:

```
{Tools} {Copy} {Table} {Foo} {Bar}
{Ask} {Bar}
```

The above will cause an error because **Ask** is not a possible menu choice. But replacing the second line with **Menu {Ask} {Bar}** would return to the main menu, thus cancelling the copy operation from the previous line, and continue executing the program. Usually, you will want the program to stop with an error (one reason to avoid **Menu** in your scripts), but there are a few situations where **Menu**'s automatic **Cancel** is useful.

Frequently, an automatic **Replace** is more useful than an automatic **Cancel**. There are also long command sequences that are repeated many times in a program, and the typing overhead becomes significant. Paradox solves both of these problems with special shortcut commands (which are simply called *commands*). **{Tools} {Copy} {Table} {*OldTable*} {*NewTable*}** is a good example, because you will use it over and over again (as a substitute for **relational assignment**). As a shortcut, PAL lets you use **Copy** *OldTable NewTable* (all of the commands generate an automatic **Replace**, if the new file already exists).

The commands require that object names (in this case, filenames) be enclosed in quotes. Thus,

```
{Tools} {Copy} {Table} {Foo} {Bar} {Replace}
```

translates to:

```
Copy "Foo" "Bar"
```

Why place object names in quotation marks? Because programming languages allow *variables*. Variables hold a name to be used in the variable's place. Thus, we could create a variable called Table1 that holds the value "Bar". A language must be able to distinguish a variable from the actual name. For text, this is accomplished by placing quotes around a name and typing a variable name without quotes. So, how do you create a variable and assign it a value? In PAL this is one step: Simply type the name of the variable followed by an equal sign (some languages require separate *declaration* and *assignment* commands).

```
Table1 = "Bar"
```

creates a variable named Table1 (unless it already existed) and assigns the value "Bar". If Table1 already held a value, the old value is replaced with "Bar".

We can now use the variable name in place of the text.

```
Table1 = "Bar"
Copy "Foo" Table1
```

makes a copy of the FOO table called BAR.

Variable names always begin with a letter. This allows an automatic distinction between numbers and variables without requiring quotation marks around numbers. In fact, it allows another distinction between numeric and alphanumeric: **12345** is the number one thousand two hundred twenty-five, but

**"12345"** is a sequence (*string*) of characters. If that's not quite clear, consider the example:

```
A = 12345 + 1
B = "12345" + "1"
```

**A** is the number 12,346, but **B** is the character string "123451". In Paradox, the additive operator (+) adds two numbers or appends one string to another. You cannot mix the two:

```
C = 12345 + "1"
```

will cause an error. The quotation marks make a clear distinction between text and numbers, just as they distinguish variable names and text. A variable may hold data of any *type* (text, numeric, or date) and Paradox will remember which type a variable holds. You can even reassign a variable with a different type, as in:

```
A = 12345
A = "12345"
```

Sometimes, you will need characters within a string that will confuse PAL or that cannot be entered from the keyboard  For example, since  a string is enclosed in quotation marks, you cannot simply include a quotation mark in the string. And other control characters, such as escape, will perform an action (such as bringing up the menu). Paradox defines special backslash sequences to enclose such characters within a string. If you know the ASCII code, you can simply type the three-digit decimal code after the backslash (e.g., \027 is Escape). The following abbreviations may be used for some of the more common characters:

| Code | Character |
|------|-----------|
| \\ | Backslash |
| \n | Linefeed (newline) |
| \r | Carriage return |
| \f | Formfeed |
| \" | Quotation mark |
| \t | Tab |

Any other character which follows a backslash will be taken literally, e.g., "\B"="B". Remember \\; you will use it frequently in directory names, e.g., "c:\\paradox\\account\\address".

Many languages require a variable to retain the same type throughout a program (such languages are called *strongly typed*); Paradox is *weakly typed*. Variables allow a section of program code to be generalized; i.e., it can then be used for several different purposes. However, to use a portion of code for many tasks, you must be able to arbitrarily *call* the fragment from anywhere in the program. Such a fragment is called a procedure. In PAL, you define a fragment as a procedure by surrounding the fragment with **Proc** and **Endproc**. Procedures are named like variables, but unlike variables, procedure names are followed by parentheses, as in Foobar ( ). The parentheses may optionally enclose a list of variables, which are *passed* to the procedure; this list is called a *parameter list*.

Following through with the table copy example, the function of the **Copy** command could be duplicated with a procedure. Call the procedure **TCopy**, and pass a source table (STable) and a destination table (DTable).

```
PROC TCopy (STable, DTable)
    {Tools} {Copy} {Table}
    Select STable
    Select DTable
    {Replace}
ENDPROC
```

The **Select** command enters a menu choice from a variable. If {STable} and {DTable} had been used, Paradox would have looked for a table called STABLE and created a table called DTABLE. Another item that you will see used in the sample programs is the comment character (a semicolon). Anything following a semi-colon is ignored by PAL, unless it is within quotation marks, where it is treated as text. This lets you document a program by adding notes as you write.

PAL also ignores extraneous space, so you can indent lines to make the program easier to read (of course, at least one space is required to separate elements such as variable names and commands). PAL also treats separate lines as space; with very few exceptions, you may start a new line any time a space would be required.

There is a problem with the TCopy procedure: It defaults to **Replace**, but if the table does not exist, the menu will not present a **Replace** option and Paradox will generate an error. The procedure needs to "look" at the menu and "decide" whether to select **Replace**. In addition to commands, PAL has *functions* that return information about Paradox. Within a program, functions look similar to procedures, but in addition to accepting parameters, they can *return* values. **Menuchoice** ( ) is a function that returns the text that is currently highlighted on the menu. If the menu is not present, it returns the string "Error".

Note: PAL variable names and function names are *case insensitive*. You may mix upper- and lowercase letters in whatever combination you please (an uppercase letter at the beginning of each new word is often helpful), and Paradox will recognize the name. Unlike names, however, values are *case sensitive*: "Error" is *not* the same as "error".

Now that you have a method for checking the menu, you need a command to alter the program execution (to select the proper response). Languages include controls called *conditional statements*. The simplest conditional is the **If... EndIf** statement (ellipses will be used to designate a control block such as **Proc... EndProc**). The condition itself is placed between an **If... Then** block. If the condition is true, the code block will be executed; if not, the code block will be skipped. Any of the comparison operators (such as <, >, =, <=, etc.) will return a value of True or False that may be used with a conditional statement. Several of the PAL functions return truth values, too.

---

*Paradox Comparison Operators:*

---

| | |
|---|---|
| = | Equal |
| > | Greater than |
| < | Less than |
| >= | Greater than or equal to |
| <= | Less than or equal to |
| <> | Not equal |

---

Several conditions may be combined to form an *expression*. Logical values (True and False) have a special set of logical operators, which combine to form a single logical value. These logical operators are: **And, Or**, and the special operator **Not**. Not takes only one operand and reverses its value; thus, **Not True** is False, and **Not False** is True (makes sense, doesn't it?).

**And** returns True only if both operands are True (**True And True=True**). **Or** returns True if either operand is True (**False Or True=True**). The results of logical operations are usually expressed in truth tables:

*AND Truth Table*

False AND False = False
False AND True = False
True AND False = False
True AND True = True

*OR Truth Table*

False OR False = False
False OR True = True
True OR False = True
True OR True = True

Of course, any conditional expression that evaluates to True or False may replace the value of True or False. Thus, statements can be expressed as:

```
If MenuChoice()="Cancel" OR McnuChoice()="Replace"
Then
    {Replace}
EndIf
```

Now, you can add a conditional block to make the procedure work just like the Copy command:

```
Proc TCopy (STable, DTable)
    {Tools} {Copy} {Table}
    Select STable
    Select DTable
    If MenuChoice()="Cancel" Then
        {Replace}
    EndIf
EndProc
```

To call a procedure, simply type its name and parameter list. The parameters in the calling statement need not have the same names as the procedure definition (you may even use string constants). The parameter (variable) names are said to be *local* to the procedure; i.e., they are not defined outside the procedure block (that's not precisely true, but close enough for now).

You may define additional local variables by placing a **Private** statement immediately after the **Proc** definition line.  Following **Private** simply list the names of the variables you want to keep local:

```
Proc DummyProc ()
    Private ThisVar, ThatVar

    ThisVar=5           ;Only defined within this procedure
    ThatVar="Local"

EndProc
```

You cannot call a procedure before it's defined, so most PAL programmers place all of their procedure definitions at the beginning of the program (until they learn to write procedure libraries).  A program that defines and uses the TCopy procedure to copy the Address table to two tables (Test1 and Test2) might look like this:

```
Proc TCopy (STable, DTable)
    {Tools} {Copy} {Table}
    Select STable
    Select DTable
    If MenuChoice()="Cancel" Then
        {Replace}
    EndIf
EndProc

TCopy ("Address", "Test1")
T2 = "Test2"
TCopy ("Address", T2)
```

You may optionally include an **Else** statement within the **If... EndIf** block.  Lines between **Else** and **EndIf** will execute only if the statement is not true.  Thus, you could test for no Cancel/Replace menu by writing the conditional block as:

```
If MenuChoice()="Error" Then
    ;Don't do anything if no menu is present
    ;By the way, as mentioned earlier,
    ;these are comments
Else
    {Replace}
```

```
EndIf
```

While many conditionals may be based on the system status (such as current menu conditions or specific data in tables), sometimes a program must get a response from the user.  The program must have a way of retrieving user *input*. And the user needs feedback from system *output*.  At its most basic level, you can instruct PAL to move the cursor to a particular location on the screen and print a line of text.  The @ symbol, followed by two numbers, gives the starting point in rows down and columns across.  The **??** prints a line beginning at the starting point (**?** will print one line below the starting point).

For example, the program could prompt the user for a table name by printing a message at the top of the screen:

```
@ 1,1
?? "Which table do you want to copy? "
```

To retrieve input, PAL provides the **Accept** command.  You must specify a data type for **Accept**: alphanumeric (and its size), numeric, and currency. These are abbreviated as in table creation:  "A#", "N", "D", and "$".  You must also specify a variable to receive the input:

```
@ 1,1 ?? "Which table do you want to copy? "
Accept "A8" To Source
```

Paradox will display the question and wait for the user to enter a response (which must be eight or fewer alphanumeric characters).  Note the space after the "?" in the prompt—this keeps the response one space away from the "?". If no response is given, or the user hits the Esc key, PAL will set a special reserved variable called **RetVal** (for **Return Value**) to False.  If a response is entered, **RetVal** will be True (this feature will be used soon).

You may place additional restrictions on **Accept,** if you wish.  These generally follow the same rules as the Validity Checks (see Chapter 2).  You may use as many or as few of the validity checks as you need. The following statement would force characters to uppercase, with one number or letter followed by up to five digits; check the input against the client table; default to 1; and require a response (no blank entry allowed):

```
Accept "A6" Picture "!*5[#]" Min "0" Max "Z99999"
Lookup "Address" Default "1" Required To ClientNum
```

Note that **Lookup** will only check a value against a table, it will not present a list of choices if the help key (**F1**) is pressed.

If you need direct table input and output, PAL supports a **Wait** command, which gives the user limited access to the current table. **Wait** has three forms: **Wait Field**, **Wait Record**, and **Wait Table**. These limit access to the current row and column, the current row, and any entry in the current table, respectively. All function keys are disabled; the command requires a list of **Until** keys that signal the end of the **Wait**. You should also specify a **Prompt** message to appear at the top of the screen. Additionally, you may specify a **Message**, which will appear briefly in the lower-right portion of the screen.

Prior to using **Wait**, the PAL script must place an image on the workspace (usually with **View**, **Edit**, or **CoEdit**). Paradox must be in Edit or CoEdit mode for the user to enter or alter data. After the **Wait**, you may need to process the terminating keystroke (the key pressed will be returned in the reserved variable **RetVal**).

Consider the following example, which places the INVOICE table on the workspace in Edit mode. The user is prompted to make changes and press the **F2** key to accept the changes, or **F10** to cancel. The script then processes the terminating keystroke.

```
Edit "Invoice"
Wait Table
   Prompt "Hit F2 to accept or F10 to cancel"
   Until "F2", "F10"

If RetVal = "F2" Then
     Do_It!       ;The command for the F2 key
   Else
     CancelEdit    ;The command for {Cancel} {OK}
EndIf
```

You may also place a table in form view before the **Wait** using either **FormKey** or **PickForm** *FormNumber* (see the descriptions in Appendix C). Multitable forms present a problem because they require **F3** and **F4** (**UpImage** and **DownImage**) to move from one table to the next. But the function keys are disabled by **Wait**. To work around this, you must add the **F3** and **F4** keys (or whichever keys you want to substitute) to the **Until** list. Then take the appropriate action and return to **Wait**.

You have now seen all of the elements that build a program, except one. Many tasks are repetitive in nature, as with the multitable wait process mentioned above. Rather than use **Scripts**, **Play** every time you want to repeat a task, you can build a loop.  Normally, program execution proceeds from the top of the instruction list to the bottom.  A loop returns execution to a higher position.  In some languages, you may tell execution to move to any arbitrary line (this is usually called a **Goto** instruction).  Paradox does not allow such operations: rather; you mark the beginning and end of a block (much like an **If... EndIf**), and specify a condition that repeats execution of the block.

The simplest loop is called a **While** loop, and the block is marked with **While... EndWhile**.  The loop will execute until the condition (which is placed immediately after the **While**) is false.  Sometimes, before the execution of the loop has completed, you may need to jump out past the end or loop back to the beginning.  The **Loop** command returns to the **While** statement, and the **QuitLoop** command jumps directly to the line after the **EndWhile**.

Suppose you want to place a multitable form on the workspace and loop back to the **Wait** until the process is completed or cancelled.  You could modify the preceding script as follows:

```
Edit "Invoice"
FormKey            ;Toggle the default form

RetVal=""          ;Required to enter the loop

While RetVal<>"F2" And RetVal<>"F10"

   Wait Table
      Prompt "Hit F2 to accept or F10 to cancel"
      Until "F2", "F3", "F4", "F10"

   ;There are better ways to do this than consecutive
   ;Ifs, but it will do for now

   If RetVal="F3" Then
      UpImage
   EndIf
   If RetVal="F4" Then
      DownImage
   EndIf

EndWhile

If RetVal = "F2" Then
    Do_It!          ;The command for the F2 key
   Else
```

```
      CancelEdit      ;The command for {Cancel} {OK}
EndIf
```

Note how the lines within the **While... EndWhile** have been indented. Additionally, the sections have been separated with blank lines. This makes reading the code (and finding the starting and ending points) much easier. The indentation is not required, but it is a convention followed by most programmers. As an interesting aside, you might want to compare this program to the similar multifile dBASE form manager in Chapter 9.

## dBASE Commands

Most of the programming concepts used in Paradox PAL programs apply to dBASE. The semantic aspects are a bit different, especially with respect to variable and table names within a command line. Additionally, the entire workspace concept is very different in dBASE. When working in the menus, dBASE does not even have a workspace, per se. You can access only one table or view at a time. To really use the full power of dBASE, you must work from the dot prompt (similar to running commands from the DOS command line prompt C>). Additional details about accessing and using dot prompt usage can be found in Appendix B.

Once you are at the dBASE dot prompt, the available commands are somewhat similar to the Paradox PAL script commands, but dBASE works at a much lower level than Paradox—you must explicitly instruct dBASE to perform many of the operations Paradox handles automatically. For example, a simple **View "Address"** command places the ADDRESS table on the Paradox workspace and lets you browse through it. In dBASE, you must first open the file with **Use "Address"** and then **Browse**. **Browse** does not require a name because it always applies to the table currently in use.

In other respects, **Use** is analogous to the PAL **View** command. You may still navigate through the table (e.g., move to new rows), but you will not see the results until you perform another operation such as **Browse** or **Edit**.

The dot prompt allows multiple table operations through *work areas*. dBASE has ten work areas numbered 1 through 10. Move from one to another with **Select** *Number*; optionally, use the letters A–J in place of the numbers. The default work area is 1—you would move to work area 5 with **Select 5**.

Each work area may be assigned an *alias*, a name that may be used in place of the number. If you invoke **Use** within an area, the table name becomes the default alias unless you specify another. You may also **Use** a table into a different area than the current one:

```
. use orders in 2
```

would open the ORDERS table in area 2 (and use "ORDERS" as the default alias). By itself, **Use** closes the file in the current work area. Likewise, **Use in 2** would close the file in area 2. You can close all files in all areas with **Close All**.

**Use** has several other options, but the only one that merits attention at the moment is the **Exclusive** clause. If you invoke **Use** *TableName* **Exclusive**, it will be off limits to other users on the network (much like a Paradox **Edit** as compared to **CoEdit**). Exclusive use is required when regenerating indexes, deleting marked rows, or converting a file. The latter operation, **Convert**, is one you should run for every new table you create. This converts tables from dBASE III format (the default) to dBASE IV format.

On a network, dBASE must verify that data you are about to change is up to date (for example, each time you start to edit a row). When using a dBASE III file, dBASE IV will ask you to press the spacebar to update the display. This becomes *very* annoying. dBASE IV files contain a special information area that tracks and updates such changes automatically, and dBASE stops asking for the spacebar when you edit. A sequence of **Convert**s appears in Figure 8.1. The file listing near the top of the screen was produced by **Dir**. **Convert** will add a column called _DBASELOCK to the converted table. dBASE uses this for locking information, so do not alter this column definition when modifying the structure of the table.

Now you are ready to edit the tables. Don't forget the **Use** commands, if the table is not already open. If you want the tabular format (rows and columns), simply type **Browse**. But you may associate a form with the current work area using **Set Format To** *FormName*. Then type **Edit** to edit the current data (or **Browse** if you simply want to view it). If you do not use **Set Format**, dBASE will simply build a default form with the fields in a column running down the page.

The **Edit** and **Browse** commands present the data as if the menu system had been used. In fact, you will have access to the same menus and function keys originally discussed. However, when you select **Exit** from the menu, you will return to the dot prompt rather than the main menu.

Other commands such as **Pack**, which deletes marked rows and compresses the file, show their results on the prompt screen (see Figure 8.2). Note that dBASE allows abbreviations in the command; in this case, **excl** rather than **exclusive**. Most commands and options can be abbreviated to four letters;

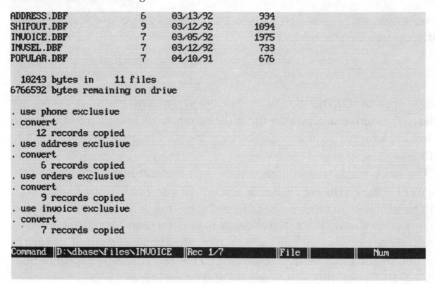

```
ADDRESS.DBF              6    03/13/92      934
SHIPOUT.DBF              9    03/12/92     1094
INVOICE.DBF             7    03/05/92     1975
INVSEL.DBF              7    03/12/92      733
POPULAR.DBF            7    04/10/91      676

  10243 bytes in     11 files
6766592 bytes remaining on drive

. use phone exclusive
. convert
     12 records copied
. use address exclusive
. convert
      6 records copied
. use orders exclusive
. convert
      9 records copied
. use invoice exclusive
. convert
      7 records copied
.
Command  D:\dbase\files\INVOICE   Rec 1/7        File       Num
```

**Figure 8.1   Converting dBASE files to include multiuser lock information.**

while this is useful for working at the dot prompt, to improve clarity in programs you should spell out the full command.

A simple program might look like the one shown on the following page:

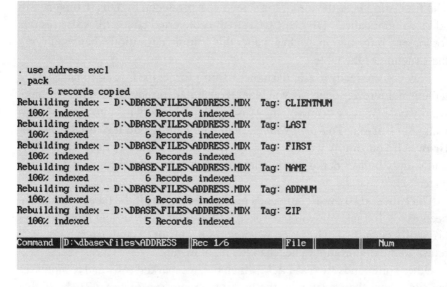

```
. use address excl
. pack
      6 records copied
Rebuilding index - D:\DBASE\FILES\ADDRESS.MDX  Tag: CLIENTNUM
   100% indexed            6 Records indexed
Rebuilding index - D:\DBASE\FILES\ADDRESS.MDX  Tag: LAST
   100% indexed            6 Records indexed
Rebuilding index - D:\DBASE\FILES\ADDRESS.MDX  Tag: FIRST
   100% indexed            6 Records indexed
Rebuilding index - D:\DBASE\FILES\ADDRESS.MDX  Tag: NAME
   100% indexed            6 Records indexed
Rebuilding index - D:\DBASE\FILES\ADDRESS.MDX  Tag: ADDNUM
   100% indexed            6 Records indexed
Rebuilding index - D:\DBASE\FILES\ADDRESS.MDX  Tag: ZIP
   100% indexed            5 Records indexed
.
Command  D:\dbase\files\ADDRESS   Rec 1/6        File       Num
```

**Figure 8.2   Using the PACK command to compress file space after deleting rows.**

```
Use Address
Set Format to Address
Edit
Use orders in 2
Select 2
Edit
Use                              &&Close Orders
Select 1
Use                              &&Close Address
```

Note that **&&** is the dBASE comment command. This program lets the user edit Address in a custom form, then loads Orders for editing in another area with its default form. It finishes by closing both tables. The **Do** command executes a program. So, the program is saved as TEST.PRG, and run with **Do test**. Notice that, unlike PAL, **Edit** pauses the program and waits for user input (Paradox requires a separate **Wait** command).

When you run a dBASE program, you'll discover another difference. dBASE compiles the program before running it. This is similar to the process Paradox uses within procedures, except that dBASE applies it to every program. And, like PAL procedure libraries, you can pre-compile a program with **Compile** *ProgName*.

dBASE also supports procedures. A procedure is placed between **Procedure** *ProcName* and **Return**. Like programs, procedures are called with **Do** **ProcName**. Actually, dBASE treats a short program as though it is a procedure with the same name as the program file, and uses the end of file as the **Return**. If the procedure must be called from another file (for example, a file that contains only procedures), use **Set Procedure To** *ProcFileName*. This functions like the PAL **AutoLib** variable, although dBASE is limited to a single open procedure library.

Because dBASE compiles all programs, it is not necessary to place the procedure definitions before the calling program (the entire file will be read and referenced before execution begins). In fact, you must place the calling program *before* the procedure definitions or dBASE will not "find" the commands.

You may have noticed another difference between dBASE and Paradox commands. When a filename is used in a dBASE command, it is not placed in quotation marks. In PAL, such an object would be a variable. Of course, dBASE needs variables, too. Within dBASE commands, variables must be *derefrenced*; i.e., you must tell dBASE that the name is a variable. Do this by placing the name in parentheses:

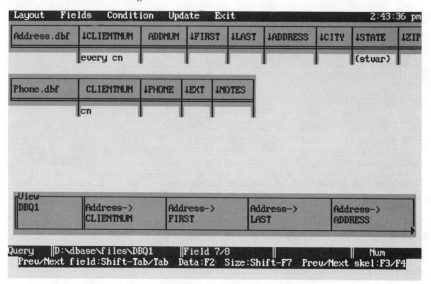

**Figure 8.3   Dereferencing variables within a dBASE query.**

```
fileName="Address"
use (FileName)
```

This dereferencing is similar to the ~ operator in Paradox queries (which tells Paradox that the next name in a query form is a variable). You must also dereference variables within a query by using parentheses. In Figure 8.3, the state name is selected from the variable **stvar**. You can avoid rewriting (or saving) multiple queries by using variables within queries. Simply change the variable, and the selected data changes, too.

As you may have noticed in the sample code, other aspects of dBASE and PAL variables are handled in the same manner. Assignment is handled with an =, and string constants within an assignment operation are delimited with quotation marks. Like PAL, dBASE is weakly typed: You may change the data type of a variable at will.

Each data type, except numeric, uses a unique delimiter. The default numeric data type for dBASE is fixed point. To select other numeric types you must use a conversion operator such as the **Float ( )** function, e.g.; **A=Float(1.23)**. In addition to the double quotation mark string delimiters, you may optionally enclose a string in single quotation marks or brackets. In this manner, you can include quotes within the string; e.g., **A=[This string includes "doubles" and 'singles']**. Date constants may be designated by enclosing the date within curly braces, as in **A={1/1/90}**. Logical values are enclosed between periods and may be designated as **.T.** or **.Y.** for true, or **.F.** or **.N.** for false (remember, dBASE is case insensitive, so you may use lowercase).

The similarity between dBASE and PAL variable assignment extends to the operators: You may use the same mathematical (and string) operations as PAL. But dBASE also adds a few operations. dBASE supports exponentiation with either ** or ^; thus, 2**5 and 2^5 both represent 2 raised to the fifth power, or 32. In string operations, you may use -, which moves blank spaces from the end of the preceding string to the end of the result string, e.g., **"1234 "-"567"="1234567 "**.

---

*dBASE Arithmetic Operators*

---

| | |
|---|---|
| + | Addition |
| - | Subtraction |
| * | Multiplication |
| / | Division |
| ** | Exponentiation |
| ^ | Exponentiation |

---

*dBASE Comparison Operators*

---

| | |
|---|---|
| = | Equal |
| > | Greater than |
| < | Less than |
| >= | Greater than or equal to |
| <= | Less than or equal to |
| <> | Not equal |
| # | Not equal |
| $ | Contained in (for string comparison) |

---

dBASE has a few inconsistencies when handling assignment. For example, you can assign from a field into a variable by using the field name. Consider a field named Address and a variable name Addr. We can use:

```
Addr=Address
```

However, you cannot go the other way (PAL, of course, can):

```
Addr="2100 N Main"
Address=Addr    && Illegal: cannot assign to a field
```

Actually, the example above would create a variable called Address and give it the same value as Addr. Instead, dBASE uses the **Replace** command:

```
Addr="2100 N Main"
Replace Address With Addr
```

If you do give the same name to an address and a field, dBASE will give precedence to the field when there is an ambiguity:

```
Addr="2100 N Main"
Address=Addr        && Assume there is a field name
Address

                    && The field is "9800 Broadway"
Test=Address        && Test is now "9800 Broadway"
```

You can override the field with **M->**, e.g., **Test=M->Address** will assign the variable to Test ("2100 N Main").

Conditional expressions are also similar to PAL. However, like the truth values **.T.** and **.F.**, the logical operators are enclosed within periods (**.AND.**, **.OR.**, and **.NOT.**). String comparisons are a bit different than PAL, too. By default, dBASE will return **.T.** if the first few characters of the left string match all of the characters in the right string (**"abc"="a"** returns **.T.**). You may change this to an exact match requirement with the command **Set Exact On**. Additionally, you may use the **$** comparison operator to search for the left string within the right, e.g., **"b"$"abc"** would return **.T.**

The dBASE **If** command is nearly identical to the PAL construct: PAL uses **Then** to end the conditional clause, dBASE uses a carriage return.

```
ThisTab="Address"
Use (ThisTab)
If RecCount ()<>0 .AND. ThisTab="Address"
      Set Format To (ThisTab)
      Edit
   Else
      Browse
EndIf
```

dBASE is much less forgiving about program file format than PAL. For example, the conditional clause of the **If** command cannot be placed on a single line, and commands cannot be split across lines without a continuation character. The continuation character, a semicolon, is particularly useful for long, convoluted logical expressions, which are easier to read on separate lines. This

convention can be confusing to C programmers who use a semicolon to *end* a
command, rather than *continue* a command on the next line.

```
If (State="NY" .AND. Company="Acme") .OR. ;
   (First="John" .AND. Last="Smith") ;
        ? "This is a very generic entry"
EndIf
```

dBASE uses **?** to print on the current line and **??** to print on the next line.
Unlike the PAL canvas, which is a static, fixed-length screen, the dBASE print
area is an extension of the dot prompt screen: It scrolls when the last line is
printed. You can reposition the cursor on the canvas with **@***row,column*, so
basic output is nearly identical to PAL (actually, PAL follows many of the
dBASE conventions since it was designed later).

The **?** command may be used to return the current value of dBASE functions.
The structure of a dBASE function is identical to PAL (including the name and
purpose in some cases):

```
. ? Upper ("change case")
CHANGE CASE
.
```

Different areas of the dBASE screen exhibit different behaviors. The first
line of the screen (line 0), does not scroll. It may be used as a static display
area to display a constant title or label. The last three lines are the status area
and will not accept data (if you try to print beyond this area, dBASE will simply
write to the last displayable line—21). If the last line is printed with **??**, the
display will remain intact; if printed with **?**, all of the lines (except 0) will scroll.
The following program produced the output in Figure 8.4.

```
Clear
@0,0
?? "This prints on the first line"
@1,0
?? "This prints on the second line"
@5,0
?? "This prints on the sixth line"
@21,0
?? "This prints on the last line"
? "This prints after the last line"
```

```
This prints on the first line



This prints on the sixth line









This prints on the last line
This prints after the last line
TEST3                                                              Num
```

**Figure 8.4   Output from the sample dBASE program.**

Omitting the final **?** would have prevented the second line (which was originally printed below the first) from scrolling off the screen.

The screen behavior may be changed with **Set Scoreboard Off** and **Set Status Off**. The former will address line 0 as a standard (scrollable) line. The latter will remove the status line at the bottom of the screen so that the last lines will be accessible. The defaults may be re-enabled with **On**.

For general user text input, dBASE provides an **Accept** command. It does not support the advance type definition (only character data is allowed) and range checking options like PAL, but is limited to a prompt and variable name:

```
Accept "Enter your name: " To Name
```

The **Input** command works just like **Accept**, but will accept data of any type. dBASE does have formatted input and output options. Both are available as extensions to the **@***row, column* command. However, these extensions handle full-screen processing and require advanced support on the part of the programmer. dBASE uses these extensions as the basis of its form and report generators. In fact, if you display the contents of the .FMT (form) and .FRG (report) files, you will see the code produced by dBASE. This subject will be returned to shortly.

The only remaining program element is the loop. dBASE has three loop structures: **Do While... EndDo, Do Case... EndCase**, and **Scan... EndScan**.

These are similar to the PAL structures **While... EndWhile**, **Switch Case...**
**EndSwitch**, and **Scan... EndScan**.  The dBASE **Do While** and **Scan** loops use
**Exit** as the optional early termination (like the PAL **QuitLoop**), and **Loop** as
the optional jump to the top of the loop.

## Functions

In a relational system, the relational language should make provisions to store
and execute functions written in the host language.  A function returns a value
that can be used as the parameter for another function or as a new column in
the table.  For example, you might want to bill the minimum of two amounts:
twenty percent over cost or five dollars, whichever is greater.  The relational
language may not have a provision for calculating the maximum of two
quantities, but it would be a simple task within a host language.  The resulting
code might resemble:

```
int max (A,B)
{
    if (A>B)
            return A;
        else
            return B;
    endif
}
```

In the "ideal" database, once the procedure has been defined and compiled
in the host language (C for this example), the query language could use the
function as one of its own.  Furthermore, the database would store the program
and the compiled code in the database catalog (this would allow for portability
to incompatible systems hardware where the code would require recompiling).
Neither Paradox nor dBASE is as sophisticated as the ideal model, however.

Paradox does not allow function definitions within query statements.  And
with dBASE, it is much simpler to write function definitions within the dBASE
language rather than linking to a general host language (though it is possible
with the Developer's Edition of dBASE and a lot of hard work).  Both Paradox
and dBASE allow function definitions within their respective programming
languages.  Again, within Paradox, function definitions can be used to work
around the query limitations.  PAL also provides quite a few pre-defined

functions that you will find useful (like user-defined functions, these cannot be used within queries).

The previous examples include several commands, but very few functions. Although a function can return data of any type, many of the frequently used functions return a logical True or False. Such functions are used within conditional statements to control the course of a program. Within mathematical procedures, you may use several functions that return numerical results. These are usually advanced mathematical operations such as exponential and trigonometric functions. Other mathematical operations work on an entire column of a table and return statistical results such as the average or standard deviation. Some functions are designed for string (text) processing. Many return information about the state of DOS or Paradox.

## User-defined Functions

When called, all function names must be followed by a set of parentheses. Many functions require a list of arguments (constants or variables) to be processed by the function. The returned value may be used in an assignment or comparison operation: Simply use the entire function as you would a variable or constant; e.g., in PAL **ThisVar = Today ( )** assigns the date to the variable ThisVar.

You may write your own functions by using a **Procedure** declaration in PAL or a **Function** declaration in dBASE. The body of the function resembles a standard program block. The primary difference comes at the end of the code. With the special command **Return Value**, the procedure will return the specified value as if it were a standard function.

PAL places the passed variable definitions within the parentheses following the **Procedure** definition. dBASE uses a separate **Parameters** command to declare the passed variables. A short example in both PAL and dBASE should illustrate the differences. First, the PAL example:

```
Procedure Sum(A,B)

   C=A+B

Return C

?? Sum(5,3)
```

and now the dBASE example:

```
? Sum(5,3)

Function Sum
    Parameters A,B

    C=A+B

Return C
```

Both programs print 8.

## Procedure Libraries

As presented thus far, functions (and procedures) exist in memory only so long as the program is running. When Paradox or dBASE comes back to the main menu or prompt, the functions are no longer available. If a database is to be extendable, incorporating features of the host language into the relational language, it must provide a link between the two languages. In theory, this link would be through catalog entries. In practice, dBASE and Paradox use *procedure libraries* to store functions for general use.

dBASE procedure libraries are more adaptable and simpler to use than Paradox libraries. Once you write a program containing functions and procedures, the command **Set Procedure To *ProgramName*** will use the named program as the procedure library. If you then call a function (such as **Sum (A,B)** from the preceding example), dBASE will first search the current program for a function called **Sum ( )**. If none is found, it will then find and execute the function defined in the library.

Functions defined within the dBASE library may be used as if they were internal dBASE functions: in queries, forms, reports, and other programs. However, only one library may be named (all common procedures must be defined within it). Paradox allows multiple procedure libraries, but the library is more difficult to set up and limited in use.

In Paradox, you must first create a library in which to store the functions and routine. Libraries are created with the command **CreateLib *LibraryName***. If the named library exists, it is erased and a new, empty library is created. If you have more than 50 procedures, the command requires a **Size** parameter:

**CreateLib** *LibraryName* **Size** *LibrarySize*.  The size may be up to 300; if you have more than 300 procedures, you will need separate libraries.

Procedures are stored in the library with the command **WriteLib** *LibraryName ProcedureList*.  Note that, although the library name is enclosed in quotation marks, the procedure names are not.  Thus, a command might resemble **WriteLib "MyLib" PrintInv, PrivErr**.  The **WriteLib** must appear *after* the procedure definition in the script.  Library-based programs require at least two scripts:  one to define the procedures and write them to the library, and another to read the library and start running the program.

**ReadLib** *LibraryName ProcedureList* reads the procedures from the library into the script that runs the program.  However, with one exception (error processing routines), you should not read procedures with **ReadLib**.  Rather, you should use the reserved variable **AutoLib** to automatically load the procedures into memory as they are required.  **Autolib** is similar to the dBASE **Set Procedure To** command.  However, you can use multiple libraries with **Autolib**.  If there were two libraries, **MyLib** and **Utilities** could be used:

```
AutoLib="MyLib, Utilities"
```

Such *automatic libraries* let PAL read procedures into memory as they are needed, and erase them when they are not.  This prevents PAL from running out of memory if you have many procedures and little memory in your computer.  If Paradox runs out of memory, and you are using libraries, you should use **SetSwap** to reserve a special memory pool.  Start with **SetSwap 15000** (as the first line of your script), and increase the size by 5000 until the problem disappears.  A setting of 25000 is optimal in most cases, but this may be too high for systems with limited memory.

Standard Paradox functions may be used in reports and forms, but not queries.  However, user-defined library functions cannot be used in reports, forms, or functions.  This is another illustration of the underlying differences between Paradox and dBASE.  Paradox forms and reports (and to a degree, queries) are objects used by the database system.  On the other hand, dBASE generates and compiles program code based on forms, reports, and queries.  Thus, just about anything that can be done within a dBASE program can be run through the other features.

# 9

# Adding Features with Programs

Now that you have a feel for how programs work, it's time to apply them to a few of the real problems you will face when managing a database. As you work with the system, try to build a set of general tools to help you manage the system: Add features that are missing from the relational tools, or design general processes that you use in all of your programming.

## Enhancing Paradox Capabilities

One of Paradox's greatest shortcomings is its lack of view support. This can be especially important when generating reports based on several tables. On the other hand, its multitable forms, while not a true relational function, provide a very useful alternative to views during input. You may also realize that many multitable forms would not be updateable, insertable, or deletable under even the "ideal" relational system (giving an advantage to the Paradox technique in some cases).

But because Paradox abandons some relational principles in the design of multitable reports and forms, management problems are compounded. As noted earlier, the basis for reports lies in the details, and the basis for forms lies in the general data. It's a fairly simple matter to match the two models when the hierarchy branches out in one direction (clear cut, one-to-many, parent-to-child relations). But many-to-many relations established through third normal form do not work very well.

You can work around some of the shortcomings of Paradox by designing your own functions and commands with procedures. This usually requires several steps to consolidate entry tables into a structure that can be used by reports. It's usually best to design the relations for form entry because modeling a system for data modification requires more constraints than simple reading (as used by reports). By writing procedures that consolidate the data for the reports, you can save much time and frustration.

The multitable form used in Chapter 5 was an invoice built from three tables: ADDRESS, INVOICE, and ORDERS. It also used a special table called INVREP, which received joined data from ADDRESS and INVOICE using third normal form. The following procedure integrates the steps used to create a report (outlined in the last chapter) based on the multitable form. Note that the INVREP table must already exist. And in a networked environment, INVREP must be located in the private directory because several users could be adding data to the INVREP table. If they don't each have their own copies of the INVREP table, managing the application would become very difficult.

```
Proc PrintInv ()
   Private PStat

   Query

      Invoice | Invoice | Date  | Client Number |
              | Check   | Check | Check _cn      |

      Invoice | Billing Address | Shipping Address |
              | _cnb            | _cns             |

      Address | Client Number | AddNum |
              | _cn           | _cnb   |
              | _cn           | _cns   |

      Address | First Name        | Last Name         |
              | Check as First B  | Check as Last B   |
              | Check as First S  | Check as Last S   |

      Address | Address          | City              |
              | Check as Add B   | Check as City B   |
              | Check as Add S   | Check as City S   |
```

```
      Address | State             | Zip               |
              | Check as St B | Check as Zip B |
              | Check as St S | Check as Zip S |


  EndQuery
  Do_It!

  Empty "InvRep"          ;should already be empty,
                          ;but make sure INVREP is
  Add "Answer" "InvRep"   ;linked to the Orders table

  PStat="Y"               ;default if printer is
                          ;ready
  While Not PrinterStatus () And PStat="Y"
     Clear
     @1,1
     ?? "Printer is not ready — 'Y' to try again,
        'N' aborts "
     Accept "A1" Picture "Y,N" To PStat
     If Not RetVal Then PStat="N" EndIf
  EndWhile

  If PStat="Y" Then
     Report "Orders" "1"
  EndIf

  Empty "InvRep"          ;let's not waste disk space

EndProc

;This error procedure will prevent an error from the
;PrivTables command if the script is run twice in one
;session
Proc PrivErr ()
   Private ErrProc

   If ErrorMessage ()="Run error: Table already used
                   in this session" Then
      Return 1           ;skip this line
   EndIf
   Return 2              ;unknown error, show
                         ;Cancel/Debug menu
```

```
EndProc

ErrorProc="PrivErr"          ;enable error procedure
PrivTables "InvRep"          ;put InvRep in the
                             ;private directory
PrintInv ()
```

Note the links used in generating the ANSWER; INVOICE links to two separate lines on the ANSWER form: the billing address through the example element **cnb**, and the shipping address through the example element **cns**. The multireport description for ORDERS then links the Invoice number from ORDERS to the keyed field of INVREP (called Invoice).

The invoice printing procedure was designed specifically for one task: to consolidate information from a multitable form into a format usable by a multitable report. It would be very difficult to generalize the procedure into one that could be used for all form to report mappings, but you will often find tasks that can be generalized. Another common problem within Paradox is the absence of a generalized report; reports are tied to a specific table format and, more important, a single table (skirting the intent of a relational system). Preparing a pre-defined ANSWER report becomes an awkward chore, and you will find yourself constantly copying reports or families from a template table to the ANSWER table. Paradox does not provide a simple command for copying the family, but you can design a general routine for use within all of your programs.

```
Proc CopyFamily (Source, Destination)
   {Tools} {Copy} {JustFamily}
   Select Source
   Select Destination
   {Replace}
EndProc
```

You could write similar procedures to copy a single form or report.

## dBASE Programs

dBASE's greatest shortcomings lie in its data entry functions. While you may use views to display consolidated data from several tables, there is no simple way to edit or enter this data, even in those cases that are theoretically updateable or insertable. Specifically, let's consider the invoice data entry that was created as a Paradox multitable form (an INVOICE control table, AD-DRESS lookup, and a list of ORDERS). You are left with few options for handling such data entry.

You could create an invoice entry table (call it INVENT). This would consist of the basic invoice information (number, date, etc.), a billing and shipping address, and several order "rows" (Number, Quantity, Description, Price, and Extended Price). These order rows could be called N1, Q1, D1, P1, E1, N2, Q2, D2, P2, E2, etc. Once the order has been entered, the program can parse out the data and send it to the appropriate tables. The problem with this approach is that it entirely circumvents the advantages of a relational system. An order is limited to an arbitrary number of items, and references (data validation) must be repeated for every "row."

You could also create a custom form, treating each area of the screen according to its source. In effect, it would act like a Paradox multitable form, but would rely on your programming to manage the keystrokes and data placement. dBASE provides some of the tools you'll need through the *@row, column* command, but there is still much you must manage yourself. The disadvantage of this approach is the programming overhead required. Nevertheless, it makes a useful example.

dBASE has many more environmental controls than Paradox; an important part of dBASE programming lies in managing the environment through various **Set** and **Window** commands. Fortunately, dBASE form and report screens generate dBASE programs based on the form or report description. Therefore, the functions used in form and report designs are available to any program. Before proceeding with this more complicated programming example, you should understand some of these concepts.

The bases of an entry form are the *@row, column* **Get** *Variable* and *@row, column* **Show** *Text* commands. These commands create data entry fields and prompts that behave like a form; i.e., you can use the cursor keys to randomly move among the fields. **Get** is a rather special input function. First, the variables must be initialized before **Get**s are called (or you may use a field name to link changes to a table). Second, you may apply default values, formatting, and range checking. Third, the **Get**s do not take immediate effect, but rather are held in a suspended state until a **Read** command is processed. The **Read** command will clear the **Get** definitions unless you retain them with **Read Save** (the option selected here). However, if you use **Read Save**, it is important that you close the definitions with **Clear Gets** when you are finished with the form.

dBASE keeps track of the key that ended the **Read** session. You can retrieve the key pressed with the **LastKey** ( ) function, but even better, you can retrieve an action code with **ReadKey ( )**. The action code returns the type of action (e.g., cursor or page movement), the direction (backward or forward), and the status of the record (whether the data was changed during the **Read**). If the status changed, 256 is added to the codes listed below:

| Code | Definition |
|------|------------|
| 0 | One character backward |
| 1 | One character forward |
| 2 | One word backward |
| 3 | One word forward |
| 4 | One field backward |
| 5 | One field forward |
| 6 | One page (screen) backward |
| 7 | One page (screen) forward |
| 12 | Terminate without save (Esc) |
| 14 | Save and terminate (Ctrl-End; actually, always 270) |
| 15 | Carriage return |
| 16 | Carriage return (from a blank record) |
| 33 | Menu (Ctrl-Home) |
| 34 | Zoom out (Ctrl-PgUp) |
| 35 | Zoom in (Ctrl-PgDn) |
| 36 | Help key |

To handle the order rows, you may be tempted to use a view file, which restricts the displayed rows to the matching ClientNum and Invoice numbers. However, like forms and reports, views are based on compiled dBASE commands. The view will create problematic side effects by altering the areas and setting filter conditions. Filters are the constraints that dBASE places on tables to limit the display. So, rather than using a view, you can set your own filter conditions. In the following example, the Invoice field in ORDERS is matched to the Invoice field in the INVOICE table:

```
Select Orders
Set Filter To Invoice=Invoice->Invoice
```

The filter applies only to the current active area, hence the initial **Select**.

You must have control over scrolling within the order rows. After all, you may have more order detail rows than will fit on the screen (the example will use three displayable rows to illustrate the technique). dBASE retains control until you try and move past the form (up at the beginning, down at the end, **Esc**, **PgUp**, **PgDn**, etc). If dBASE is managing cursor movement within the form, how is it possible to scroll up one order instead of moving into the Address data? The answer: by setting windows.

**Define Window** *WindowName* **From** *TopRow*, *LeftCol* **To** *BotRow*, *RightCol* defines a rectangular window. The window will have a single-line border unless you override with **Double**, **Pane**, or **None** (for double lines, inverse video, or no borders). You may also set custom border characters and custom colors (through a **Color** option) should you so desire.

Once a Window has been defined, you may use it with **Activate Window** *WindowNames*. If you list several window names, all will be displayed, but only the last will be active. The active window determines cursor movement in and out of bounds, as if it were a separate screen, so the order rows will be placed in a separate window called **wOrders**. Note that the @ coordinates are relative to the area *within* the window; e.g., **@0,0** is one down and one right of the upper left-hand corner of the window.

Now it's time to look at the sample program. If you've worked through the preceding chapters, you should understand the programming concepts. This example is quite long—it emulates the functions of a Paradox multitable form, though it is not perfect. Key usage is not quite consistent (**PgUp** and **PgDn** move from invoice to invoice in the first section, and between sections in the other sections), and record management could stand some improvement. Note that the general techniques involved are useful in both Paradox and dBASE programming when you want to gain additional control over data entry.

```
Do InvEnt

Procedure InvEnt
   Private ShowFirstOrd, RV

   Set Talk Off        && Don't display
                       && variable assigns
   Set Status Off      && Don't display status line

   Use Invoice In 1
   Use Address in 2
   Use Orders in 3

   Select Invoice
   Goto 1              && Move to the first record
   CurCli=ClientNum
```

```
Select Orders
Set Filter To Invoice=Invoice->Invoice
Select Address
Set Filter To ClientNum=Invoice->ClientNum

Declare CatNo[7], Qu[7], Dsc[7], UPr[7], EPr[7]

Clear

Define Window wInvoice From 0,0 To 4,79
Define Window wAddress From 5,0 To 11,79
Define Window wOrders From 12,0 To 20,79

Activate Window wInvoice
@0,2 SAY "Invoice: "
@0,20 SAY "Date: "
@1,2 SAY "Client: "
@1,20 SAY "Bill: "
@1,30 SAY "Ship: "

Do SetInvoice    && Display GET contents
Clear Gets       && Clear data entry for next window

Activate Window wAddress
@0,1 SAY "Bill To:"
@0,40 SAY "Ship To:"

Do SetAddress
Clear Gets

Activate Window wOrders
@0,2 SAY "Cat No"
@0,9 SAY "Quan"
@0,15 SAY "Description"
@0,37 SAY " Price"
@0,46 SAY "  Total"

RV=0                && Start with Invoice screen
ShowFirstOrd=.T.    && Start with first Orders row
Do While RV<>99

    Do Case
```

```
         Case RV=0
             RV=MngInvoice()
         Case RV=1
             RV=MngAddress()
         Case RV=2
             RV=MngOrders()      && Control movement
                                 && in Orders
     EndCase

EndDo
DeActivate Window All

Select Invoice
Use
Select Address
Use
Select Orders
Use

Use Orders Exclusive
Pack                     && Get rid of blank rows
Use
Use Invoice Exclusive
Scan For Invoice=" "   && Erase blank
                       && numbered invoices
    Delete
EndScan
Pack
Use

Select 1
Set Talk On
Set Status On

Return

Function MngInvoice
    Private RK, RC
    && Apply GETs to the Invoice section and control
    && movement to next Invoice or Orders section
    && Returns:
    &&   99 = Terminate
    &&    0 = Move to next table
```

```
Do While .T.
   Select Invoice
   CurCli=ClientNum       && CurCli restricts
                          && OrdLink view to the
                          && current client

   ShowFirstOrd=.T.    && This variable tells
                       && SetOrders to start
                       && the rows with the first
   Do SetOrders        && Display GET contents
   Clear Gets          && Clear data entry for
                       && next window

   Do SetAddress
   Clear Gets

   Do SetInvoice
   If RecNo()>RecCount()
      Append Blank
   EndIf
   Read Save

   RK=ReadKey()
   If ReadKey()>=256
      && Data in GETs has changed
      RK=RK-256
   EndIf
   Do Case
      Case RK=7    && Forward one screen
         If Invoice<>" "
            Skip 1    && Next row
         EndIf
      Case RK=6    && Backward one screen
         Skip -1  && Previous row
      Case RK=5    && Forward one field
         RC=1     && Move to Address
         Exit
      Case RK=12 .OR. RK=14      && Terminate
         RC=99
         Exit
   EndCase
EndDo
```

```
    Clear Gets

Return RC

Function MngAddress
    Private RK, RC
    && Apply GETs to the Address section and control
    && movement to next Invoice or Orders section
    && Returns:
    &&   99 = Terminate
    &&    0 = Move to Invoice section
    &&    2 = Move to Orders section

    Do While .T.
       Select Invoice

       Clear Gets          && Clear data entry
                           && for next window

       Do SetAddress
       If RecNo()>RecCount()
          Append Blank
       EndIf
       Read Save

       RK=ReadKey()
       If ReadKey()>=256
          && Data in GETs has changed
          RK=RK-256
       EndIf
       Do Case
          Case RK=7    && Forward one screen
             RC=2      && Move to Orders
             Exit
          Case RK=6    && Backward one screen
             RC=0      && Move to Invoice
             Exit
          Case RK=4    && Backward one field
             RC=0
             Exit
          Case RK=5    && Forward one field
             RC=2
             Exit
```

```
            Case RK=12 .OR. RK=14        && Terminate
               RC=99
               Exit
         EndCase
      EndDo
      Clear Gets

Return RC

Function MngOrders
   Private RK, RC
   && Apply GETs to the Orders section and control
   && movement to next Invoice or Orders section
   && Returns:
   &&   99 = Terminate
   &&    1 = Move to Address

   Do While .T.

      Do SetOrders
      Activate Window wOrders
      If RecNo()>RecCount()
         Append Blank
      EndIf
      Read Save
      ShowFirstOrd=.F.          && Now allow scrolling

      RK=ReadKey()
      If ReadKey()>=256
         && Data in GETs has changed
         RK=RK-256
         Do SaveOrders
      EndIf
      Do Case
         Case RK=7          && Forward one screen
            RC=0            && Move to Invoice
            Exit
         Case RK=6          && Backward one screen
            RC=1            && Move to Address
            Exit
         Case RK=5          && Forward one field
            Skip 1
         Case RK=4          && Backward one field
```

```
            Skip -1
            If BOF()        && If Beginning of File
               RC=1          && Move to Address
               Exit
            EndIf
         Case RK=12 .OR. RK=14  && Terminate
            RC=99
            Exit
      EndCase

   EndDo
   Clear Gets

Return RC

Procedure SetInvoice

   Activate Window wInvoice
   Select Invoice
   If Date={}
      Replace Date with Date()
   EndIf
   @0,11 GET Invoice
   @0,26 GET Date
   @1,11 GET ClientNum
   @1,26 GET BillAdd
   @1,36 GET ShipAdd

Return

Procedure SetAddress
   Private LU

   Activate Window wAddress
   Select Invoice
   If SFirst=" " .AND. SLast=" " .AND. ;
      SAdd=" " .AND. ;
      SCity=" " .AND. SSt=" " .AND. SZip=" "

      Replace SFirst With ;
         Lookup (Address->First,ShipAdd, ;
                 Address->AddNum)
      Replace SLast With ;
```

```
        Lookup (Address->Last,ShipAdd, ;
             Address->Addnum)
   Replace SAdd With ;
     Lookup (Address->Address,ShipAdd, ;
             Address->Addnum)
   Replace SCity With ;
     Lookup (Address->City,ShipAdd,Address->Addnum)
   Replace SSt With ;
     Lookup (Address->State,ShipAdd, ;
             Address->Addnum)
   Replace SZip With ;
     Lookup (Address->Zip,ShipAdd,Address->Addnum)

EndIf

If BFirst=" " .AND. BLast=" " .AND. ;
   BAdd=" " .AND. ;
   BCity=" " .AND. BSt=" " .AND. BZip=" "

   Replace BFirst With ;
      Lookup (Address->First,BillAdd, ;
             Address->AddNum)
   Replace BLast With ;
     Lookup (Address->Last,BillAdd, ;
             Address->Addnum)
   Replace BAdd With ;
     Lookup (Address->Address,BillAdd, ;
             Address->Addnum)
   Replace BCity With ;
     Lookup (Address->City,BillAdd,Address->Addnum)
   Replace BSt With ;
     Lookup (Address->State,BillAdd, ;
             Address->Addnum)
   Replace BZip With ;
     Lookup (Address->Zip,BillAdd, ;
             Address->Addnum)

EndIf

@1,1  GET BFirst
@1,17 GET BLast
@2,1  GET BAdd
@3,1  GET BCity
```

```
@3,17 GET BSt Picture "!!"
@3,20 GET BZip Picture "99999"
@1,41 GET SFirst
@1,57 GET SLast
@2,41 GET SAdd
@3,41 GET SCity
@3,57 GET SSt Picture "!!"
@3,60 GET SZip Picture "99999"

Return

Procedure SetOrders
   Private I

   Activate Window wOrders
   Select Orders
   If ShowFirstOrd
     Goto Top
   EndIf
   && The following "trick" checks for an empty set in
   && the filter (i.e., dBASE points to one row past
   && the last row)
   If RecNo()<=RecCount()
        InitRec=RecNo ()
     Else
        InitRec=0
   EndIf
   I=1
   Scan For RecNo()=>InitRec .AND. .NOT. Deleted();
        While I<=3
     && Read values starting with the initial record
     && Continue reading up to three records (no room
     && to display more)

     CatNo[I]=Part
     Qu[I]=Quan
     Dsc[I]=Desc
     UPr[I]=UPrice

     Do ShowOrders
     I=I+1

   EndScan
```

```
    If InitRec>0
       Goto InitRec
    EndIf

    && Now add blank entries for new information
    && (if any)
    Do While I<=3
       CatNo[I]=Space(6)
       Qu[I]=0
       Dsc[I]=Space(20)
       UPr[I]=0
       Do ShowOrders
       I=I+1
    EndDo

Return

Procedure SaveOrders

    If RecNo()<=RecCount()
         InitRec=RecNo ()
    Else
         InitRec=0
    EndIf
    I=1
    Scan For RecNo()=>InitRec While I<=3
       && Write values starting with the initial record
       && Continue writing up to three records (no room
       && to display more)

       If CatNo[I]>" " .AND. Qu[I]>0 ;
          .AND. Dsc[I]>" " .AND. UPr[I]>0

            If Deleted()
               Recall      && If marked as deleted,
                           && unmark
            EndIf
            Do WrOrder     && Write an order row to
                           && table

         Else
            Delete         && Mark row for deletion
       EndIf
```

```
      I=I+1

   EndScan

   Do While I<=3

      If CatNo[I]>" " .AND. Qu[I]>0 ;
         .AND. Dsc[I]>" " .AND. UPr[I]>0

         Append Blank     && Make new order row
         Do WrOrder       && Write new order row
                          && to table

      EndIf
      I=I+1
   EndDo
   If InitRec>0
      Goto InitRec
   EndIf

Return

Procedure WrOrder

   Replace ClientNum With Invoice->ClientNum
   Replace Invoice With Invoice->Invoice
   Replace Part With CatNo[I]
   Replace Quan With Qu[I]
   Replace Desc With Dsc[I]
   Replace UPrice With UPr[I]

Return

Procedure ShowOrders

      @1+I,2 GET CatNo[I] Picture "XXXXX"
      @1+I,9 GET Qu[I] Picture "9,999"
      @1+I,15 GET Dsc[I] Picture ;
                 "XXXXXXXXXXXXXXXXXXXX"
      @1+I,37 GET UPr[I] Picture "9,999.99"
      @1+I,46 SAY Qu[I]*UPr[I] Picture "99,999.99"

Return
```

As you can see, managing multiple files under dBASE can be more work than Paradox. To be fair, the program could have jumped from one form to another, keeping invoice and order information on separate screens (and a different format since ORDERS would show all rows only in a **Browse** type data entry mode). Although form design is quite complicated, reporting can be much simpler under dBASE. Assuming the appropriate view has been designed (FULLINV in this example) and a matching report defined (INVREP), the following program will print the consolidated report:

```
Set View To FullInv
Report Form InvRep To Printer
```

Now you're probably interested in some of the details behind these commands. dBASE has many more control commands than Paradox. For example, dBASE has a full set of page handling commands and system variables for designing a page layout complete with headers, footers, and margins. Additionally, dBASE commands tend to have many options. Many of the common commands and functions are listed and described in the Appendices. The lists are not complete, but include the more common commands and options, and focus on those commands that help manage the systems. You can find more detail in the dBASE manual or a book devoted to dBASE programming.

## Procedure Libraries Revisited

Procedure libraries were introduced in the previous chapter. Now that you have seen a few applications for the procedures and functions, you should be able to place them within a library. This will improve the performance of most PAL code, as the library storage method is similar to the compiling technology used in other database systems. As an example, consider an invoice report for an accounting system:

```
CreateLib "MyLib"

Proc PrintInv ()
   Private PStat

   Query

      Invoice | Invoice | Date  | Client Number |
```

```
           | Check    | Check  | Check _cn       |

   Invoice | Billing Address | Shipping Address |
           | _cnb            | _cns             |

   Address | Client Number | AddNum |
           | _cn           | _cnb   |
           | _cn           | _cns   |

   Address | First Name       | Last Name       |
           | Check as First B | Check as Last B |
           | Check as First S | Check as Last S |

   Address | Address          | City            |
           | Check as Add B   | Check as City B |
           | Check as Add S   | Check as City S |

   Address | State          | Zip             |
           | Check as St B  | Check as Zip B  |
           | Check as St S  | Check as Zip S  |

EndQuery
Do_It!

Empty "InvRep"            ;should already be empty,
                          ;but make sure
Add "Answer" "InvRep"     ;Invrep is linked to the
                          ;Orders table

PStat="Y"                        ;default if printer
                                 ;is ready
While Not PrinterStatus () And PStat="Y"
   Clear
   @1,1
   ?? "Printer is not ready—'Y' "
   ?? "to try again, 'N' aborts "
   Accept "A1" Picture "Y,N" To PStat
   If Not RetVal Then PStat="N" EndIf
EndWhile

If PStat="Y" Then
   Report "Orders" "1"
EndIf
```

```
   Empty "InvRep"            ;let's not waste disk space

EndProc

WriteLib "MyLib" PrintInv
Release Procs PrintInv

Proc PrivErr ()
   Private ErrProc

   If ErrorMessage ()=
      "Run error: Table already used in this session"
      Then
          Return 1        ;skip this line
   EndIf
   Return 2                ;unknown error, show
                          ;Cancel/Debug menu

EndProc

WriteLib "MyLib" PrivErr
Release Procs PrivErr
```

Note the **Release Procs** statements after writing the procedures to the library: This erases the procedures from memory. If the script that defines the library contains many procedures, this prevents PAL from running out of memory before the script ends. The script that actually runs the procedures might look like this:

```
SetSwap 25000
AutoLib="MyLib"

ReadLib "MyLib" PrivErr    ;explicitly load the
error handler
ErrorProc="PrivErr"        ;use the error handler

PrintInv ()
```

One last thought about libraries: There are procedures that you may use in several different programs. These might be handy utilities that create shortcut commands for menu selections (copying all family members, sending a report to a file, etc). You should keep such utilities in a separate library (and separate directory), such as "Utility". Then, you can use the library in all of your programs by adding the statement **Autolib="Utility"**. This allows you to work without copying the procedure from one script to the next. Additionally, if there are any bugs to fix, you can fix them in one place. The only overhead involved is the DOS copy command, e.g.,

```
copy c:\paradox\original\utilities.lib c:\paradox\new\
```

## Summary

The programming features of a database can help you overcome the limitations within the system. Whenever possible, you should try to generalize your database structures and programs so you can use them within several different databases. Although this requires additional work the first time, it is an investment that will help you in the next design. You should try your hand at some simple models first, especially when designing a new system.

Keep the initial base tables simple, including only as many fields as necessary. For example, an ADDRESS table could include the key plus one Address line. Once the initial model is working, and the programs have integrated the basic information, you can expand the model to include the details. It is far simpler to change the entire structure of a few basic tables and programs than to reorganize a complete set.

# 10

# Manipulative Queries

You now have all of the tools necessary to develop a database application, and you should be able to write useful programs at this point. The tabular nature of some operations has been emphasized, e.g., queries and batch table commands. Remember, the strength of a database is its ability to effectively manage large chunks of data in one fell swoop.

By Codd's definitions, table operations should remain consistent whether done one row at a time or many rows at a time. Thus, batch operations (such as update queries) are a fundamental property of RDBMS. Chapter 3 made reference to four manipulative operators: **insertion, deletion, update**, and **primary key update**. The first two alter the number of rows in a table, the latter two change only existing entries. The insert and delete operators are very similar to **Add** (or **Append**) and **Subtract** commands, but query-based operations are much more adaptable. Whereas the commands apply only to similarly structured tables and allow only a single source and destination, an update query may use several tables as a source (only one target is allowed).

Neither Paradox nor dBASE support a **primary key update**. This operation, which updates all matching key values in related tables, requires both domain assignments and a formal declaration of the relationships between tables. Paradox and dBASE do not make provisions for such declarations and neither package supports domains, but both packages support **insertion, deletion**, and **update**.

dBASE calls manipulative queries *update queries*. In many respects, an update query resembles a standard query (or view definition), but rather than displaying a new table or view, the update query makes changes to existing tables. As a safety measure, Paradox also creates a new, temporary table when an update query is executed. The temporary tables contain the information that was altered in the target base table; in most cases, you can use this information to reverse a mistake.

In the course of performing update operations, the database should check the integrity of the altered data in order to keep the tables in a consistent state. Unfortunately, full consistency is not available in Paradox or dBASE. For example, Paradox does not apply integrity checks to update queries; and, of course, dBASE has no integrity checks.

## Paradox Manipulative Queries

To create a manipulative query in Paradox, you must use the keyword **insert**, **delete**, or **changeto** within the target table's query form (the target table is the one that will be altered). **Insert** and **Delete** are placed in the far-left column since they affect entire rows (just as an **F6** in the far left checks all rows). **Changeto** (the Paradox name for **update**) is entered under every column that will be affected.

A simple **Changeto** and its results appear in Figure 10.1. Note how a condition and example element have been combined with the update. The

```
Viewing Changed table: Record 1 of 3                          Main

ADDRESS         Client Number              AddNum        First Name
       <"4", cn, changeto "000"+cn


ADDRESS  Client Number  AddNum  First Name  Last Name    Address      City
   1     0001           1       Frank       Smith        345 Weiner Way   Minneapol
   2     0002           1       Bob         Schmidt      978 Grill Lane   Bloomingt
   3     0003           1       Robin       Jones        888 Egg Drive    New York
   4     4              1       Chuck       Schmitt      555 Bit Ave      Rochester
   5     5              1       Jack        Spratt       1212 Steak Ave   Bloomingt
   6     5              2       Jack        Johnson      2121 Mechanic    Bloomingt


CHANGED  Client Number  AddNum  First Name  Last Name    Address      City
   1     1              1       Frank       Smith        345 Weiner Way   Minneapol
   2     2              1       Bob         Schmidt      978 Grill Lane   Bloomingt
   3     3              1       Robin       Jones        888 Egg Drive    New York
```

**Figure 10.1   A Paradox Changeto query using a conditional statement and example element.**

features of a standard query are still available in update queries—this is what gives the update query its power. The query simply selects all Client Numbers less than "4" and appends "000." The temporary table, CHANGED, records the old values before the update query was executed. You can then restore the database if you made a mistake. In fact, that's how the following examples illustrate **Delete** and **Insert** queries.

If you want to restore the old keys, a simple **Subtract** command could not delete the new entries from ADDRESS because the primary keys (the Client Numbers) of the ADDRESS and CHANGED tables do not match. However, the remaining columns are identical, so you can use a query to match the rows by placing example elements in each column (except the Client Number) of ADDRESS and CHANGED. Placing the **Delete** keyword in the left-hand column of the ADDRESS query form tells Paradox to delete rows from the ADDRESS table. Figure 10.2 shows the query and result. Paradox always removes temporary tables, such as CHANGED, from the query form after processing. So, if you perform this query on your system, the resulting screen will be different (for the purpose of this example, the query had to be restored). The DELETED temporary table contains the rows that were removed—a simple **Add** command could restore the ADDRESS table from this change (**Tools**, **More**, **Add**, **Deleted**, **Address**, **Update**).

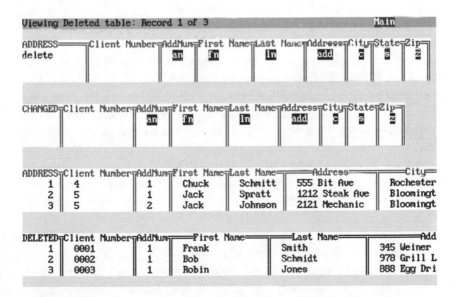

**Figure 10.2   The Delete query can match rows between ADDRESS and CHANGED even though the key (Client Number) has changed.**

```
Viewing Inserted table: Record 1 of 3                          Main ═▼

ADDRESS══════Client Number═AddNum═First Name═Last Name═Address═City═State═Zip═
insert        cn            an     fn         ln        add     c    s      z



CHANGED═Client Number═AddNum═First Name═Last Name═Address═City═State═Zip═
         cn            an     fn         ln        add     c    s      z



INSERTED═Client Number═AddNum══════First Name════════Last Name════════════Ad
   1        1            1       Frank            Smith              345 Weiner
   2        2            1       Bob              Schmidt            978 Grill
   3        3            1       Robin            Jones              888 Egg Dr


ADDRESS═Clie═AddNum═First Name═Last Name═══════Address═══════City═══════State
   1    1    1       Frank     Smith      345 Weiner Way  Minneapolis    MN
   2    2    1       Bob       Schmidt    978 Grill Lane  Bloomington    IN
   3    3    1       Robin     Jones      888 Egg Drive   New York       NY
   4    4    1       Chuck     Schmitt    555 Bit Ave     Rochester      MN
```

**Figure 10.3   An Insert query will restore the old keys (and matching columns) from CHANGED to ADDRESS.**

Finally, you can insert the rows from the CHANGED table to the ADDRESS table. Optionally, you could use the Add command since there are no conditions on the insertion, and the table structures match. With the update query, the example elements select the columns to include in the target. Therefore, you must include the key Client Number. You could also leave ADDRESS columns blank by omitting example elements in columns of the target. In Figure 10.3, ADDRESS has been completely restored.

You must be a bit careful with temporary tables. If you exit Paradox, they will be erased; or repeating the operation (e.g., a second **Insert**) will replace the temporary table with a new copy. Other operations may also replace the temporary tables. **Add** will sometimes create a CHANGED table when the destination is keyed (but **Add** will not create an INSERTED table). Using the temporary tables for recovery from mistakes is not foolproof. For example, when using Insert, primary keys in the target table may be overwritten by data from the source(s), and no CHANGED table will be created to help you get out of the resulting mess.

You can put the temporary tables to many creative uses other than error recovery. For example, when processing invoices, you could first Delete all current entries, copy the family from INVOICE to DELETED, and run the invoice reports from the DELETED table. Then, you could archive the processed invoices into another table with an **Add** or **Insert**. Such a process would allow other users on a network to change invoices that had not yet been processed. And it would not require an additional column or query to determine which invoices were still available for modification.

Sometimes, you may need to use programming instead of an update query. A **Changeto** query is very similar to scanning a table while in Edit mode, but is usually much faster. As noted in the programming chapters, Paradox does not allow PAL functions within its query calculations. Unlike queries, **Scan** loops can use functions (both standard and user-defined), so you should learn both techniques. For example, you could replace the previous **changeto** with the script:

```
Edit "Address"
Scan For [Client Number]"4"
   [Client Number]="000"+[Client Number]
EndScan
Do_It!
```

The other disadvantage of the script is that no CHANGED table is created, although you could add another table in the scan and use **CopyToArray** and **CopyFromArray** at the cost of even slower performance. Although any **Scan** will be slower than the equivalent query, if you need a PAL function, such as **Match** ( ) to process the changes, a **Scan** loop may be your only option. Consider an example where you add a Prefix code to an existing database. You want to separate a prefix such as "Dr." from the first name:

```
Edit "Address"
Scan For Match ([First Name], "Dr. ..",FN)
   [First Name]=FN
   [Prefix]="Dr."
EndScan
Do_It!
```

The more complex multitable update queries are more difficult to emulate with a **Scan** loop, although there are still times when they are useful. Even so, the beauty of an update query is that it is easier to understand: You can see a fairly simple picture of what will happen. With a program, there will be many nested loops and movements from table to table. A typical example would be an **Insert** query that consolidates information from many sources.

The query in Figure 10.4 creates a list for which more than $20.00 worth of parts have been ordered, and includes the name and phone numbers of the clients. You might want to try writing the equivalent script as an exercise. The

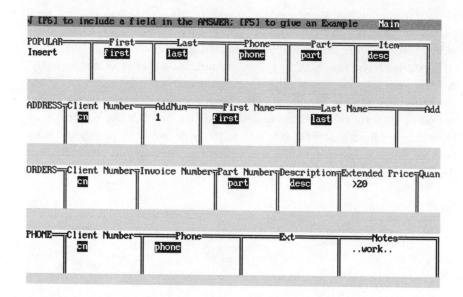

**Figure 10.4    An Insert query using multiple source tables.**

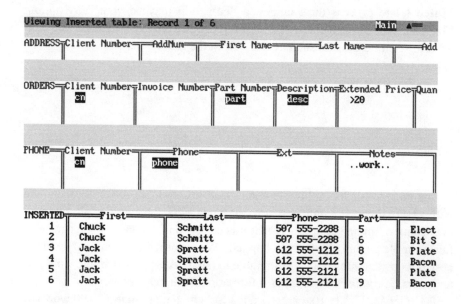

**Figure 10.5    The result of the query from Figure 10.4.**

result (based on the sample tables) is shown in Figure 10.5. Note this exception to duplicate suppression: Unlike the standard queries, the Paradox update queries do not eliminate duplicate rows; in this case, there were two work phone numbers for the same client.

The dBASE update queries are fairly similar to the Paradox queries, but the keywords are different: **Append**, **Mark**, **Unmark**, and **Replace**. As with interactive dBASE operations, rows are not actually deleted by queries. Rather, they are marked for later deletion when you **Pack** the table. Therefore, dBASE gives you an **Unmark** update query to reverse all or part of a **Mark** query. This gives you a way to undo the damage if you inadvertently delete the wrong rows. The **Append** query adds new rows (like the Paradox **Insert** query), and **Replace** changes a column value (like the Paradox **Changeto** operator).

Compared to their Paradox equivalents, the dBASE **Replace** query is the least similar to **Changeto**. It requires the keyword **Replace** in the far left column, and the keyword **With** to designate the modified column. Thus, in Figure 10.6, the UPRICE column will be increased by 5 percent for clients who do not have offices in Minnesota. Note that dBASE labels the query form for the updated table as the Target. Unlike Paradox, dBASE does not report the modifications made during an update; therefore, you should use a little extra caution when writing dBASE **Replace** queries.

| Layout   Fields   Condition   Update   Exit | | | | | | 6:59:08 pm | |
|---|---|---|---|---|---|---|---|
| ─Target─ Orders.dbf | CLIENTNUM | INVOICE | PART | DESC | QUAN | UPRICE | EPRICE |
| replace | CN | | | | | U, with U*1.05 | |

| Address.dbf | CLIENTNUM | ADDNUM | FIRST | LAST | ADDRESS | CITY | STATE | ZIP |
|---|---|---|---|---|---|---|---|---|
| | CN | | | | | | <>"MN" | |

```
Query    ||D:\dbase\files\INFLATE  ||Field 2/8           ||          || Num    Ins
         ||Prev/Next field:Shift-Tab/Tab  Data:F2  Size:Shift-F7  Prev/Next skel:F3/F4
```

**Figure 10.6    A dBASE Changeto query.   Note the location of Changeto; the With operator selects the column.**

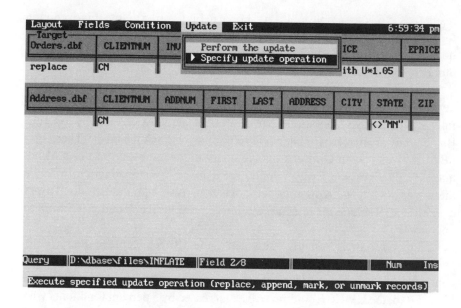

**Figure 10.7** Activating the update operation with Update, Perform the update.

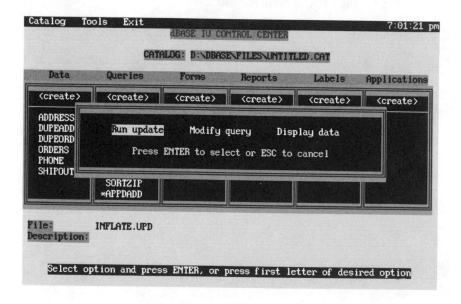

**Figure 10.8** Activating an update query through the Control Center.

There are several ways to run a dBASE update query. From within the query design screen, you may select **Update, Perform the update**, as shown in Figure 10.7. If you are working from the main dBASE menu, the update queries are designated with an asterisk (see Figure 10.8). You may select the query, and choose **Run update** from the menu, or you may execute the update from within a program. When you create an update query, dBASE compiles the query to a .UPD file. Thus, in the previous examples, the INFLATE query was compiled to INFLATE.UPD. You may run the program with a **Do** command, e.g., **Do Inflate.upd**. Note that you must include the .UPD extension to prevent dBASE from assuming a .PRG extension.

Because dBASE **Mark, Unmark,** and **Append** queries are nearly identical to their Paradox counterparts, you should be able to construct the dBASE **update** queries based on the Paradox examples. Rather than repeat a sequence of queries, which would be similar to the Paradox examples, let's look at another useful function of the insertion (**Append**) query. You can create a table that is essentially similar to a base table, with one extra column: This will be used as a selection field. Say, for example, that you want to select a limited set of invoices for printing. First, create a table like INVOICE with an extra column called Select. You needn't include all of the INVOICE columns, just enough to identify the invoice.

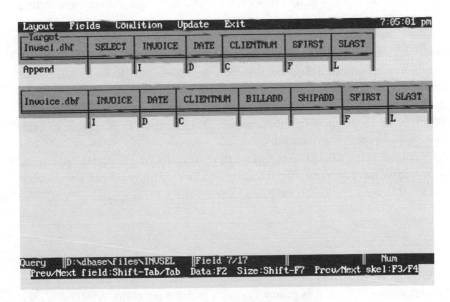

**Figure 10.9   Using a query to create a selection field.**

| Records | Organize | Fields | Go To | Exit | | |
|---|---|---|---|---|---|---|

| SELECT | INVOICE | DATE | CLIENTNUM | SFIRST | SLAST |
|---|---|---|---|---|---|
| | 1 | 10/22/90 | 4 | Chuck | Schmitt |
| | 2 | 10/22/90 | 2 | Bob | Schmidt |
| | 3 | 10/22/90 | 2 | Bob | Schmidt |
| | 4 | 10/22/90 | 3 | Robin | Jones |
| | 5 | 10/22/90 | 5 | Jack | Johnson |
| | 6 | 03/15/91 | 3 | Robin | Jones |
| | 8 | 03/15/91 | 5 | Jack | Johnson |

Browse    D:\dbase\files\INVSEL    Rec 1/7    File    Num

**Figure 10.10   A table with a selection column.**

Then, create an **Append** query to copy the relevant information. Figure 10.9 shows such a query. Even though the structures do not match, the **Append** query will insert the rows. This operation would still work if the corresponding column names were different or the source data came from different tables (the columns are mapped through example element names rather than column names or table structures). The result of the insertion is shown in Figure 10.10. The user can then place an "X", or some other mark, next to the invoices that should be printed. Another view can then select the full information for printout. Such a selection method may also be used to select rows for other actions such as deletion or modification. This method is adaptable to both dBASE and Paradox applications.

Of course, using dBASE there are methods for handling the same operations from within the programming language. Indeed, with a simple single-table extract, this would be much simpler in a program:

```
use invsel
append from invoice
```

As long as updates are limited to single source files (and especially when column names match), it is generally easier to use a program. Under dBASE, such operations are also safer. When dBASE runs low on memory, query operations may return incomplete results. dBASE does not return an error

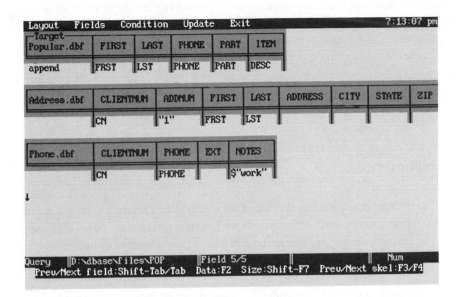

**Figure 10.11** **The top portion of the multiple source dBASE Append query modeled after Figure 10.4.**

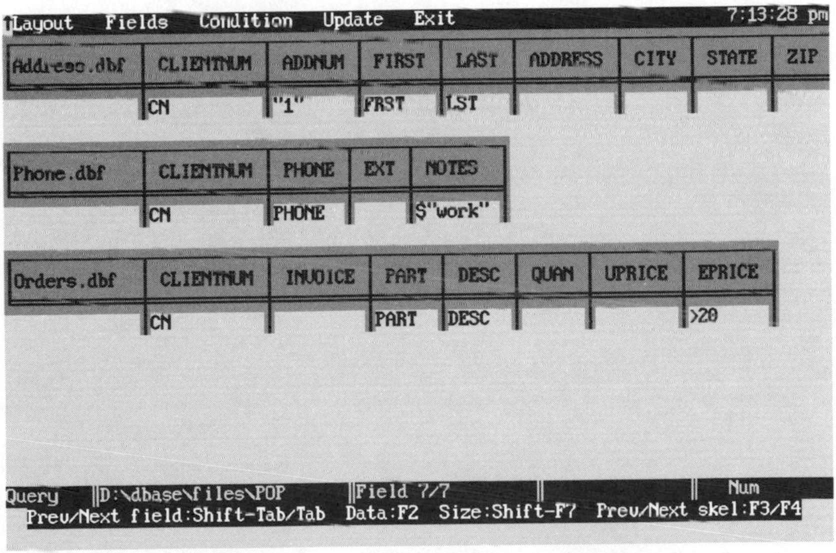

**Figure 10.12** **The bottom portion of the multiple source dBASE Append query.**

message under such circumstances, so you must use extreme caution when working with queries under tight memory constraints such as network workstations or DOS-based multitasking systems.

On the other hand, update queries that require several source tables are easier to manage with update queries. The dBASE query corresponding to the Paradox example (Figure 10.4) is shown in Figures 10.11 and 10.12.

## Summary

Update queries are an essential piece of the relational database toolkit—a piece that is often overlooked. Once you learn to write programs, it is sometimes tempting to use the programming language as a powerful tool to manage your application because a programming language is much more adaptable than database operations. But a database is designed to handle much of the work that has traditionally been the domain of custom programming; you should first look to the database features to manipulate data. Then, if the queries do not provide enough features, you can turn to custom programming.

# 11

# Final Words

By now, you should be familiar with many of the basics involved in building database applications on IBM-compatible computers. You have seen relational features (and lack of features) in the two most popular database packages. You should be able to write simple programs with these packages, and with some practice and attention to the reference manuals, to expand those simple programs into complete applications. If you are looking for a database package, you should have a good concept of what you need and which environment might best fit those needs.

There are many details of dBASE and Paradox that have not been covered in this book. But you should now have a good basis from which to learn the additional features. You should be able to glean much of this information from the manuals, or you could use one of the many books written specifically for the database you will be using. When looking for such references, it is useful to know what details you may need. For either system, if you are using a network, you should learn more about network particulars.

With Paradox, you will want to focus on the issues of private directories, temporary (or private) tables, and shared directories. With both Paradox and dBASE you should study "deadlock" or "deadly embrace" (this is where two or more network sessions can no longer proceed because each has locked resources the other needs). dBASE has an entire set of SQL commands which you may find helpful. Some of these commands help overcome the relational shortcomings of dBASE.

Both dBASE and Paradox have SQL components to their systems, though the Paradox method is more tightly integrated with the system. SQL will probably be more important in the next few years as network servers begin to handle database requests directly. In this mode, the database processing becomes more distributed: One portion is handled by the local computer (the client) and the other portion by the remote computer (the server).

For example, most network applications use the server as a remote, shared disk drive. All of the data would be sent across the network; in a query Paradox or dBASE would read every byte of a file and select only that portion which matched the conditions. However, with an SQL server, dBASE or Paradox could send an SQL query to the server. The server would select only the data matching the request and send it back to the local computer, cutting network traffic and improving performance. Such distributed databases are an important component of Codd's RDBMS design, though most systems fall far short of the mark. As of this writing, Paradox includes a program called SQL Link, which accesses data on an SQL server. Borland has announced, but not yet delivered, a product called dBASE Server, which would support the same capabilities.

Most of the discussion has focused on features which are similar to Codd's model, listing the shortcomings only when they are directly related to a supported feature. There are, however, several features that the packages do not support at all (or support in name, with very little resemblance to Codd's concepts). For example, neither package really supports a catalog, which contains all information about the database, as such a catalog must store information in tables. Although Codd refers to the catalog as a single object, it would probably be implemented as a special collection of tables. The catalog should be updated as tables are created, modified, and destroyed. It would store information about names (tables, domains, columns), integrity constraints, data types, statistics, etc.

With Paradox, you can retrieve information about table names, column definitions, and so forth, through the **Tools, Info** menu. But this places much of the responsibility on the programmer. And Paradox cannot group arbitrary tables into a single database. dBASE has a catalog and unlike Paradox, it *may* be automatically updated as arbitrary objects are created, deleted, or moved. At the menu (**Assist**) level this is automatic, but it must be explicitly set (**Set Catalog To** *CatName*) at the dot prompt. It is limited to only the object names, type, and description. There is no direct listing of column names, data types, and relations. Like Paradox, this information must be retrieved through commands.

Why is such a catalog important? Because as a system grows, you want to be able to find what types and ranges of data are stored, and where they are located. Does the database have vendor part numbers? Which tables and views contain this information? Ideally, such questions could be answered with a simple query. With dBASE or Paradox, such questions require a special program (or a great deal of determination when working with the menus).

Statistics are an important part of the catalog because they can help the DBMS make more efficient use of resources. For example, if part of a distributed database lies over a slow communications line, the DBMS should be able to design an appropriate query to minimize communication time. To do this, the catalog must contain information about the relative data transfer times and approximate quantity of data to transfer.

Data security is another important issue, especially as an application is moved to network operation. Both dBASE and Paradox have password protection available. While this is certainly useful for restricting access to sensitive data, it does little to prevent destruction of data. Although you can prevent table deletion from within an application, a user need only drop out to DOS and erase the file there. Under Codd's definitions, you would not have the option of bypassing the database system to alter an object because the database itself would be an integral part of the operating system.

As your programs take on more sophisticated features, you may have uses for other features such as transaction logging. Ideally, an RDBMS traces all changes to the data. At any time, it should be possible to restore the system to an earlier state. This could be especially important in the case of a power failure or system crash. Both Paradox and dBASE have autosave features that at least help prevent such disasters, but they are not perfect. A badly timed power outage can still corrupt the tables. At this level, it is important to make regular backups of the system.

Transaction logging is, in some respects, similar to a system backup. But, it has a limited scope. Generally, a command initiates a transaction. Then, at any point, you may *rollback* or *commit* a transaction. In the former case, any changes since the beginning of the transaction are reversed. In the latter case, the changes are made permanent so that they cannot be reversed. A transaction operates across many tables and programming statements. A typical case is a banking transaction—money is transferred from one account to another. But after processing the deposit, it's discovered that the withdrawal is too large. A rollback insures that both accounts are restored to their original state.

Paradox initiates a transaction every time Edit mode is begun. From the interactive (menu) level, the changes may be reversed one at a time with the **Undo (Ctrl-U)** command. Or, all of the changes may be abandoned with the **Cancel** selection from the menu. Paradox gives even more options from within PAL: **EditLog Revert** does a rollback and **EditLog Permanent** accepts the current changes (without ending edit mode). But you may also **EditLog Mark** to set subtransactions (each **Revert** will return to the next earlier **Mark**).

Unfortunately, transaction logging does not work within multitable forms or CoEdit mode, so there are some fairly severe limitations to this method.

dBASE uses a transaction structure similar to a control loop (such as **Do While... EndDo**). However, nesting is not allowed with **Begin Transaction... End Transaction** blocks. A **Rollback** command will restore the tables to their pre-transaction state and skip to the instruction following the **End Transaction** command. dBASE transactions are much more comprehensive than PAL; as is proper, a **Rollback** affects all changes to the database, independent of the mode used. In fact, a dBASE **Rollback** will delete any tables which were created during the transaction.

As you can see, a database environment can give you great control over data management. You can start from simple beginnings—small data organizers of perhaps one or two files—and grow to a system including many (perhaps hundreds) of related files with sophisticated management and reporting options. Fortunately, such projects can be built in an orderly fashion if the underlying concepts are understood. Hopefully, you now have a firm basis on which to build. With some help from the manuals and more advanced books on the subject, you should be well on your way to developing an important asset.

# Appendix A

# Report Design

Chapter 7 outlined report usage and report integration within the database modeling techniques used by dBASE and Paradox. However, the details about creating the reports were not included. This Appendix outlines the process of creating the reports for Chapter 7. The sample reports required the part number, quantity, description, and price to print line-by-line details of an invoice. The default Paradox report would include the invoice number and client number on each line (see Figure A.1), so this information must be removed. To do this, move to the lines with Client Number and Invoice Number and hit **Ctrl-Y** to remove them.

The blank lines at the top and bottom of the form band should be removed, too. Next, remove the field descriptions by moving to the first character in the line and hitting Del until the first character of the field (e.g., **AAAAAA**) is flush against the left margin. Remove the Extended Price line with **Ctrl-Y**. The result should look like Figure A.2.

Now the fields must be moved to the same line. Place the report in Insert mode with Ins (the default is Overtype mode). Now move to the first character of the last field and hit backspace. This will move the field up to the previous line as in Figure A.3. Use a space to separate the fields. Now string the remaining fields together in the same manner.

As with forms, you can use a calculated field to print the extended price. Move the cursor to the right of the last field and select **Field**, **Place**, **Calculated**, **[Quantity]\*[Unit Price]**. The field is located and sized with the cursor keys (just like placing a field within a form). For this particular report, the unit price field should be shortened by placing the cursor on the Unit Price field and

```
Designing report R for Orders table                      Report    1/1
Report Header
....+...10....+...20....+...30....+...40....+...50....+...60....+...70....+...8*

 ▼page

mm/dd/yy                        Invoice                          Page 99

 ▼form

Client Number: AAAAAA
Invoice Number: AAAAA
Part Number: AAAAA
Description: AAAAAAAAAAAAAAAAAAAA
Quantity: 999999
Unit Price: (999,999,999.99)
Extended Price: (999,999,999.99)

 ▲form
```

Figure A.1    The default Paradox INVOICE report.

```
Designing report R for Orders table                      Report    1/1
Form Band                                                     Part Number
....+...10....+...20....+...30....+...40....+...50....+...60....+...70....+...8*

 ▼page

mm/dd/yy                        Invoice                          Page 99

 ▼form
AAAAAA
AAAAAAAAAAAAAAAAAAAA
999999
(999,999,999.99)
 ▲form

 ▲page
```

Figure A.2    Blank lines within the form band have been removed with
Ctrl-Y.  Extended Price has been removed, too.

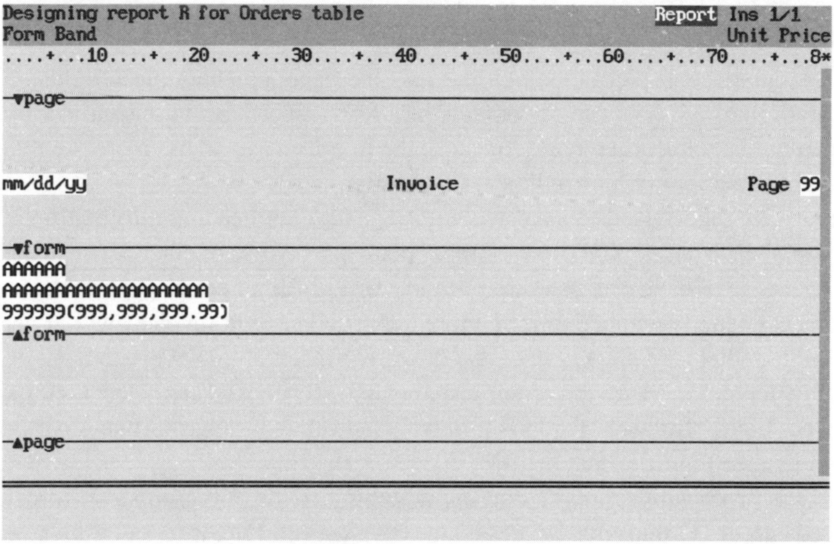

```
Designing report R for Orders table                    Report Ins 1/1
Form Band                                                     Unit Price
....+...10....+...20....+...30....+...40....+...50....+...60....+...70....+...8*

 ▬▼page─────────────────────────────────────────────────────────────────


mm/dd/yy                          Invoice                      Page 99

 ▬▼form─────────────────────────────────────────────────────────────────
AAAAAA
AAAAAAAAAAAAAAAAAAAAAA
999999(999,999,999.99)
 ▬▲form───────────────────────────────────────────────────────────────



 ▬▲page─────────────────────────────────────────────────────────────────
```

Figure A.3  The Unit Price field has been moved to the same line as
Quantity by placing the cursor at the start of Unit Price and hitting the
backspace key (insert mode must be on).

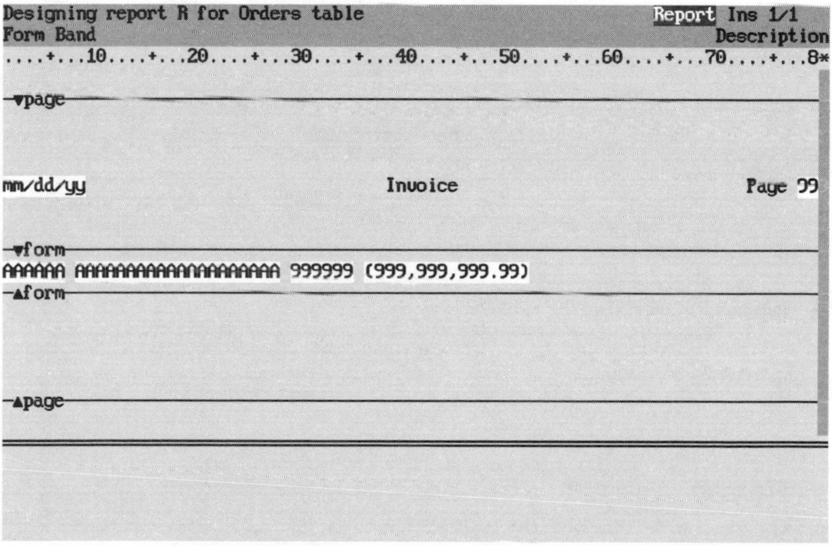

```
Designing report R for Orders table                    Report Ins 1/1
Form Band                                                     Description
....+...10....+...20....+...30....+...40....+...50....+...60....+...70....+...8*

 ▬▼page─────────────────────────────────────────────────────────────────


mm/dd/yy                          Invoice                      Page 99

 ▬▼form─────────────────────────────────────────────────────────────────
AAAAAA AAAAAAAAAAAAAAAAAAAAAA 999999 (999,999,999.99)
 ▬▲form───────────────────────────────────────────────────────────────



 ▬▲page─────────────────────────────────────────────────────────────────
```

Figure A.4  All fields have been moved to the same line.  This is similar
to a Tabular Report.

selecting **Field**, **Reformat**, **Digits**. The result (Figure A.4) is nearly identical to a tabular report.

A tabular report places the fields across the page; it cannot place fields on separate lines as shown in the default free-form report. So in this case, why bother with a free-form report? Because the free-form report has more flexible formatting options, which will be used shortly.

Next the report needs an invoice number and other heading information at the top of each page. You cannot simply place the invoice number between the form and page bands; if you did, Paradox would fill an entire page with the contents of the form band in base table order and several invoices would get mixed together. To prevent this, you must first insert a special group band on the invoice field: Move the cursor just above the form band and select **Group**, **Insert**, **Field**, **Invoice**. Paradox inserts a new band called Group Invoice Number (see Figure A.5).

In the process of grouping data by matching fields, the group also forces sorted output. Groups may be nested to sort on several fields (e.g., Last Name and First Name). The outermost Group takes the highest precedence; thus, to alphabetize by last name and break the ties with first names, the Last Name group should be on the outside.

To print the invoice number once for each group (and hence, once for each invoice), place the Invoice Number field between the group and form bands

```
Designing report R for Orders table                          Report  Ins 1/1
Group Header for Invoice Number
....+...10....+...20....+...30....+...40....+...50....+...60....+...70....+...8*

  ─▼page─────────────────────────────────────────────────────────────────────


mm/dd/yy                           Invoice                              Page 99

  ───▼group Invoice Number────────────────────────────────────────────────────

  ─▼form─────────────────────────────────────────────────────────────────────
AAAAAA AAAAAAAAAAAAAAAAAAAAA 999999 (999,999,999.99)
  ─▲form─────────────────────────────────────────────────────────────────────
  ───▲group Invoice Number────────────────────────────────────────────────────




  ─▲page─────────────────────────────────────────────────────────────────────
```

**Figure A.5   The Invoice Number group bank will sort the output by Invoice Number.**

with **Field, Place, Regular, Invoice Number**. You will also want each invoice on a separate page. To force a page break before the page is filled with invoices, type PAGEBREAK (it *must* be in all capital letters) just above the bottom Group Invoice Number band. To improve the appearance, put some space between the invoice number (at the top) and the form band.

Groups are useful for another purpose—summary totals. An invoice requires a total for the entire order. In this example, you must calculate the total extended price. Create a new line just below the form band, move the cursor under the extended price, and select **Field, Place, Summary, Calculated, [Quantity]*[Unit Price], Sum, PerGroup**. The last two selections (**Sum, PerGroup**) choose a total (as opposed to the **Average, Count, High,** or **Low** value), which is set to 0 after every group (as opposed to **Overall**, which would use a running total). The complete report, thus far, resembles Figure A.6. This figure also includes descriptive labels just above the form band. These labels are simple text entries typed from the keyboard.

Now it's time to add details from other tables, and this is where you run into the first major stumbling block: inserting the billing and shipping address. The billing and shipping address codes are located in the INVOICE table, but the actual addresses are stored in the ADDRESS table. As with forms, reports cannot nest links. There is no address number link in the order table, so the link cannot be made. This is a major problem in Paradox—the conceptual

```
Designing report R for Orders table                    Report  Ins 1/1
Group Footer for Invoice Number      Total for [Quantity]*[Unit Price], per group
....+...10....+...20....+...30....+...40....+...50....+...60....+...70....+...8*

   ─▼page────────────────────────────────────────────────────────────

mm/dd/yy                           Invoice                         Page 99

     ─▼group Invoice Number──────────────────────────────────────────
AAAAAA

                             Unit
Part # Description           Quan  Price    Total
  ─▼form──────────────────────────────────────────────────────────────
AAAAAA AAAAAAAAAAAAAAAAAAAAA 999999 (999.99) (9,999.99)
  ─▲form──────────────────────────────────────────────────────────────
                                             (9,999.99)
PAGEBREAK
     ─▲group Invoice Number──────────────────────────────────────────
```

**Figure A.6  The PAGEBREAK will force a formfeed after each invoice. Summary Invoice numbers and total price (per invoice) have been added.**

models for form and report design do not match: The former is based on a general table and the latter on a detail table. Before you can continue, you must save the current state of the report with **F2**.

There are ways to patch around the problem. You can write a query to join INVOICE and ADDRESS, use it as the basis of the report, and then empty the table (to save space on the disk). This approach can be automated through programming, as outlined in Chapter 9. In order to show how the multitable report works, the manual process will be described here. The query and resulting ANSWER are shown in Figure A.7. Note that the query avoids a many-to-many join by separating the address fields into billing and shipping addresses.

The ANSWER table is not keyed (a requirement for summary tables used by multitable reports). You could use **Modify**, **Restructure** and add a primary key to the Invoice Number. But this would be awkward and slow when later automated. Creating an empty dummy table is a better approach. First, create a table called INVREP (for Invoice Report): **Tools**, **Create**, **Invrep**. Rather than manually entering the field descriptions, you may use **Borrow**, **Answer**. Paradox enters the field descriptions automatically, as shown in Figure A.8. Key the Invoice field by placing an "*" after the "A6" and hit **F2**.

Now, you can create a multitable report by linking fields from Invrep into the Orders report. You can start editing where you last left off with **Report**,

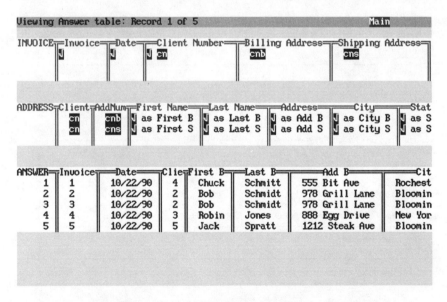

**Figure A.7    A query to produce summary information for linkage to the INVOICE table.**

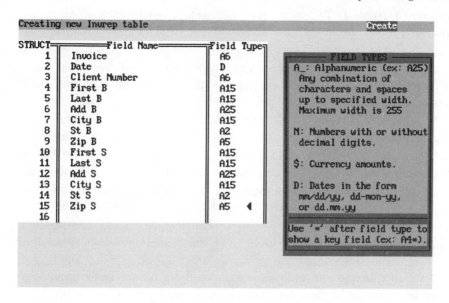

Creating new Inurep table                                    Create

```
STRUCT══════════Field Name══════════Field Type═
  1 ║ Invoice                    A6        ┌─────── FIELD TYPES ───────
  2 ║ Date                       D         A_: Alphanumeric (ex: A25)
  3 ║ Client Number              A6        Any combination of
  4 ║ First B                    A15       characters and spaces
  5 ║ Last B                     A15       up to specified width.
  6 ║ Add B                      A25       Maximum width is 255
  7 ║ City B                     A15
  8 ║ St B                       A2        N: Numbers with or without
  9 ║ Zip B                      A5        decimal digits.
 10 ║ First S                    A15
 11 ║ Last S                     A15       $: Currency amounts.
 12 ║ Add S                      A25
 13 ║ City S                     A15       D: Dates in the form
 14 ║ St S                       A2        mm/dd/yy, dd-mon-yy,
 15 ║ Zip S                      A5   ◀    or dd.mm.yy
 16 ║
                                          Use '*' after field type to
                                          show a key field (ex: A4*).
```

**Figure A.8** From the Create menu, select Borrow, Answer to replicate the ANSWER structure. The table will then be keyed on Invoice.

```
Field to place                                      Report    1/1
◀ Part Number  Description  Quantity  Unit Price  Extended Price  [Invrep->]
....+...10....+...20....+...30....+...40 ..,+,..50....+...60....+...70....+...8*

▼page─────────────────────────────────────────────────────────


mm/dd/yy                        Invoice                        Page 99

────▼group Invoice Number───────────────────────────────────────────
AAAAAA

                         Unit
Part # Description       Quan  Price    Total
─▼form────────────────────────────────────────────────────────────
AAAAAA AAAAAAAAAAAAAAAAAAAAAA 999999 (999.99) (9,999.99)
─▲form────────────────────────────────────────────────────────────
                                       (9,999.99)
PAGEBREAK
────▲group Invoice Number───────────────────────────────────────────
```

**Figure A.9** Once the link has been established, [Invrep->] appears as one of the field choices.

**Change**, **Orders**, **1**. To link the INVREP table, select **Field**, **Lookup**, **Link**, **Invrep**, **Invoice Number**. Now, when you select **Field**, **Place**, one of the menu choices will be **[Invrep->]** (see Figure A.9). As you may have noticed in the calculated fields, square brackets are sometimes used to indicate a field name. If an arrow appears within the square brackets, the name ahead of the arrow is a table name, and the (optional) name after the arrow indicates a specific field.

If you select **[Invrep->]**, the fields within INVREP are displayed, as in Figure A.10. If you ever want to see a list of the linked tables from within this menu, simply hit "[." Now you can finish the invoice by placing the billing and shipping addresses on the report form (see Figure A.11). The current date and page number fields have been removed from the header with **Field**, **Erase**.

The results from ANSWER must be added to the dummy table by using **Tools**, **More**, **Add**, **Answer**, **Invrep**, **NewEntries**. To print the report, select **Report**, **Output**, **Orders**, **1**, **Printer**. You can also test the output by sending it to the screen (**Screen**) or a file (**File**, *filename*). If you try this example, you will see that there are several items that could use fixing: better alignment, more labels, etc. You can return to **Report**, **Change** to make some modifications. Particular attention should be focused on the space between first and last names, and cities and states—there is simply too much. Free-form reports have a feature that can remove the extra space. **Setting**, **RemoveBlanks**, **FieldSqueeze**, **Yes** will close space between fields, and **Setting**,

```
Field to place                                          Report      1/1
Invoice  Date  Client Number  First B  Last B  Add B  City B  St B  Zip B ▶
....+...10....+...20....+...30....+...40....+...50....+...60....+...70....+...8*

 ▼page

mm/dd/yy                            Invoice                         Page 99

    ▼group Invoice Number
AAAAAA

                             Unit
Part # Description      Quan  Price    Total
 ▼form
AAAAAA AAAAAAAAAAAAAAAAAAAAA 999999 (999.99) (9,999.99)
 ▲form
                                       (9,999.99)
PAGEBREAK
    ▲group Invoice Number
```

**Figure A.10  The fields from INVREP are displayed within the IN-VOICE report after selecting [Invrep->].**

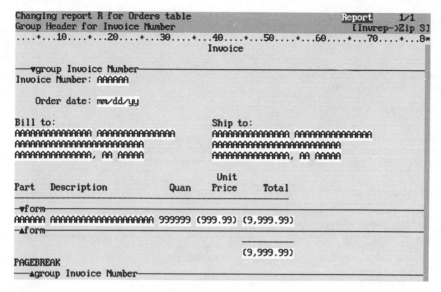

```
Changing report R for Orders table                          Report    1/1
Group Header for Invoice Number                        [Invrep->Zip S]
....+...10....+...20....+...30....+...40....+...50....+...60....+...70....+...8*
                              Invoice

     ─▼group Invoice Number────────────────────────────────────────
Invoice Number: AAAAAA

     Order date: mm/dd/yy

Bill to:                              Ship to:
AAAAAAAAAAAAAAA AAAAAAAAAAAAAAA       AAAAAAAAAAAAAAA AAAAAAAAAAAAAAA
AAAAAAAAAAAAAAAAAAAAAAAAAAA           AAAAAAAAAAAAAAAAAAAAAAAAAAA
AAAAAAAAAAAAAAA, AA AAAAA             AAAAAAAAAAAAAAA, AA AAAAA

                                          Unit
Part   Description            Quan     Price    Total
──────────────────────────────────────────────────────────────────
─▼form────────────────────────────────────────────────────────────
AAAAAA AAAAAAAAAAAAAAAAAAAAA 999999 (999.99) (9,999.99)
─▲form────────────────────────────────────────────────────────────

                                       (9,999.99)
                                      ──────────
PAGEBREAK
     ─▲group Invoice Number────────────────────────────────────────
```

**Figure A.11   The finished INVOICE report with fields linked from IN-VREP.**

**RemoveBlanks, LineSqueeze, Yes, Fixed|Variable** will remove unprinted lines (for example, two-line addresses with only one line).

However, **FieldSqueeze** and **LineSqueeze** have several disadvantages. They will not work in group bands (where our addresses are located) and they will close up all spacing. Thus, all of the order lines would be thrown out of alignment and the addresses would not be affected. Even if the group bands were affected by the squeeze options, you would have problems because the billing address and shipping address are printed side by side (the shipping address would then be thrown out of alignment).

Fortunately, there is a feature that you can use to overcome some of these limitations: calculated fields. For example, in Figure A.12, the First and Last billing names have been replaced with **Field, Place, Calculated, [Invrep->First B]+" "+[Invrep->Last B]**. Similarly, the city, state, zip code line was replaced with **[Invrep->City B]+", "+[Invrep->St B]+" "+[Invrep->Zip B]**. The new format also includes separator lines and right-aligned labels over numbers. Before saving the changes, you can check the results with **Output, Screen** as shown in Figure A.13. The report is now complete.

```
Changing report R for Orders table                          Report    1/1
Group Header for Invoice Number          [Invrep->first b]+" "+[Invrep->last b]
....+...10....+...20....+...30....+...40....+...50....+...60....+...70....+...8*
                              Invoice

    ─vgroup Invoice Number───────────────────────────────────────────────
Invoice Number: AAAAAA

    Order date: mm/dd/yy

Bill to:                              Ship to:
AAAAAAAAAAAAAAAAAAAAAAAAAAAAAAAAA     AAAAAAAAAAAAAAAAAAAAAAAAAAAAAAAAA
AAAAAAAAAAAAAAAAAAAAAAAAAAA           AAAAAAAAAAAAAAAAAAAAAAAAAAA
AAAAAAAAAAAAAAAAAAAAAAAAAAA           AAAAAAAAAAAAAAAAAAAAAAAAAAA

                                           Unit
Part    Description             Quan      Price     Total

─vform──────────────────────────────────────────────────────────────────
AAAAAA  AAAAAAAAAAAAAAAAAAAAA 999999  (999.99)  (9,999.99)
─Δform──────────────────────────────────────────────────────────────────
                                                 ───────────
                                                  (9,999.99)

PAGEBREAK
    ─Δgroup Invoice Number───────────────────────────────────────────────
```

**Figure A.12**   The composite field entries (name and city, state, zip) have been replaced with calculated fields.

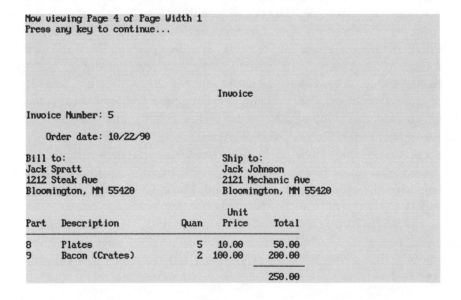

```
Now viewing Page 4 of Page Width 1
Press any key to continue...




                              Invoice

Invoice Number: 5

    Order date: 10/22/90

Bill to:                              Ship to:
Jack Spratt                           Jack Johnson
1212 Steak Ave                        2121 Mechanic Ave
Bloomington, MN 55420                 Bloomington, MN 55420

                                           Unit
Part    Description             Quan      Price     Total

8       Plates                    5      10.00      50.00
9       Bacon (Crates)            2     100.00     200.00
                                                  ─────────
                                                    250.00
```

**Figure A.13**   Using Output, Screen to preview the report on the display.

# Labels

Labels are a special modification of free-form reports. Thus far, the sample reports have used a single report width. In the figures, the right margin of the report can be seen as a dark line down the right side of the screen. If the text or fields extend beyond this margin, Paradox will first print all pages of the first leftmost section, then print the next section for all pages, and continue printing sections until the rightmost section has finished. Paradox calls these side-by-side sections *page widths.*

Normally, you will avoid multiple page widths. Placing several sections side by side makes organizing and viewing the data difficult. But some labels come in sheets with several columns (e.g., four-across labels). Although Paradox usually prints only one record per line (or page widths), you can override this default to print successive records side by side in each page width.

As an example, consider labels for the orders from the invoice application. Since the order information is not needed for the labels, you can use the INVOICE table as the label basis. First make a new free-form report (number 1) for the INVOICE table and remove all spaces between the form band and page band. It's also important to remove the first blank line before the page

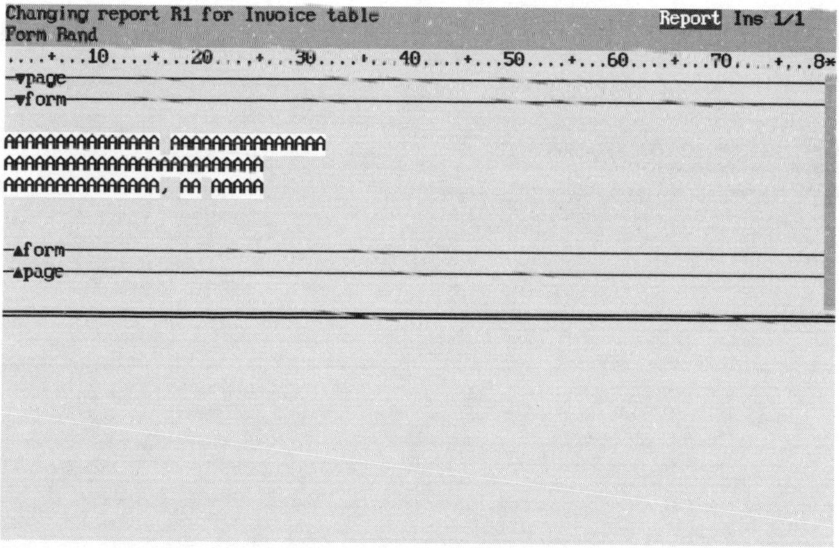

**Figure A.14    A basic label format for INVOICE.**

band to make label alignment (in the printer) easier. Otherwise, the report will always print one extra line at the beginning of each print job.

Next link the ADDRESS table to the INVOICE table with **Field**, **Lookup**, **Link**, **Address**, **Client Number**, **Shipping Address**. The Shipping Address selection links the shipping address number to the AddNum in the ADDRESS table. Thus, it will print *only* the shipping addresses. The basic layout is shown in Figure A.14. We'll use a four-across layout with 1 × 3.5-inch labels (a fairly common format). One inch high is six lines, so the top and bottom of the form band have been padded with extra blank lines to make a total of six lines.

To narrow the right margin for a 3.5-inch wide label (with ten characters per inch), select **Setting**, **PageLayout**, **Width**, **35**. In Figure A.15, note that additional page widths have been automatically added. The 1/3 in the upper right-hand corner of the screen indicates that the cursor is in the first width of three. When the right margin is narrowed, Paradox converts the extra width from the original page into new page widths.

Watch out! In the process of fine-tuning your layout, you may often discover an additional page width where none was wanted. Then, when you try to print your labels, you'll get a very messy result as the printer attempts to print extra labels off the end of the page (frequently wrapping text to the next line as the printer hits the right margin).

```
Changing report R1 for Invoice table                        Report Ins 1/3
Form Band                                              [Address->First Name]
....+...10....+...20....+...30....*....+...10....+...20....+...30....*....+...10
 ─▼page─
  ─▼form─

 AAAAAAAAAAAAAAA AAAAAAAAAAAAAAA
 AAAAAAAAAAAAAAAAAAAAAAAAAAA
 AAAAAAAAAAAAAA, AA AAAAA


 ─▲form─
 ─▲page─
```

**Figure A.15   Setting the width lower creates two new page widths for a total of three across (note the 1/3 in the upper right-hand corner).**

```
Changing report R1 for Invoice table                    Report  Ins 1/4
Form Band                                            [Address->First Name]
....+...10....+...20....+...30....*....+...10....+...20....+...30....*....+...10
 ─▼page─
 ─▼form─

 AAAAAAAAAAAAAA  AAAAAAAAAAAAAA
 AAAAAAAAAAAAAAAAAAAAAAAAAAAA
 AAAAAAAAAAAAAA, AA AAAAA


 ─▲form─
 ─▲page─
```

**Figure A.16   A new page width has been added for a total of four across.**

Page length must also be adjusted. Labels work best with a continuous length setting, rather than a specific number of lines. This is set with **Setting**, **PageLayout**, **Length**, **C** (the "C" stands for "continuous"). This report also needs another page width (for a total of four), so select **Setting**, **PageLayout**, **Insert** (Insert and Delete refer to inserting and deleting page widths). The new layout appears in Figure A.16.

If you attempt to print the labels at this point, you will still get only one-across labels. Since no fields are in the three new page widths, nothing will print there. However, if you place fields in the additional page widths, Paradox will simply make four copies of the same label. **Setting**, **Labels**, **Yes** tells Paradox to print the format from width one in the other widths, but access sequential records for each width. The image does not change in appearance from Figure A.16. The only way to later confirm the label setting is to print the labels, or select **Setting**, **Labels**. In the latter case, the default will appear as **Yes** if the label setting is enabled and **No** if the label setting is disabled (see Figure A.17).

The current output from **Output**, **Screen** appears in Figure A.18. Note that, as with the invoices, the names and cities are followed by unsightly space. This time, you can remove the space with **Setting**, **RemoveBlanks**, **FieldSqueeze**, **Yes**. You should also set **Setting**, **RemoveBlanks**, **LineSqueeze**, **Yes**, **Fixed**. Then, if you later add a second address line (or other information), you will not have blank lines printed between other lines when some fields are blank. The **Fixed** setting prints the same number of lines for each label (six in this case).

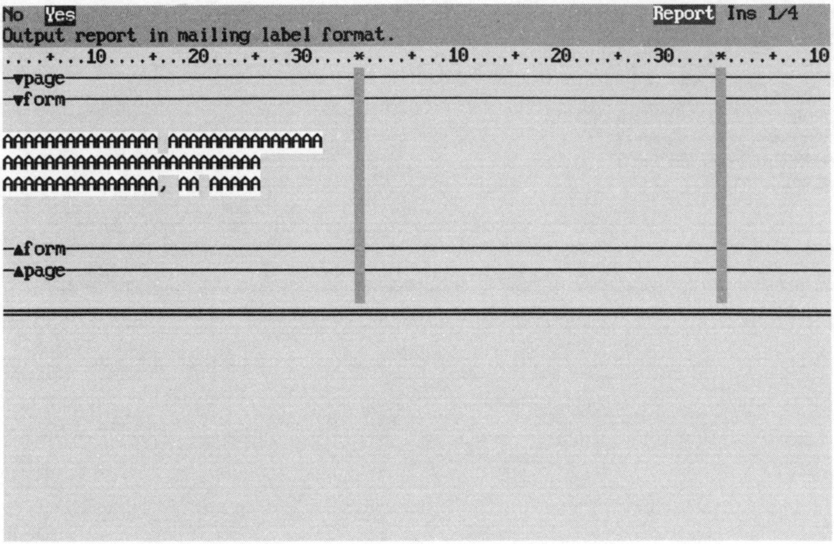

```
No  Yes                                                      Report  Ins 1/4
Output report in mailing label format.
....+...10....+...20....+...30....*....+...10....+...20....+...30....*....+...10
—▼page
—▼form

AAAAAAAAAAAAAA AAAAAAAAAAAAAA
AAAAAAAAAAAAAAAAAAAAAAA
AAAAAAAAAAAAA, AA AAAAA


—▲form
—▲page
```

Figure A.17   The Yes default under Setting, Labels indicates that label format has already been selected.

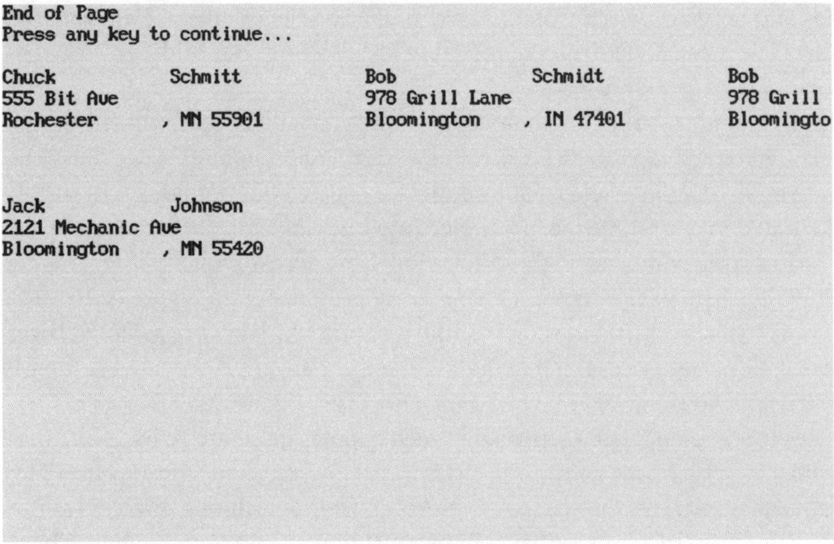

```
End of Page
Press any key to continue...

Chuck         Schmitt        Bob            Schmidt         Bob
555 Bit Ave                  978 Grill Lane                 978 Grill
Rochester     , MN 55901     Bloomington    , IN 47401      Bloomingto


Jack          Johnson
2121 Mechanic Ave
Bloomington   , MN 55420
```

Figure A.18   The screen output shows that the labels need a few refinements to remove the extra space.

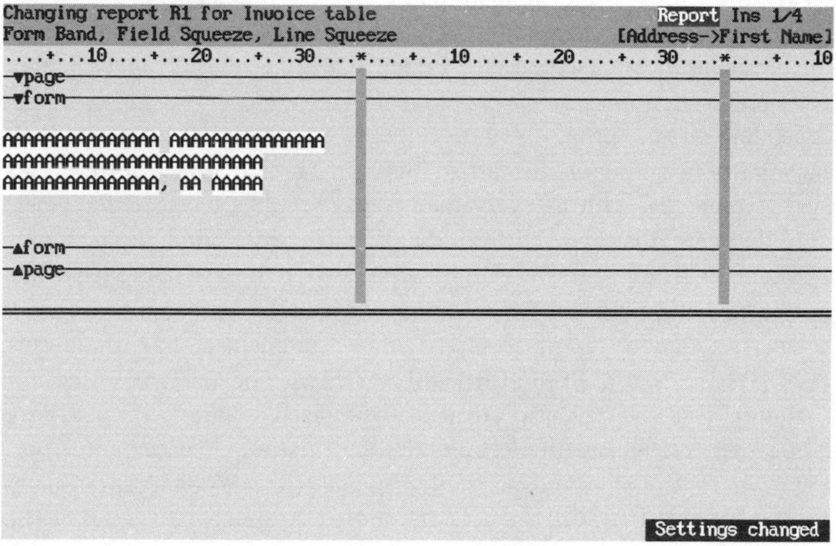

```
Changing report R1 for Invoice table                     Report  Ins 1/4
Form Band, Field Squeeze, Line Squeeze             [Address->First Name]
....+...10....+...20....+...30....*....+...10....+...20....+...30....*....+...10
 ▼page
 ▼form

AAAAAAAAAAAAAAAA AAAAAAAAAAAAAA
AAAAAAAAAAAAAAAAAAAAAAAAAA
AAAAAAAAAAAAAA, AA AAAAA



 ▲form
 ▲page



                                                          Settings changed
```

Figure A.19    The FieldSqueeze and LineSqueeze indicators in the upper
left-hand corner indicate that these options have been turned on.

```
End of Page
Press any key to continue...

Chuck Schmitt              Bob Schmidt                 Bob Schmid
555 Bit Ave               978 Grill Lane             978 Grill
Rochester, MN 55901       Bloomington, IN 47401      Bloomingto


Jack Johnson
2121 Mechanic Ave
Bloomington, MN 55420
```

Figure A.20    The new screen output with squeeze enabled is much easier
to read.

The **Variable** setting would simply omit the line and ruin the label alignment. Unlike the labels setting, **FieldSqueeze** and **LineSqueeze** are confirmed at the top of the report design screen (see Figure A.19; the revised screen output appears in Figure A.20).

Depending on your printer, you may need to adjust the left margin to keep characters from printing on the carrier (**Setting**, **Margin**, *MarginSize*). This can cause problems with the very narrow page widths required for labels because the margin is removed from the printable area. Some printers have control commands for setting a margin—this is often the best approach if it is supported on your printer (check your printer manual).

You can set Paradox reports to send a control command at the beginning of a report. **Setting**, **Setup**, **Predefined** will present a list of standard settings for font control. But you can also create a customized setting (as a hardware margin would require) with **Setting**, **Setup**, **Custom**, *PrinterPort*, *CommandString*. The printer port specifies where the printer is connected (usually LPT1, but LPT2, LPT3, COM1, COM2, and AUX are also available). The command string is the string of characters that must be sent to the printer to set the desired feature.

For example, to set a margin, an IBM Proprinter uses Esc X#1#2 (where #1 is the left margin and #2 is the right margin). The escape character cannot be entered into the string, but Paradox allows a backslash followed by three digits representing the ASCII encoding. Thus, Esc can be represented as \027. Similarly, the margin sizes can be encoded. Thus, \027X\004\255 would send Esc X with a left margin of 4 and a right margin of 255 (the maximum). A few of the more common codes have abbreviations:

| *Code* | *Character* |
|--------|-------------|
| \\ | Backslash |
| \n | Linefeed (newline) |
| \r | Carriage return |
| \f | Formfeed |
| \" | Quotation mark |
| \t | Tab |

You should avoid setup strings wherever possible since they limit reports to a single printer. It also helps to set the page length to 60 lines (**Setting**, **PageLayout**, **Length**, **60**) and use formfeeds, rather than linefeeds to eject the page. By using these settings and avoiding setup strings, the report will work with almost every printer in use today (except PostScript-compatible printers).

The length should be limited to 60 lines because most laser printers have a maximum printable length of 60 lines on a letter-size page. Both the default length and the page eject option may be set through the Paradox Custom Configuration Program (see Appendix E).

Even if you must use setup strings for something such as compressed print, you can override the defined string through the main menu **Report, SetPrinter, Override, Setup**. In fact, you may override the printer port and/or page eject option by using **PrinterPort** or **EndOfPage** in place of **Setup**. Once an override is set, it will affect *all* reports printed until the override is cancelled with **Reports, Override, Regular**.

If you are *certain* that the report will always go to the same type of printer, you can place control codes within the report: Simply place a calculated field with the control codes. For example, on Epson-compatible printers, Esc E places the printer in bold strike. **Field, Place, Calculated, "\027E"** will create a field that switches the type style to bold. This, however, will cause spacing problems: The report form will show the field as using up space, but it will not take any space on the printed page and the row will print several characters to the left (relative to the other rows). This technique will also cause problems when the margins are very narrow: There may not be enough room in which to place the calculated field.

## dBASE Reports

From the main menu, select the query to use (in this case, FULLINV), and then select **Create** under **Reports**. The report layout is similar to Paradox (see Figure A.21). Note: Unlike Paradox, where the active area for a band lies between the lines (below the first marker and above the last), the active area for dBASE bands lies *below* each marker. Thus, there is only a single detail band line—the equivalent of the double-line form band in Paradox.

You must create a group band for the invoice so that the invoice number and addresses will print only once. Select **Bands, Add a group band, Field value, Invoice**. Now you can place the fields with **Fields, Add field** (or **F5**). The basic process is similar to form design. As with Paradox, you can use a calculated field to combine fields such as First and Last; and City, State and Zip. Select **<create>** under the **Calculated** column from the **Add Field** menu (see Figures A.22 and A.23). Note that the **Trim ( )** function is required to remove the trailing spaces from CITY; STATE does not require **Trim ( )** since it will always be two characters without space, and ZIP is at the end so it doesn't

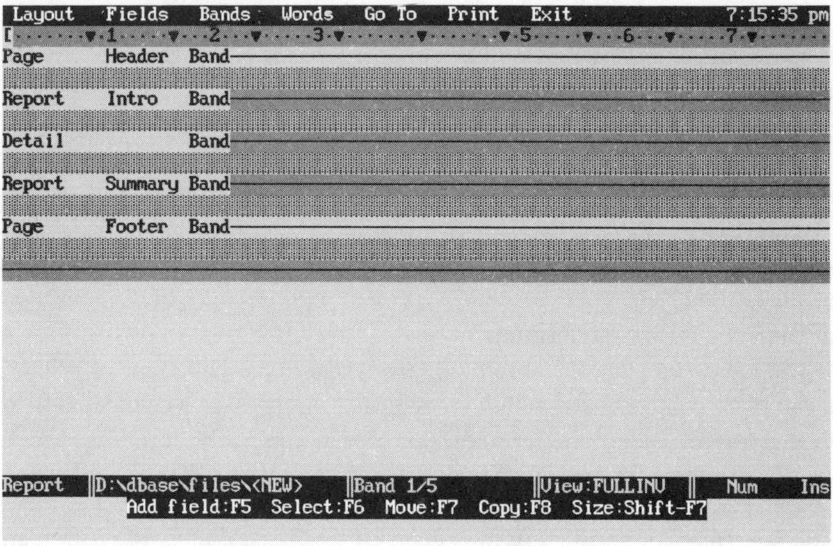

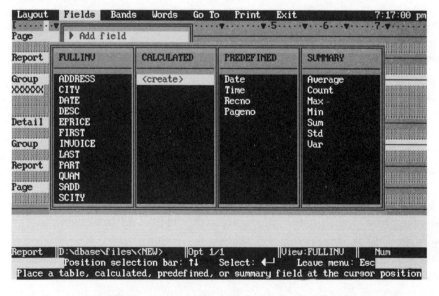

**Figure A.21    The default dBASE report description.**

require trimming, either. Although dBASE allows "-" rather than a "+" to remove the trailing spaces, the operator would also remove the spaces from the constants ", " and " ".

**Figure A.22    Creating a calculated field in a dBASE report.**

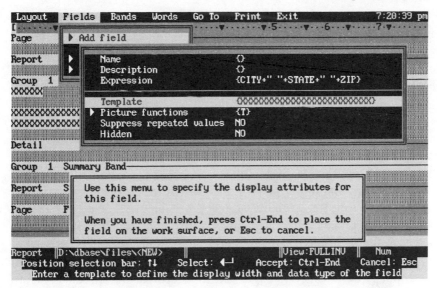

**Figure A.23** Note the expression used to combine city, state, and zip code information in a single field.

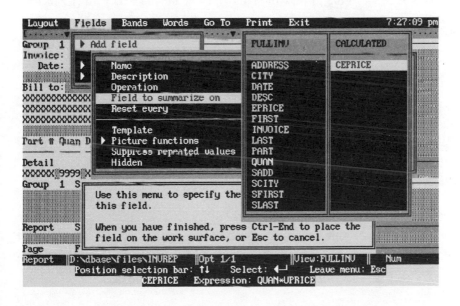

**Figure A.24** Selecting a summary field based on CEPRICE.

Don't forget to use QUAN*UPRICE for the extended price. The extended price may be named so that it may be used as a summary field (CEPRICE was used in the **Name {}** selection). To total the order on CEPRICE, select **Sum** from the **Summary** column of the **Fields**, **Add Field** menu. Then select CEPRICE, as shown in Figure A.24.

Only some fine-tuning remains. In the Group 1 Intro Band, select **Bands**, **Begin band on new page**, **Yes** to start each invoice on a separate page. You can create a header that says "Invoice" on each page by adding the text under the Header Band. dBASE supports text attributes, so you may create boldface letters by selecting **Words**, **Style**, **Bold**, **On** (dBASE also supports underline, italic, superscript, and subscript, plus user-customized attributes).

The line below the Report Intro Band should be removed. If it is not, a blank invoice will be printed at the beginning of each print run. The Report Intro Band is useful for designing cover sheets (it only prints on the first page), but its placement is a bit confusing since it appears *after* the Page Header Band, which prints at the top of *every* page. The final report layout appears in Figure A.25. As with Paradox, you may print to the screen (or printer or file) directly from the report design screen. A screen view (**Print**, **View report on screen**) for the invoice is shown in Figure A.26.

Report editing is much easier in dBASE than in Paradox. The **F6** key selects fields or sections of the form, which may then be moved or copied (**F7** or **F8**,

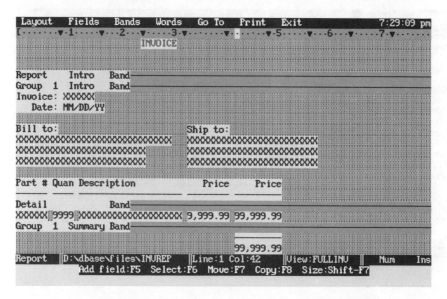

**Figure A.25   The final report definition for the INVOICE view.**

```
                    INVOICE

Invoice: 5
   Date: 10/22/90

Bill to:                 Ship to:
Jack Spratt              Jack Johnson
1212 Steak Ave           2121 Mechanic Ave
Bloomington, MN 55420    Bloomington, MN 55420

Part # Quan Description      Price    Price
_____ ____ _____      _____    _____
8        5 Plates            10.00    50.00
9        2 Bacon (Crates)   100.00   200.00
                                     _____
                                      250.00




          Cancel viewing: ESC,  Continue viewing: SPACEBAR
```

**Figure A.26    Print, View report on screen sends the output to the display for format verification.**

respectively). dBASE also supports search and replace functions through the **Go To** menu.

You may set the printer type (or filename for saving to disk) in the **Print, Destination** menu. The **Print, Control of printer** menu selects font size, the method for ejecting pages (linefeed or formfeed), and any custom control codes sent at the beginning and/or end of the report. The **Print, Page dimension** menu sets the page length, left margin, and line spacing (usually single spaced).

Note that you cannot override many of the default report parameters (other than the default printer). However, you can save the general settings from the **Print** menu through **Print, Save settings to print form**, *FormName*. The settings may be recalled for another report with **Print, Use print form**, *FormName*.

## dBASE Labels

Rather than changing a report setting to generate labels, dBASE uses a separate report generator. It is accessed by selecting **<create>** under the **Labels** column of the main dBASE menu. dBASE begins with a standard size: 1 × 3.5, and one across (see Figure A.27). Other standard sizes are available through

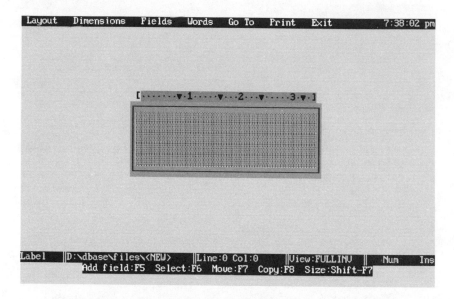

**Figure A.27** The default label format under dBASE (note that labels and reports are separate objects under dBASE).

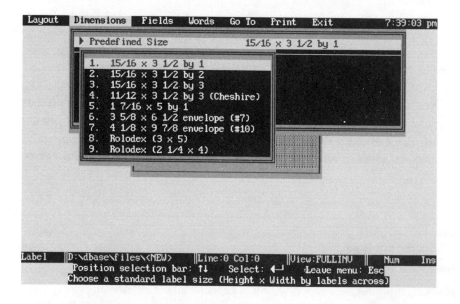

**Figure A.28** Dimensions, Predefined Size presents a list of standard label formats.

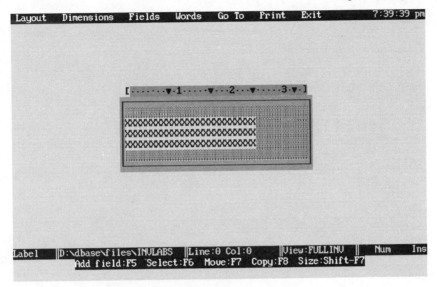

**Figure A.29    A completed label definition.**

**Dimensions, Predefined Size** (see Figure A.28). Or you may customize any of the dimensions through the other settings under **Dimensions**. These include the number of labels across the page (**Columns of labels**), the number of spaces between each column (**Spaces between label columns**), the **Width of label**, **Height of label**, and the number of **Lines between labels**. Field placement and text styles are set as with standard reports. Figure A.29 shows a complete label definition.

Appendix **B**

# The dBASE Dot Prompt

The dot prompt can be intimidating to non-programmers using dBASE, but dBASE works best from the dot prompt, and it would be well worth your effort to learn how to use it. If your copy of dBASE starts at the menu level, you can get to the dot prompt by selecting **Exit, Exit to dot prompt**. You will see a blank screen with a single . at the bottom and a status line underneath. The dot is very similar to the DOS C> prompt: It tells you that dBASE is ready and waiting for the next command. You can return to the menus by typing **Assist** at the dot prompt. To return to DOS (exit dBASE), type **Quit**.

The commands you type at the dot prompt are the same commands you would use within your programs. The dBASE dot prompt works very much like a continuous **Miniscript** in Paradox, with the advantage that each command may be immediately followed by another without going through the menus. Most of the commands in the Command Reference (Appendix C) may be used directly from the dot prompt.

The advantage of using the dBASE dot prompt over the menu interface is its intuitiveness. dBASE was originally command based, and it shows in the structure. For example, non-exclusive and exclusive editing are approached in very different manners under dBASE menus (the former is in the **Display data** menu and the latter in the **Modify structure** menu). These very different approaches to performing two related commands are not very intuitive. But, from the dot prompt, it is a simple command line option under **Use**: Use *Table* or **Use** *Table* **Exclusive**.

Contrast this to Paradox, which uses very similar keystrokes and menu selections for similar commands: **Edit** and **CoEdit** (commands), **F9** and **Alt-F9** (keys), or **Modify**, **Edit** and **Modify**, **CoEdit** (menus). In addition to the dot prompt's more consistent structure, there are several commands and options available from the dot prompt that are not accessible from the menus (**Convert** and the SQL commands are examples).  Paradox has relatively few commands and options that are not available from the menus (e.g., **Index**).

Writing programs is a simple extension of the dot prompt.  At its most basic, you simply type the commands in a file, pretending that each new line (after a carriage return) is another dot prompt from dBASE.  You can either write this program with a text editor or word processor (it should be saved with a .PRG extension).  To use the dBASE editor, select **Applications**, **<Create>**, **dBASE program** from the menus, or enter **Modify command** *ProgName* from the dot prompt.  If you use your own word processor to create the program, you may add the file to the catalog with **Catalog**, **Add file to catalog**.  The program may be run from the dot prompt even if it does not appear in the catalog.

# Appendix C

# Command and Function Reference

## Common Paradox Commands

Although there are over 160 PAL commands, there are far fewer that you will use regularly. This reference highlights some of the more important commands by category, including a brief category description. Complete command and function lists can be found in the Paradox manuals.

### Batch Table Commands

The batch table commands (such as Copy), create or alter several rows with a single command. Most of these commands are also abbreviated forms of menu commands. The italicized parameters should be replaced with table names. These commands may be used only in Main mode (i.e., not during an Edit or CoEdit).

Every relational operation in Paradox creates new tables, so commands that operate on entire tables become very important under PAL. You can build your own temporary work tables and **Add** the final results to the main tables. You can query tables, producing temporary tables such as ANSWER, DELETED, INSERTED, and CHANGED, which you can **Rename** for later use. You should learn these batch commands well, and use them frequently.

| *Command* | *Description* |
|---|---|
| Add *Source Destination* | Adds the records in the source into the destination. If the destination table is keyed, any records in the source table that have an identical key will update the destination records (and create a CHANGED that contains the old values). This is a shortcut command for **{Tools} {More} {Add}**. |
| Copy *Source Destination* | Creates an identical copy of the source table. This is a shortcut for **{Tools} {Copy} {Table}**. |
| Delete *TableName* | Deletes the named table. This command is a shortcut for **{Tools} {Delete} {Table}**. |
| Empty *TableName* | Removes all rows from the named table. This command is a shortcut for **{Tools} {More} {Empty}**. |
| Index *TableName* on *ColumnName* | Creates an index on the named column for the designated table. If a table has many rows, and the values in a column vary widely, an index can speed sorting and query operations *based on the indexed column*.<br><br>Thus, if you have many different zip codes in an Address table (e.g., not all in the same city), and often query a report by zip code, **Index "Address" On "Zip Code"** would help Paradox quickly find and sort the results. Once an index has been created, Paradox will use it and update it automatically. |
| Index Maintained *TableName* on *ColumnName* | **Index Maintained** may be used to index a column in a keyed table (see **Index** for a description of indexes). If a table has changed since the last index regeneration, a normal index is com- |

pletely regenerated whenever needed (e.g., sorting a report or performing a query on the indexed column).

Maintained indexes are updated as they are changed (e.g., after every Edit or Changeto query), and regenerates only the portion of the index affected by the changes.

Rename *OldName NewName*

Changes the name of a table from the OldName to the NewName. This is a shortcut for **{Tools} {Rename}**.

Subtract *Source Destination*

Removes the records in the source table from the destination. If the destination table is keyed, all records that match the key in Source will be removed, even if the non-keyed columns do not match. If the destination table is not keyed, only the rows that match the source exactly will be removed. This is a shortcut for **{Tools} {More} {Subtract}**.

## Workspace Management

Several PAL commands manage the workspace. The workspace includes those tables that would normally appear on the lower portion of the screen when working interactively. Many of these commands replace function key operations. Most do not take any parameters.

*Command*                      *Description*

CancelEdit

If Paradox is in Edit mode, this command cancels all changes and returns the tables to their state before the editing session began.

ClearAll

Removes all tables and query images from the Paradox workspace. **ClearAll** must be used from Main mode.

ClearImage

Removes the current table from the workspace. **ClearImage** must be used from Main mode.

CoEdit *Table*

Places the named table on the workspace and toggles CoEdit mode. Any other tables currently on the workspace will also be placed in CoEdit mode. Use the **Do_It!** command to return to Main mode. If you do not want to place a new table on the workspace, use **CoEditKey**, which has the same effect as **Alt-F9**.

Do_It!

Acts as the **F2** key. It is typically used to return to Main mode or process a query.

DownImage

Moves down the workspace (to the next table or query form).

Edit *Table*

Places the named table on the workspace and toggles Edit mode. Any other tables on the workspace will also be placed in Edit mode. The CancelEdit command will cancel any changes from the current Edit session. The **Do_It!** command will accept changes. If you do not want to place a new table on the workspace, use **EditKey**, which has the same effect as **F9**.

FirstShow

Places the current image (table or query form) at the top of the workspace.

Moveto *TableName*

Moves to the named table or query form. Query forms should be marked with **"(Q)"** as in **"Address(Q)"**. If more than one view of a table is on the workspace, you may use a number, e.g., **"Address(2)"**. Moveto may also be used with field names and record numbers (see Movement Within Tables).

UpImage
: Moves up the workspace (to the previous table or query form).

View *Table*
: Places the named table on the workspace.

## Movement within Tables

There are several ways to move within a table under PAL control. Some commands move to absolute row number (these will not be listed since they are unreliable in some situations such as network applications where the record numbers could change). Several of these commands control movement as if you were using the cursor keys.

| *Command* | *Description* |
| --- | --- |
| CtrlEnd | Move to the last column |
| CtrlHome | Move to the first column |
| Del | Delete the current row (only in Edit or CoEdit mode). |
| Down | Move down one row. |
| End | Move to the last row. |
| FormKey | Toggles current table to the default form (or the current form to the row/column table view). You may want to use this command with the function **IsFormView ( )**, e.g., **If Not IsFormView ( ) Then FormKey EndIf**. (See PickForm.) |
| Home | Move to the first row. |
| Ins | Create a blank row at the current cursor position (only in Edit or CoEdit mode). |

Left

Move left one column (or one character in FieldView mode).

Locate *Value*

Locates the first occurrence of the specified value in the current column. Optionally, the keyword Next may be used to start the search at the current row (e.g., **Locate Next "John"**). If you want to include the ".." or "@" wildcard characters, you must include the Pattern keyword (e.g., **Locate Pattern "John.."**). RetVal is set to True if a match is found, or False if not found. This form of **Locate** is the command equivalent of **Ctrl-Z**.

Locate *ValueList*

Locate may be used with a list of several column values. In this special case, the first *N* fields of the table will be searched. Normally, this form would be used to locate a multiple column key (e.g., **Locate "0009", "02"**). The Next keyword may be included to start the search at the current row. RetVal is set to True if a match is found, or False if not found.

Moveto *ColumnName*

A column name may be enclosed in square brackets to move the cursor to the desired column (e.g., **Moveto [Last Name]**). Both a table and column name may be combined to move to a specific column within a separate image (e.g., **Moveto [Address->Last Name]**). Optionally, the keyword Field may be included to specify a column by a quoted name or variable (e.g., **Moveto Field "Last Name"** or **A="Last Name" Moveto Field A**).

PickForm *FormNumber*

Toggle the current table in form view. The form number may be expressed either as a number or an alphanumeric value. For example **1**, **"1"**, **"R"**, and **3** are all valid form numbers. Likewise, variables may contain either a number or an alphanumeric value.

Right                                          Move right one column (or one charac-
                                               ter in FieldView mode).

Up                                             Move up one row.

## Input/Output

PAL provides a very rich set of commands for input and output (I/O). The programming chapters included examples of rudimentary I/O commands—@, **??**, and **Accept**—and one example of a more advanced sequence using **Wait**. PAL has commands that help you build menus like those used within Paradox. And there are several other methods for editing tables; these require that the table be on the workspace in Edit mode (see Batch Table Commands, above).

Many of the examples have made reference to the Paradox workspace. This is simply the area in which Paradox places and displays query forms and tables. Paradox has a separate display area called the *canvas*, which displays information printed to the screen from PAL. For example, the **??** command displays output on the canvas.

Paradox automatically switches between the canvas and workspace based on the commands you select (for example, to execute **Wait**, which displays a table, Paradox switches to the workspace). Usually, this switch is quite natural and has few side effects. However, there are commands that paint a copy of the underlying workspace onto the canvas. When this happens, especially in the middle of an edit, the image on the canvas may not match the workspace; i.e., the image on the canvas reflects an earlier table state. If you see side effects, such as data in a table that keeps flickering between two values (particularly in Debug mode), you're probably seeing the switch from canvas to workspace.

| *Command* | *Description* |
|---|---|
| *@ RowNumber, ColumnNumber* | Positions the cursor at the specified row number and column numbers. The numbering starts with 0,0 at the top left side of the screen, and ends with 24,79 at the lower right. |

| | |
|---|---|
| **? *TextData*** | Displays the text starting at the first column below the current cursor location. The text may include constants and variables separated by commas, e.g., **Print "Hello ",[First Name], " ",LastNVar**. |
| **?? *TextData*** | Similar to **?**, but displays the text beginning at the current cursor location. |
| **[*FieldName*] = *Value*** | In addition to creating and assigning variables, the assignment operator will work with field names. If a table is in Edit mode, this is as simple as using **[Last Name] = "Smith"**. Optionally, you may use - to specify the table name using **[Address->Last Name] = "Smith"**. You may also select the current field with **[ ]**. |
| **Accept *DataType OptionalSpecs* To *VariableName*** | Stores data entered at the keyboard in the named variable. (See the example in Chapter 8 for details.) |
| **Array *ArraySpec*** | Creates a special variable called an array. The array specification is a variable name with a number from 1 to 1500 as the size. Thus, **Array B[5]** would create an array called **B** of size 5—this array can hold five different values. Each element is accessed by a number from one up to the dimension selected: **B[2] = 6** or **?? B[4]**. Note that each element of the array may be a different type (**B[1]="A character string"** and **B[2]=5**). Arrays are mentioned in this section because of the **CopyToArray** and **CopyFromArray** commands (see **CopyToArray** and **CopyFromArray**). |
| **Beep** | Makes a sound like the error beep. |

Clear

Erases the canvas. Although this clears all text, it does not affect the underlying workspace (all Viewed tables remain). Optionally, you may specify **Clear EOL**, which clears from the cursor to the end of the line; or **Clear EOS**, which clears the area of the screen below and to the right of the cursor.

Close Printer

See **Open Printer**.

CopyFromArray *ArrayName*

Copies the values from the named array into the current row of the current table (Paradox must be in Edit or CoEdit mode).

CopyToArray *ArrayName*

Copies the current row of the current table to the named array. The elements in the array may be addressed either by the column number+1 or the column name. For example, if Last Name is the fourth column of the row stored in **CurRow**, you may address it either as **CurRow[5]** or as **CurRow["Last Name"]**. The first array element contains the name of the base table (in this case, the row was from the ADDRESS table and **CurRow[1]** is **"Address"**).

Message *TextData*

Displays the text in the lower-right portion of the screen (similar to a Paradox error message). Many commands that affect the workspace will erase the message. You may want to use the **Sleep** command to delay the next command long enough for the user to read the message.

Open Printer

If you send text directly to the printer with the **Print** statement, you should open each job with the **Open Printer** command and close each job with the **Close Printer** Command. This keeps

Local Area Networks from interpreting each **Print** statement as a separate job, and possibly separating every line of print with a header page. It also keeps the network from printing jobs from other computers between lines of the PAL output (which would result in a very messy situation). Although these statements are not required on a machine not connected to a network, it's generally a good idea to include them for easy conversion to a network environment.

Print *TextData*

Similar to the **??** command, **Print** sends output to the printer (rather than the screen). As with **??**, you may mix variables and constant text in a comma delimited list, e.g., **Print "Hello ", [First Name], " ", LastNVar**. See **Open Printer** for important information about job processing.

Print File *FileName TextData*

Opens the named file (e.g., "C:\\PARADOX\\TEXT.OUT") and writes the output to the file. Otherwise, it is similar to **Print**.

Report *TableName ReportNumber*

Sends a report for the named table to the printer. The report number may be expressed either as a number or an alphanumeric value. For example **1**, **"1"**, **"R"**, and **3** are all valid form numbers. Likewise, variables may contain either a number or an alphanumeric value.

SetPrinter *Port*

Sends all printer output to the specified port, regardless of the setting defined in the report specification. The override may be cancelled only through the menus: **{Report} {SetPrinter} {Regular}**.

ShowArray, ShowFiles, ShowMenu, and ShowTables

These four commands create menus that resemble the Paradox menu, and record the selected item to a named variable. (They are discussed in detail at the end of the Input/Output section.)

Sleep *TimeInterval*

Creates a pause in program execution for a specified number of milliseconds. Usually, the **Sleep** command should follow any **Message** commands. Otherwise, the message may be erased by the next PAL command. The interval may extend up to 30 seconds with the maximum value of 30000.

Wait Field, Wait Record, Wait Table

Allows the user to interact directly with an object on the Paradox table until a specific key is pressed. (See the discussion in Chapter 8 for details.)

The discussion of the various **Show...** commands was saved until the end of this section because they are so useful and powerful that more thorough coverage is warranted. These commands emulate the Paradox menu bar, giving both a selection on the first line and a description on the second. In its most basic (and most often used) form, **ShowMenu**, these options set with text constants. Like the **Wait** command, the **Show...** commands specify a **To** variable, which receives the keystroke, or in this case, the name of the item selected. The **ShowMenu** command lists the menu choice, a colon, and the menu description. Each set (choice and description) is followed by a comma, except for the last. Watch out for that final comma; it's easy to cause an error by accidentally using one!

The menu in Figure C.1 was created with the following script:

```
ShowMenu
    "View":"View a table",
    "Edit":"Modify a table",
    "Report":"Print a report"
    To MenVal
```

The variable MenVal will contain "View", "Edit", or "Report". Additionally, there is one special value, "Esc", which will be returned if the **Esc** key was hit.

**Figure C.1 A custom menu created with the ShowMenu command.**

The special value RetVal is also set by **ShowMenu**: True if a menu item was selected, or False if the **Esc** key was hit.

With **ShowMenu** (and **ShowArray**) you may specify a **Default** value just prior to the **To**. This may be used to highlight an item other than the first. For example, if you want to process the **Esc** key, return to the previous menu level, and highlight the last item selected from the previous menu level. To save development time, you may want to avoid **Default** because it often adds significant overhead to the program. On the other hand, the application will have a more polished feel if you use the **Default** option.

All of the **Show...** commands allow **Until** and **KeyTo** options. The **Until** works like the **Until** in the **Wait** command: It specifies a list of keys to process (e.g., **"F10"**, or **"F2"**). The **KeyTo** option specifies the variable that stores the returned keystroke (just like the **To** in **Wait**). RetVal will be False if a key from the **Until** list or Esc was pressed, and **True** if a menu selection was chosen. You can use this option to emulate Paradox standards like F10 returning to the base menu. But, like the **Default** option, this adds significant overhead to the program. It's best to avoid the options: Keep it simple and add the polish later if you really want it (and have the time).

**ShowArray** reads the menu items from one array, and the menu description from another. We could write the **ShowMenu** example as follows:

```
Choose a table:
Address  Orders  Invr2  Client  A2  Phone  Addbak  T  S  At  P2  Ir  Phbak ▶
```

**Figure C.2    A menu created with the ShowTables command.**

```
Array Choice[3]
Array Desc[3]
Choice[1]-"View" Desc[1]="View a table"
Choice[2]="Edit" Desc[2]="Modify a table"
Choice[3]="Report" Desc[3]="Print a report"
ShowArray Choice Desc To MenVal
```

Note how the two assignment operations have been combined on a single line. PAL doesn't really "care" much about formatting. Likewise, the **ShowMenu** example could have been placed on a single line (if you think about it, you'll realize that's why the commas are necessary between lines).

**ShowTables** creates a display similar to the Ask and View table name menus by listing the tables in the specified directory. You must specify a prompt description for the first line. Figure C.2 was created from the following command (the directory contains the sample tables for this book).

```
ShowTables "E:\\Word\\PCDB\\Tables\\"
            "Choose a table: "
             To TabChoice
```

The **ShowFiles** command is similar to **ShowTables**, but it displays all matching files rather than tables only. You may use a file mask with ?s and *s (as in DOS commands), and may optionally exclude the file extension from the display with the **NoExt** option.   The **ShowTables** example could be written as:

```
ShowFiles NoExt
    "E:\\Word\\PCDB\\Tables\\*.db" "Choose a table: "
    To TabChoice
```

## Control Structures

The result variable of a menu command, such as **ShowFiles**, can be processed by sequential **If** statements, but Paradox has several more convenient structures for flow control.   One of the most useful is the **Switch... EndSwitch** command. **Switch** lists several conditions, labeled **Case**, only one of which is executed. The program thus selects one list of instructions from several alternatives. Optionally, an **Otherwise** may be used in place of the final **Case** to execute if none of the other conditions are True.

   Each **Case** specifies a conditional statement followed by a colon, and forms an individual instruction block.   The instruction block is terminated with the next **Case**, **Otherwise**, or **EndSwitch**.   The following **Switch** statement could be used with the preceding **ShowMenu** example:

```
While True
    ShowMenu
        "View":"View a table",
        "Edit":"Modify a table",
        "Report":"Print a report"
        To MenVal
    Switch

        Case MenVal="View":
            ClearAll      ;Remove any existing images
            View "Address"
            Wait Table
                Prompt "Hit F2 when done viewing"
                Until "F2"

        Case MenVal="Report":
            Report "Address" "R"

        Case MenVal="Edit":
            ClearAll      ;Remove any existing images
            Edit "Address"
```

```
Wait Table
    Prompt "Hit F2 when done viewing"
    Until "F2"
    Do_It!

Case MenVal="Esc":
    QuitLoop

    EndSwitch
EndWhile
```

Note how the continuous **While** (the condition is always True) keeps the menu at the same level until the **Esc** key is pressed. At that point the program ends. If this were a procedure or script called by another, similar menu, the program would have dropped down to the previous menu level.

The **For... EndFor** command is similar to a **While** loop, but the **For** command takes a special condition, which specifies the number of repetitions. You may specify a counter variable, starting number, ending number, and increment: **For *Counter* From *Start* To *End* Step *Increment***. If the starting number is omitted, the count will start with the current value of the counting variable. If an increment is omitted, the default of 1 will be used. Omitting the ending number will cause an infinite loop (**QuitLoop** would be required to terminate the loop). Usually, the starting value is smaller than the ending value, but you can reverse them and count backwards by specifying a negative increment. The following program prints the even numbers from 2 to 10 across the top of the screen.

```
@1,1
For I From 2 To 10 Step 2
    ?? I," "
EndFor
Sleep 5000
```

At first glance, the **For** command might seem like a good choice for stepping through the values in a table: Start with one and use the last record number in the **To** portion. But this is not an advisable practice. If a table is shared on a network, the final record number could change before the loop completes.

Paradox provides a much better alternative: the **Scan... EndScan** loop. **Scan** begins at the start of the current table on the workspace, executes all of the instructions up to the **EndScan**, then moves to the next row and repeats the instruction block. Optionally, you may include a **For** conditional instruction, which skips matching rows.  For example, the following script would append a "0" to the beginning of any client number except "2".

```
Edit "Address"
Scan For [AddNum]<>"2"
    [AddNum] = "0" + [AddNum]
EndScan
Do_It!  ;End Edit Mode
```

## Query Commands

PAL has a few query commands.  You had a very brief encounter with one in Chapter 4: **Scripts**, **QuerySave**. If you look at the script created with this command, you will see a **Query... EndQuery** command that resembles:

```
Query

  Orders | Quantity | Unit Price | Extended Price |
         | _q       | _p         | changeto _q*_p |
         |          |            |                |
         |          |            |                |

Endquery
```

   Essentially, PAL stores a visual image of the query you designed with **Ask** (this is akin to a relational language statement called from within the host language).  The vertical bars separate the columns, and the table name appears in the left column.  The top row defines the field names.  Each successive row contains the items entered within the query form (commands such as **Delete** or **Insert** would appear under the table name).  If multiple query forms were present, each image would be separated by a blank line.  Likewise, if there are too many columns for a single block, the **Query** statement allows the same table name in separate blocks.

   The items preceded by an underscore (such as _q) are the example elements. This allows a word processor or editor to display a query without resorting to special formatting such as reverse video.  You may include another code to reference variables within a query. A variable is preceded by a tilde; e.g., **~ThisVar**. The variable code may be included in both a query image on the Paradox workspace or entered within a query script by using a tilde.  The final code is **Check**, which appears as the first entry in the column that has been selected for inclusion in the Answer table.

PAL tends to include extraneous characters within the query image. For example, the two empty rows (which include only vertical bars) are not really necessary. It's sometimes easier to view (and read) a large query if you remove these extra lines. You can avoid query images entirely by using {**Ask**} **Select** *TableName* within your scripts; this is often more readable than a large form description. There is, however, a major advantage to the query form: It clears any existing query images off the workspace. This prevents errors such as, "Query appears to ask two unrelated questions," if a query form from a previous query is on the workspace. Such query errors are not reported to PAL, and the script will keep executing until the resulting sideeffects create a more serious error.

On the other hand, you may want to work with a query form from a previous query. In this case, the {**Ask**} command is your best option for adding additional images. You can move to an existing query image by appending a **"(Q)"** after the table name, e.g., **Moveto "Invoice(Q)"**. If you decide to record {**Ask**} statements in your scripts, there are several commands that emulate the function keys used in building queries. And there are other commands which alter the final result.

| *Command* | *Description* |
|---|---|
| Check | Toggles a check mark in the current column (**F6**). Use **Moveto** [*fieldname*] to move to a field before using **Check**. By using **Check** under the table name, you may check all columns in the current query form (an advantage over the **Query** statement, which must list every column with the word **Check**). |
| CheckDescending | Like **Check**, but sorts the selected column in descending order (**Ctrl-F6**). The sort is subject to higher order check marks (any columns to the left in the ANSWER take higher precedence—see the **SetQueryOrder** command). |
| Do_It! | Begins query processing (**F2**). |

Example

Toggles the state of the example key (**F5**).

GroupBy

Uses the current column as part of the ANSWER table sort order, although the column does not appear in AN-SWER (**Shift-F6**).

SetQueryOrder Order

Alters the column order in the AN-SWER by overriding the default in the Paradox Custom Configuration Program (see Appendix E). The order may be either **ImageOrder** (which follows the order in the query forms if the columns have been rotated) or **TableOrder** (which follows the order of the base tables regardless of any rotation). **TableOrder** is usually the safest approach if you typically select every column of a table (the ANSWER will always look like the original base tables). **ImageOrder** is particularly useful when you must change the sort order of a table (by rotating a column into the first position) or require an ANSWER to retain a constant structure. The latter case may be necessary if the structure of the base tables changes and you use another empty table as a form and report template for the ANSWER. Note: The order name is *not* placed in quotes; e.g., **SetQueryOrder ImageOrder**.

## Access Commands

Although these commands are primarily intended for network use, several are useful on single-computer installations. For example, **PrivTables** and **SetPrivDir** can alter the behavior of special Paradox tables. These *private* or temporary tables are unique to each user on a network (ANSWER, CHANGED, and DELETE are a few examples). On a network installation, these tables are usually stored on a local hard disk or a special directory on the network server available only to the designated user. Unlike the temporary Paradox tables, the tables you define as private will not be deleted when you exit Paradox.

On a single-user installation, Paradox places these tables in the working directory by default. But even on a single-user installation, you may force Paradox to place the temporary tables in a separate directory. Why would you want to do this? There are several reasons. For example, you might want to mimic network behavior. Or, if you have two separate drives, you can improve performance by using separate drives for the work area and temporary tables. Or you might prefer separating empty template tables (in the private directory) from full data tables (in the working directory).

| *Command* | *Description* |
|---|---|
| ImageRights *Restriction* | Places further restrictions on a table (beyond the default of full access or protections placed with **Tools**, **More**, **Protect**, **Password**, **Table**). **ImageRights UpDate** prevents the user from adding or deleting rows, or from changing a primary key. |
| | For the best control over your applications, you should make data entry and data modification separate operations. **ImageRights Update** gives you a simple method for making these distinctions. **ImageRights ReadOnly** will prevent any changes to the underlying data. To cancel **ReadOnly** or **Update**, issue **ImageRights** by itself. |
| Lock *List* | Explicitly locks the listed tables with the designated locks. **Lock** statements are particularly useful at the beginning and end of procedures that will be using several different workspace configurations (different files loaded on the workspace at different times). In this case, all tables used throughout the procedure should be listed in the **Lock** list. The list is a comma delimited list of tables and lock attributes (each table name followed by its locks). The locks |

available are FL (full lock), PFL (prevent full lock), WL (write lock), and PWL (prevent write lock).

FL prevents any other network user from accessing the table (including viewing the table).

PFL keeps another user from issuing an FL.

WL prevents other users from changing a table, although they may still view it.

PWL prevents other users from issuing WL or FL.

Locks may be combined (**Lock "Address" WL, "Address" PFL**). Locks of the same type are cumulative: For each **Lock** placed, a corresponding **Unlock** must be used, e.g., **Lock "Address" WL, "Invoice" FL Lock "Address" WL Unlock "Address" WL, "Invoice" FL Unlock "Address" WL**. (See **LockRecord** for individual row locks.)

LockRecord

Locks the current row of the current image. Although only one record may be locked within an image, several rows may be locked by performing **LockRecord** on several images on the workspace. The locks are removed with **UnlockRecord**.

PrivTables *List*

Stores the listed tables in the user's private directory. If the table already exists in the working directory, it will be hidden from view. When a named table is created (or renamed to a listed name) it will be placed in (or moved to) the private directory.

Note: Unlike the Paradox temporary tables, which also reside in the private directory (KEYVIOL, CHANGED, DELETED, etc.), the private tables are *not* deleted when you exit Paradox. When you are done working with a private table, you should include instructions to **Empty** or **Delete** the table to conserve disk space.

**PrivTables** can fail under several conditions—it should always be one of the first commands in a script (before any tables are actually used). If you have problems while executing the same script several times within the same session, you may need to trap errors by the message name "Run error: Table already used in this session" and continue with the next line. (See Error Processing in Appendix D.)

SetPrivDir *Directory*

Uses the named directory as the private directory. The default private directory may be set through the Paradox Custom Configuration Program (see Appendix E).

## PAL Functions

This is not a complete listing of PAL functions, but rather the functions that you will use most frequently in your programs, reports, and forms. A more complete listing can be found in the Paradox manuals.

## Status Functions

The status functions return information about the current system state. Many return truth values (does a table or file exist?). Others return descriptive information about the environment (version numbers or directory names).

| *Function* | *Description* |
| --- | --- |
| AtFirst ( ) | Returns True if the current row is the first in the current view. When moving through a table with a **Skip**, or **Moveto** command, you should use **Bot ( )**. |
| AtLast ( ) | Returns True if the current row is the last in the current view. When moving through a table with a **Skip**, **Moveto**, or **Locate** command, you should use **EOT ( )**. |
| BOT ( ) | Returns True if the last **Skip** or **Moveto** command attempted to move the pointer before the first row (**B**eginning **O**f **T**able). To test if the pointer is *on* the first row, use **AtFirst ( )**. |
| CharWaiting ( ) | Returns True if a character is waiting in the type-ahead buffer, False if no character is waiting. The characters may be retrieved, one at a time, with **GetChar ( )**. |
| CheckMarkStatus ( ) | Returns the type of check mark or an empty string if none is present. The possible check values are: "Check", "CheckDescending", "CheckPlus", and "GroupBy" (capitalized as shown, use **Upper ( )** or **Lower ( )** from the String section to eliminate case dependence). |
| Directory ( ) | Returns the name of the current directory. Paradox may use either upper- or lowercase letters, depending on how the entry was originally typed. Use **Upper ( )** or **Lower ( )** from the string section to eliminate case dependence. The directory name always ends with a backslash. |

DirExists (*DirName*)

Returns 1 if the named directory exists, 0 if it does not exist, and -1 if the name is invalid (e.g., two colons or illegal characters in the name). Note that unlike many similar status functions, this does not return a value of True or False.

EOT ( )

Returns True if the last **Skip**, **Moveto**, or **Locate** command attempted to move the pointer past the last row (**End Of T**able). To test if the pointer is *on* the last row, use **AtLast** ( ).

Field ( )

Returns the name of the current field. Note: Although PAL ignores case differences when field names are entered in programs, it always returns the name exactly as it appears in the table definition. Use the **Upper** ( ) or **Lower** ( ) string function to create similar case independence within your scripts.

GetChar ( )

Returns the ASCII code of the next character waiting in the type-ahead buffer. Use **CharWaiting** ( ) to determine whether any characters are in the buffer. Special keys, such as function and cursor keys, will be returned as negative numbers representing keyboard scan codes (see **Asc** ( ) in the string functions).

IsAssigned (*VariableName*)

Returns True if the named variable (or array element) exists. Since PAL does not create a variable until it is assigned a value, the status may be checked to skip portions of a script that might access a value before it is defined (for example, a **While** loop that checks a value near the beginning of the block and changes the value near the end).

IsBlank (*Name*)

Returns True if the named item is a blank value. The item may be a variable, field name, or expression such as **[First]+[Last]**.

IsBlankZero ( )

Returns True if the Custom Configuration Program has been set to treat blank values as zeros when used in arithmetic expressions.

IsEmpty (*TableName*)

Returns True if the named table is empty (contains no rows). This is often useful before printing a report or after a query, to make sure data was found, e.g., **IsEmpty ("Answer")**.

IsFile (*FileName*)

Returns True if the named file exists.

IsFormView ( )

Returns True if the current table is in Form mode.

IsShared (*TableName*)

Returns True if the named table is in a shared (network) directory.

IsTable (*TableName*)

Returns True if the named table exists. This is especially important for determining the presence of temporary tables such as Answer, Changed, and Deleted. Because PAL will not always report query errors you may need **IsTable ("Answer")** after some query operations. Note that the Answer table may exist from a previous query unless it was deleted or renamed. (See **IsEmpty ( )**.)

IsValid ( )

Returns True if the contents of the current field match **ValCheck** restrictions. This may be especially important for field data entered under script control.

Monitor ( )

Returns "B&W", "Color", or "Mono" depending on the current monitor type defined in the Custom Configuration Program (see Appendix E).

NImageRecords ( )

Returns the number of records in the current image. In an imbedded multi-record form (multirecord inside a multitable form) it will count only the number of rows linked to the current master. (See **NRecords ( )**.)

NImages ( )

Returns the number of images currently on the workspace.

NRecords (*TableName*)

Returns the number of rows in the named table. This command should be used only where necessary; many people use it where other options would be better. For example, if you are using **NRecords ( )** in a **For** loop, a **Scan** loop might be a better choice because the number of records might change between the beginning and end of the loop. (See **NImageRecords ( )** for a restricted count when working with multitable forms.)

PrinterStatus ( )

Returns True if the printer is ready to accept output from a report or PAL. It checks only the default printer; to temporarily enable another printer as the default, use the **SetPrinter** command.

PrivDir ( )

Returns the name of the private directory. On a network, the private directory is unique to each user. The temporary tables (such as ANSWER, CHANGED, KEYVIOL, and DE-LETED) are stored in this directory to prevent conflicts (one user's AN-SWER from overwriting another's).

QueryOrder ( )

Returns the current query order: either "TableOrder" or "ImageOrder". (See the **SetQueryOrder** command for more details.)

RecNo ( )

Returns the current record (row) number. You should avoid references to record numbers wherever possible, especially in shared environments such as networks.

SysMode ( )

Returns the name of the current mode (as normally indicated in the upper right-hand corner of the screen). The most common mode names returned during script execution are "Main", "Edit", "CoEdit", and "DataEntry".

Table ( )

Returns the name of the current table. The name will be returned with an initial uppercase character followed by lowercase characters. Use **Upper** ( ) or **Lower** ( ) to remove case dependence.

Version ( )

Returns the version number of Paradox under which the script is currently running.

## String Functions

Because most database information is represented as strings, these functions often form the core of programs. Certainly, numeric information such as dates, quantities, and amounts are important. But most descriptive information and labels are stored as strings, and hence, many retrieval and matching functions are string-based.

Paradox, and by extension, PAL, allow two special string operations in queries and the **Match** ( ) function: ".." and "@". ".." is similar to the DOS *; it matches any combination of characters. Unlike DOS, characters may follow the "..", as in "..ight", which would match "fight", "fright", "blight", etc. "@" will match any single character, like the DOS counterpart, **?**. Either operator will remove case sensitivity from a match; thus, "frank.." will match "Frank", where "frank" would not (this can be handy in queries when you're not sure about the capitalization).

| *Function* | *Description* |
|---|---|
| Asc (*Character*) | Converts a single letter to the equivalent ASCII number. Thus **Asc("A")** returns 65. **Asc ( )** can also convert key names and function keys such as "Do_It!" and "F2" to their equivalent extended ASCII codes. Normally, DOS uses a double byte code: 0 followed by a one-byte scan code. However, PAL uses a negative number instead of an initial 0. Thus, "F2", keyboard scan code 60, converts to -60. |
| Chr (*AscVal*) | Converts a numeric ASCII code to the equivalent character. Thus, **Chr(65)** returns "A". |
| Fill (*Character, RepeatCount*) | Returns a string that repeats a single character a designated number of times. Thus, **Fill ("b",10)** returns "bbbbbbbbbb". |
| Format (*FormatCodes, Data*) | **Format ( )** takes text or numeric data and returns a fixed-length text string that conforms to the specified formatting codes. In essence, it is an enhanced **StrVal ( )** function, which is used when a fixed-length result or enhanced formatting (such as leading 0s, commas, or dollar signs) is required. There are several codes that may be combined in a comma-delimited list— the list is itself a string and must be enclosed in quotation marks. A list of codes and examples is included at the end of this section. |
| Len (*String*) | Returns the number of characters in the string. |
| Lower (*String*) | Returns a string in which uppercase letters are converted to lowercase. |

| | |
|---|---|
| Match (*String, Pattern, Variables*) | Given a pattern of fixed characters and wildcard elements (@ and ??), **Match ( )** will return True if the designated string matches the pattern and False if the string does not match. Optionally, you may include a list of variables: up to one for each wildcard specified; the variables will then be set to the corresponding wildcard portion. For example, **Match ("PO Box #499", "PO..B..#..", a, b, c)** would return True and set a=" ", b="ox ", and c="499"). With the string "POB#499", the return value would be True with a="", b="", and c="499". |
| NumVal (*String*) | Converts a string of numerals into the number they represent. For example, **NumVal ("12345")** would return the number 12,345. If the string cannot be converted, "Error" is returned. |
| Search (*Fragment, String*) | If the specified string fragment occurs in the string, **Search ( )** returns a number corresponding to the position of the first match. If the fragment does not occur within the string, **Search ( )** returns 0. Thus, **Search ("ad","Bradley")** returns 3 since the fragment begins at the third position of the string. |
| Spaces (*Number*) | Returns the designated number of spaces (similar to the **Fill ( )** function). |
| StrVal (*Data*) | Converts the number, date, or logical value to the equivalent string. This is frequently used to concatenate data: **YesterDate="Yesterday was "+StrVal(Today( )-1)**. |
| SubStr (*String, Position, Length*) | Returns the portion of a string starting at the designated position and includes the number of characters specified by the length. Thus, **a="This" b=a+" "** |

**+SubStr(a,3,2)+" "+SubStr(a,2,3)**
would set b="This is his".

Upper (*String*)                    Returns a string in which lowercase
                                     letters are converted to uppercase.

The **Format** ( ) command allows you to specify special formatting codes to enhance the appearance of text or numeric data, and returns the formatted data in a fixed-length string. Although it is chiefly used with numbers, currency, and data in order to force a particular format, text may be forced into a particular location within a fixed-length field. You might use this feature to write fixed-length fields to an ASCII file, or design custom reports with **Print** commands.

The key to fixed-length fields is the width specifier: **W**. This is followed by a number representing the width or, in the case of numeric data, a decimal number that represents the full width and decimal places. Thus, "W9" would return a nine-character string, and "W9.2" a nine-character string with two decimal positions (one character for the sign, one for the decimal point, five for the whole portion, and two for the fraction). All data is truncated (numbers are *not* rounded). If the whole portion of a number exceeds the full width, it is converted to a string of *s. Although the width specifier is optional, most applications will require it for proper alignment on the output device (screen, printer, or file).

The alignment specifiers, **AL**, **AC**, and **AR**, align the characters within the specified width. The codes set the characters to the left, center, or right, respectively.

The case specifiers, **CU**, **CL**, **CC**, convert upper- and/or lowercase characters to match the designated pattern: **CU** converts all characters to uppercase, **CL** converts all characters to lowercase, **CC** converts the first letter of each word to uppercase, and any other characters remain the same.

Alignment and width specifiers may be used with any data type. The remaining specifiers work with numeric data only (with a few restricted to dates and logical values). The edit specifiers, which start with **E**, add special characters to a numeric string: **EC** adds commas (or periods) between the groups of thousands; **EZ** fills in leading 0s when a number doesn't fill the entire width specification; **EB** and **E\*** work similarly, but specify leading blanks or asterisks, respectively. **EI** specifies international format (commas and periods reversed from the American convention); **ES** specifies scientific notation (mantissa and exponent); **E$** adds a leading "$" to the number.

The sign specifier alters the default convention for positive and negative notation. **S+** forces a leading + when the number is positive. **S-** prints a leading sign (-) only when the number is negative. **SP** places parentheses around negative numbers, typically used in financial applications. Or **SD** may be used to specify debit/credit notation (DB follows positive number, CR follows negative numbers). **SC** is the debit/credit complement to the **S-** option, printing CR after negative numbers.

Logical values usually print as True or False. You can override this with **LY**, which substitutes Yes and No, or **LO** which substitutes On and Off.

The date specifier, **D**, is followed by a number that selects the format, according to the following chart. Mon refers to a three-letter month abbreviation, Month to the full name, mm to the month number, dd to the day, yy to a two-digit year, and yyyy to a four-digit year.

| Date Code | Format |
|-----------|--------|
| D1 | mm/dd/yy |
| D2 | Month dd, yyyy |
| D3 | mm/dd |
| D4 | mm/yy |
| D5 | dd-Mon-yy |
| D6 | Mon-yy |
| D7 | dd-Mon-yyyy |
| D8 | mm/dd/yyyy |
| D9 | dd.mm.yy |
| D10 | dd/mm/yy |
| D11 | yy-mm-dd |

Consider the following script:

```
SetPrinter "LPT1"
Open Printer

Print Format ("W10,AC", "Title")," ",
      Format ("W10,AC","Amount"),
      "\n"                              ;PAL code for
                                        ;linefeed

Print Format ("W10,AC",Fill("-",10))," ",
      Format ("W10,AC",Fill("-",10)),
      "\n"
Print Format ("W10,AR", "Line 1:")," ",
      Format ("W10.2,AR,E$C",1234.56),
```

```
      "\n"
Print Format ("W10,AR", "Line 2:")," ",
      Format ("W10.2,AR,E$ZC",-12.34),
      "\n"
Print "\f"                           ;PAL code for
                                     ;formfeed


Close Printer
```

which creates the following output (followed by a formfeed):

```
   Title     Amount
---------- ----------
  Line 1:  $1,234.56
  Line 2: $-00012.34
```

## Time and Date Functions

These functions return information about the current time and date (as set in the system clock). Because Paradox does not support Time as a field type, such information is returned as a text string.

| *Function* | *Description* |
|---|---|
| BlankDate ( ) | Returns the blank value in date format (typically designating an unknown date). |
| DateVal (*String*) | Converts a string such as "2/1/90", into date format. |
| Day (*Date*) | Returns the day in number format. **Day (2/1/90)** would return the number 1. |
| DOW (*Date*) | Returns the day of the week: "Mon", "Tue", "Wed", "Thu", "Fri", "Sat", or "Sun". |
| Month (*Date*) | Returns the month in number format. |
| MOY (*Date*) | Returns the month of the year as a three-letter string: "Jan", "Feb", |

"Mar", "Apr", "May", "Jun", "Jul", "Aug", "Sep", "Oct", "Nov", or "Dec".

Time ( )

Returns the current time in hours, minutes, and seconds as a string: e.g., "15:22:25".

Today ( )

Returns the current date.

Year (*Date*)

Returns the year in number format.

## Mathematical Functions

PAL has two types of mathematical functions: those that take one or two arguments, and summary functions that operate on table columns. The summary operations are covered in the next section. Several mathematical functions are quite specialized and are more useful for scientific and engineering applications. These include the trigonometric functions **Sin ( )**, **Cos**, **Tan ( )**, and their inverses **ASin ( )**, **ACos ( )**, **ATan ( )**. As befits their application, radians are used for angular measurements. Similarly, **Pi ( )**, **Exp ( )**, **Ln ( )**, and **Log ( )** are of more technical than general interest, so they are not covered in-depth (though the latter may be of occasional value in financial applications).

PAL supports a few financial functions including amortization and present-value calculations. However, these functions are limited to regular payment schedules; i.e., they do not operate on a column of irregular payment amounts and/or intervals, and are thus somewhat limited in a database application.

*Function*

*Description*

Abs (*Number*)

Returns the absolute value of a number (negative numbers are made positive).

BlankNum ( )

Returns the blank value in number format (typically designating an unknown number). Normally, mathematical operations on blank numbers will return blank results. However, Paradox may be set to treat blanks as zeros in mathematical operations (see the discussion of the Custom Configuration Program in Appendix E).

Int (*Number*)

Returns the integer portion of a number (everything after the decimal point is truncated). **Int (5.9)** returns 5.

Max (*Number1, Number2*)

Returns the larger of two numbers. **Max (9,5)** and **Max (5,9)** return 9.

Min (*Number1, Number2*)

Returns the smaller of two numbers. **Min (9,5)** and **Min (5,9)** return 5.

Mod (*Dividend, Divisor*)

Returns the remainder (modulus) of the dividend divided by the divisor. **Mod (5,3)** returns 2.

Pow (*Base, Exponent*)

Returns the base raised to the exponent. **Pow (5,3)** returns 125.

Rand ( )

Returns a random number between 0 and 1. PAL does not use a fixed initial seed value, so the sequence is not guaranteed to repeat from one session to the next.

Round (*Number, Place*)

Rounds a number to the specified inverse power of 10 (decimal place). **Round (5.91,0)** returns 6, **Round (5.91,1)** returns 5.9, and **Round (5.91, -1)** returns 10.

SqRt (*Number*)

Returns the square root of a number. **SqRt (9)** returns 3.

## Summary Functions

The summary functions operate on a column of a table. These functions come in two flavors: The standard column functions and the image functions. The standard functions operate on a named table/column combination and the image functions operate on the current table and column (on the workspace).

When viewing a tabular format, the two variations return the same result. But, when the image functions are applied to a linked multitable/multirecord column, they apply only to the current linked data. For example, when viewing the multiple order amounts linked to a particular invoice, **ImageCSum ( )** would return the sum for the current invoice rather than the entire table. On the other hand, a statement like **CSum ("Orders","Extended Price")** would total the amounts for the entire table.

| *Function* | *Description* |
|---|---|
| CAverage (*Table, Column*) | Returns the average of the values in the designated column. **CAverage ( )** excludes blank values from the average, regardless of the **Blank=Zero** setting (see the discussion of the Custom Configuration Program in Appendix E). |
| CCount (*Table, Column*) | Counts the entries in the designated column. Like **CAverage ( )**, **CCount ( )** never counts blank values. (For a count of all rows, see **NRecords ( )** in the Status Functions section.) |
| CMax (*Table, Column*) | Returns the largest value in the designated column. |
| CMin (*Table, Column*) | Returns the smallest value in the designated column. |
| CNPV (*Table, Column, Rate*) | Returns the Net Present Value of the designated column at the specified periodic rate. The calculation assumes that each row represents a fixed period (for example, weekly) and the rate is scaled to match the period (in this case, a weekly interest rate). The returned value will not be correct if the column contains any blank values. |
| CStd (*Table, Column*) | Returns the population ($n$-weighted) standard deviation of the values in the designated column. Like **CAverage ( )**, **CStd ( )** does not include blank rows in the calculation. This assumes that the column contains all data for the group (the population), rather than a portion of the data (a sample). To convert to sample deviation, multiply the result of **CVar( )** by **CCount(***Table,*** |

*Column*)/(**CCount(***Table*, *Column*)-**1**), and take the square root: **SqRt ( )**.

CSum (*Table, Column*)

Returns the sum of the values in the designated column.

CVar (*Table, Column*)

Returns the population (*n*-weighted) variance of the values in the designated column. This assumes that the column contains all data for the group (the population), rather than a portion of the data (a sample). To convert to sample variance, multiply the result by **CCount (***Table*, *Column*) **/ (CCount (***Table*, *Column*)**-1)**.

ImageCAverage ( )

Returns the average of the current column. Blank rows are not included. Calculations are subject to linked form restrictions (see the introduction to this section).

ImageCCount ( )

Returns the count of entries in the current column. Blank rows are not included. (For a count of all rows, see **NImageRecords** ( ) in the Status Functions section.) The count is subject to linked form restrictions (see the introduction to this section).

ImageCMax ( )

Returns the largest value in the current column. The result is subject to linked form restrictions (see the introduction to this section).

ImageCMin ( )

Returns the smallest value in the current column. The result is subject to linked form restrictions (see the introduction to this section).

ImageCSum ( )

Returns the sum of the entries in the current column. Blank rows are not included. Calculations are subject to

linked form restrictions (see the introduction to this section).

## dBASE Commands

dBASE commands typically have many more options than Paradox commands.
The descriptions follow the standard convention of placing a vertical bar
between alternate selections. Thus, **Set Printer On|Off** specifies two distinct
options: **Set Printer On** and **Set Printer Off**. Ellipses (...) indicate that the
elements may be repeated several times; the ellipses *should not* be typed as part
of the command. This section also follows the convention of placing optional
elements in brackets. For example, **Append From** *Source* [**Type** *FileType*]
[**For** *Condition*] has two optional elements: a **Type** specifier and a **For** clause.
Either or both may be used in a single command line. Many optional elements
are common to several commands; a description of these global elements
follows.

| *Global Specifier* | *Description* |
|---|---|
| Color *Attributes* | Specifies color codes for write opera-tions to the display. The attribute con-sists of one or two color codes separated by a slash. The first code is the foreground color, and the second the background color. The color codes are W, N, R, G, B, RG, RB, GB, and RGB for White, Black (None), Red, Green, Blue, Brown (Red + Green), Magenta (Red + Blue), Cyan (Green + Blue), and White. You may include a trailing + for intense colors. Thus, B+/N would specify bright blue on a black background. |
| Fields *FieldList* | Limits the operation to those fields des-ignated in the list. |
| For *Condition* | The **For** clause limits the action of a command to those elements (usually rows of a table) that match the condi- |

tion.  Elements (rows of a table) that do not match are skipped.

Function *FuncList*

The function list is a formatting string that applies to data as a whole rather than a specific character position (as in **Picture**).  The **R** option could use clarification:  When used with a picture, it strips literal characters from input (**@...Get**).  Thus, **@1,1 Get Picture "999-99-9999" Function "R"** would display an entry like "123-45-6789", but would return a value of "123456789".

| Code | Description |
|---|---|
| ! | Convert lowercase to uppercase |
| ^ | Use scientific notation |
| $ | Use currency format |
| ( | Place parentheses around negative numbers |
| A | Use only alphabetic characters |
| B | Left alignment during input (**@...SAY**) |
| C | Use CR after negative numbers |
| D | Use the current date format |
| E | Use the European date format |
| I | Center alignment during input (**@...SAY**) |
| J | Right alignment during input (**@...SAY**) |
| L | Use leading 0s |
| M | Specify an option list for input (e.g., **M Red,White,Blue**) |
| R | Remove literal characters from input |
| S*n* | Create a scrolling field *n* characters wide |
| T | Remove leading and trailing blanks |
| X | Use DB after negative numbers |
| Z | Use blank for the number 0 |

NoAppend

Blocks the addition of new rows to a table.

NoClear

Leaves the image of a table on the workspace after data entry or browsing has been completed.

| | |
|---|---|
| NoDelete | Blocks the addition of new rows to a table. |
| NoEdit | Blocks the modification of table rows. |
| NoInit | Applies the same options specified the last time a command was used. Thus, if **Browse NoDelete NoAppend** were used, and if the next **Browse** were **Browse NoInit**, the second **Browse** would prevent the user from adding or deleting rows. |
| NoMenu | Block access to the menu bar. |
| Picture *PictureSpec* | The picture specification is a string of characters. Generally, these follow a character-by-character basis, e.g., **Picture "!!!"** would print only three characters and capitalize any lowercase. Or you may prefix a function with @ to apply general formatting, e.g., **Picture "@!"** would print any number of characters and convert all to uppercase. (See **Function**.) Characters not listed below will be printed as a literal; i.e., the character will appear in the output. |

| *Code* | *Description* |
|---|---|
| # | a digit, space, decimal point, or sign |
| ! | Any single character and convert it to uppercase |
| 9 | Only a single digit |
| A | Any single letter |
| L | T, F, Y, or N |
| N | Any single letter or digit (or "_") |
| X | Any single character |
| Y | Y or n (and convert lowercase to uppercase) |

If the data is numeric:

| Code | Description |
|------|-------------|
| . | Sets the decimal position |
| , | Includes separators for thousands |
| * | Uses leading *s |
| $ | Uses leading $s |

With Production

Creates matching index files when creating or copying data from a table.

Style *Font*

Selects font specifications such as **B**, **I**, **U**, **R**, or **L** (for bold, italic, underline, superscript, or subscript respectively). This may be combined with a number, 1–5, to designate font control codes. Generally, these codes affect only printer output (some screen attributes may be affected depending on the display adapter).

While *Condition*

The **While** clause halts the execution of a command when the condition becomes false (.F.).

## Batch Table Commands

dBASE applies batch commands to the table in the current work area (i.e., the current table in **Use** acts as the source or destination). Some batch operations allow a scope. This limits the number of records to a specific set:

**Record** *N* limits the operation to the *N*th row.
**Next** *N* starts at the current row and uses *N* rows.
**All** selects all rows.
**Rest** selects the rows from the current row to the last row.

| Command | Description |
|---------|-------------|
| Append From *Source* [Type *FileType*] [For *Condition*] | Appends records from the designated Source file to the current table. If a **Type** is not specified, the source must |

be a dBASE III or IV table. **Append From** can convert other specified types: **dBASEII**, **Delimited** (standard ASCII data format), **Delimited With Blank** (ASCII with blanks separating records), **Delimited With** *Delimiter* (ASCII, you specify the record separator), **DIF**, **FW2** (Framework II), **RPD**, **SDF** (fixed-length ASCII), **SYLK**, and **WKS** (Lotus 1-2-3, version 1A). The For condition is evaluated on the destination table (i.e., after data conversion), *not* the source file.

Append From Array *ArrayName*
[For *Condition*]

Appends records from the designated array to the current table. The For condition is evaluated on the source (array) contents.

Convert [To *Size*]

Converts the current table to dBASE IV network format (i.e., **Convert** adds a field to the table to manage record locking). You may override the default column width of 16 characters by entering a number from 8 to 24.

Copy Structure To *Destination*
[Fields *FieldList*] [[With] Production]

Creates a new empty table, which matches the column definitions in the current table.

Copy To *Destination* [Type
*FileType*] [[With] Production]
[Fields *FieldList*] [*Scope*] [For
*Condition*] [While *Condition*]

Copies the current table to a new file. Optionally, you may convert the data to a new **Type**. The types are the same as **Append From** with the addition of **DBMemo3**, which coverts to dBASE III-compatible files.

Count [To *Variable*] [*Scope*] [For
*Condition*] [While *Condition*]

Counts the rows in the current table that match the specified condition. The result is then stored in the designated variable (or simply displayed on screen if **To** is not included and **Set Talk On** is the current talk status).

Create *TableName*

Places the user in the table definition screen and creates the named table. If a table of the same name already exists, you will be asked if you want to overwrite the existing table. If you want to modify a table's structure, you must use **Modify Structure**.

Delete [*Scope*] [For *Condition*] [While *Condition*]

By itself, **Delete** marks the current row for deletion (you must use **Pack** to actually remove the marked rows). If conditions are specified, **Delete** scans through the table and marks all matching rows. You may unmark rows with **Recall**.

Delete Tag *TagName* [Of *IndexName*]

Removes a tag from the named index file.

Index On *ColNames* Tag *TagName* [Of *IndexName*] [For *Condition*] [Unique] [Descending]

Creates a tag within the production (or named) index file. A *tag* is the name given to a particular sort order. For example, you could **Index On Last+ First Tag LF** to define a sort order based on last name, breaking ties with a first name sort. In the example, the name of this tag is **LF**. A single index file may contain several tags: You may select a tag through the **Use** command or **Set Order To** *TagName*. **Caution:** If an index is not open when a table is modified, the index will be corrupted (out of date). The production index (which has the same name as the table) is automatically opened with the table; usually you should work with the production index to avoid problems.

Join With *AliasName* To *TableName* For *Condition* [Fields *FieldList*]

Creates a new table from the relational **JOIN** of the current table to the table in the designated area (by Alias name). The **For** condition specifies the type of join (equi-join, theta-join, etc.), and the optional field list selects a subsct of the complete field list. For example, if the current table were ADDRESS and the INVOICE table were in another work area, **Join With Invoice To ShAdd For ClientNum=Invoice->ClientNum .AND. AddNum=Invoice-> ClientNum** would create a new table called SHADD with the combined columns from ADDRESS and INVOICE.

Modify Structure

Places the current table in the table definition screen and allows the user to modify the structure.

Pack

Removes rows marked for deletion. The current table must be in exclusive use before **Pack** will execute.

Recall [*Scope*] [For *Condition*] [While *Condition*]

By itself, **Recall** unmarks the current row (so that **Pack** will no longer remove the row). If conditions are specified, **Recall** scans through the table and marks all matching rows. You may mark rows for deletion with **Delete**.

Reindex

Rebuilds all open indexes in the current work area. The table must be in exclusive use.

Replace *FieldName* With *Variable* [*Scope*] [For *Condition*] [While *Condition*]

Assigns the named variable (or any legal dBASE expression) to the specified field of the current row. If conditions are specified, the **Replace** command scans through the table and changes the specified field in all matching rows. **Replace** may have undesirable side effects if key fields are replaced during a scan. If you must alter key fields, you should first deactivate the index with **Set Order To** (without any tag name).

Replace From Array *Array* [*Scope*] [Fields *FieldNames*] [For *Condition*] [While *Condition*]

Assigns the values from the named array to the first *N* fields of the current row (where *N* is the number of columns in the array). You may alter the fields selected by naming the specific fields to be changed. If conditions are specified, the **Replace Array** command scans through the table and changes all matching rows.

Sort To *TableName* On *FieldName1* [/Al/Dl/Cl/ACl/DC] [... ,*FieldNameN*] [/Al/Dl/Cl/ACl/DC] [Ascending|Descending] [*scope*] [For *Condition*] [While *Condition*]

Creates a new table from the current table sorted on the listed field(s). You may specify either Ascending or Descending as the default, and may override the default on a field-by-field basis with /A or /D. The /C option (which may be combined with the Ascending/Descending overrides) forces the sort to ignore case—by default dBASE sorts with all uppercase letters before lowercase.

Sum *FieldOpList* To *VariableList*|To *Array* [*Scope*] [For *Condition*] [While *Condition*]

Sums the field(s) or field operations to the designated variable(s) or array. Field operations may include any valid arithmetic expression using fields, e.g., **Sum Quan\*UPrice To GTotal**. If conditions are not specified, the sum will include all rows in the table. (For grouping operations, see **Total**.)

Total On *Key* To *TableName* [Fields *FieldList*] [*Scope*] [For *Condition*] [While *Condition*]

Creates a new table that totals field values for each *Key* value in the current table. The current table must be sorted or indexed on the key field. Operationally, this is similar to a Paradox Calc Sum query with the key field checked.

Update On *Key* From *Source* Replace *FieldName1* With *FieldOp1* [... ,*FieldNameN* With *FieldOpN*] [Random]

Matches the key in the named table (*Source*) to the key in the current table and replaces the designated fields in the current table with the values in the source table. If the source table is not currently in the orders specified by the key, it must be indexed on the key, and the **Random** option must be specified. The current (destination) table must be in key order or indexed on the key. **Caution:** If the key field of the destination table is not indexed (or sorted on the key field), the results may be unpredictable.

Zap                           Empties the current table of all rows.

## Work Area Management

*Function*                    *Description*

Assist                        Activates the dBASE Control Center (the default dBASE controlling menu system).

Browse [NoInit] [NoAppend]    Places the current table in Browse
[NoMenu] [NoEdit] [NoDelete]  mode. For advanced users, there are
[NoClear]                     several additional options that restrict access to fields, alter presentation order, and specify calculated fields (these options are not covered). The table will remain under user control until the user terminates Browse mode (Esc or Ctrl-End).

Clear                         By itself, **Clear** clears the screen and
[AlllGetslMemorylMenuslPopupslType  deactivates all @**...Get**s. **Clear Type-**
AheadlWindows]                **ahead** removes all characters from the keyboard type-ahead buffer. **Clear Memory** removes all variables (but not arrays) from memory. The remaining commands clear the specific object type set through the **Define** commands (see **Define...**).

Close                         Closes files of the designated type in all
AlllAlternatelDatabaseslFormatl  work areas. If you want to close a
IndexeslProcedure

single table in a single work area, use **Use** by itself in the desired work area.

Edit [NoInit] [NoAppend]
[NoMenu] [NoEdit] [NoDelete]
[NoClear] [*RowNumber*] [Fields
*FieldList*] [*Scope*] [For *Condition*]
[While *Condition*]

Places the current table in Edit mode (use the default or current form—see **Browse** for row/column format). For advanced users, there are several additional options that restrict access to fields, alter presentation order, and specify calculated fields (they are not covered). The table will remain under user control until the user terminates Edit mode (Esc or **Ctrl-End**). If a row number is listed, the cursor will move to the specified row before editing begins.

Rename *OldName NewName*

Renames any file. Unlike the PAL version, the dBASE **Rename** command renames *only* the designated file, not all associated files. Thus, objects associated with a table must be individually renamed. Note that production indexes should not be renamed—the name of a production index is stored with the dBASE table files and is not affected by the **Rename** command.

Select *Area\Alias*

Changes the active work area. You may specify either the internal area name (by number or single letter), or the alias assigned to the work area (typically, the name of the table in use).

Use [*TableName*] [In *Area*] [Index
*IndexList*] [Order [Tag] *IndexTag*
[Of *IndexFile*]] [Alias *AliasName*]
[Exclusive] [NoUpdate]

Opens a file in the current (or designated) work area. Although the .mdx index that matches the program name—the production index—is automatically opened when the table is opened, you may designate a list of index files to open. And you may select which tag within the index is used for the current sort order (...**Tag *IndexTag* Of *IndexFile***). **Exclusive** prevents other network users from accessing the table. **NoUpdate** treats the table as a Read-Only file. By itself, **Use** closes the table in the current work area. To open a view, use **Set View To** *ViewName*—this will close open dBASE tables and clear the work areas.

## Movement within Tables

| *Command* | *Description* |
|---|---|
| Append | Places dBASE in Edit mode and allows the user to enter new data at the end of the file. |
| Append Blank | Creates a blank row at the end of the file (without entering Edit mode). |
| Continue | Continues searching for the next matching value (see **Locate**). If a match is found, the **Found ( )** function will return **.T.** |
| Find *SearchVal* | See **Seek** (which is designed for handling variables). |
| Goto BottomlTop [In *Area*] | Moves the table pointer either to the first or last row in the table according to the currently defined sort order. For example, if the table is using a last name index, **Goto Top** would move to the first name in an alphabetical list. |
| Goto [Record] *RowNumber* [In *Area*] | Moves to the specified row number. **Caution:** dBASE does not change the row numbers to match the current sort order. Thus, if an index is in use, **Goto 1** and **Goto Top** may not have the same effect. Likewise, **Goto RecNo( )+1** may not move to the next row as shown in the current sort order (see **Skip** for the proper method). Generally, you |

should avoid using **Goto** in your programs.

Locate [For *Condition*] [*Scope*] [While *Condition*]

Scans through the table until a matching row is found. If the locate is successful, the **Found** ( ) function will return **.T.** To locate the next match, use the **Continue** command. If you are searching a key column, **Seek** is more efficient than **Locate**.

Seek *SearchVal*

Moves to the record whose key value (based on the current index tag in use) matches the designated value. If the current tag (sort specifier) is based on the Last column, **Seek "Smith"** would move to the first row with the last name Smith. **Set Exact Off** will make partial matches (only the first few characters need match), **Set Exact On** will locate only exact matches. If the seek is successful, the **Found( )** function will return **.T.** (similar to PAL's **Ret-Val**). (See the **Seek** ( ) function in Chapter 10 for an alternative method.) If the search value includes several columns, you must pad the full field length with spaces, e.g., **Seek "Smith John"**. (See **Locate** for searching on non-key columns.)

Skip *Size* [In *Alias*]

Moves the record pointer by the number of records specified: Positive numbers move forward and negative backward. You may optionally specify a table alias to move the pointer in a work area other than the current one. **Skip** follows the current index order. You may use the **BOF( )** and **EOF( )** functions to check for attempted moves past the beginning or end of the file. .

## Input/Output

| *Command* | *Description* |
|---|---|
| ? *Data* [Picture *PictureSpec*] [Function *FuncList*] [At *Column*] [Style *Font*] | Prints a carriage return and then prints the data to the current device. Unlike PAL which sends **?** output only to the screen, dBASE can send **?** output to the screen (**Set Console On**), a printer (**Set Printer On**), and/or a file (**Set Alternate To** *FileName*, **Set Alternate On**). The functions may include **H, V,** and **;** (see Chapter 2). The column specifies an offset from the left margin. |
| ?? *Data* [Picture *PictureSpec*] [Function *FuncList*] [At *Column*] [Style *Font*] | Prints the data to the current device without sending a carriage return. (See **?** for details.) |
| ??? *Data* | Prints the data directly to the printer without modification (no control codes added). This command is primarily intended for writing special control codes to the printer. Therefore, it supports special abbreviations for the control codes: {NULL}, {CTRL-A} through {CTRL-Z}, {DEL}, {TAB}, {LINEFEED}, {RETURN}, {BACKSPACE}, {ESC}, {CTRL-[}, {CTRL-@}, {CTRL-\}, {CTRL-]}, {CTRL-^}, and {CTRL-_}. Thus, to send a reset to a LaserJet, you would use **??? "{ESC}E"**. |
| @ *Row, Column* | Moves the cursor to the specified row and column. |
| @ *Row, Column* Clear [To *Row, Col*] | Clears the screen from the designated row and column to the end of the line, or optionally clears the box between the designated corners. |
| @ *Row, Column* Fill To *Row, Col* [Color *Attribute*] | If a color is not specified, this command works like **@...Clear**. If a color |

is specified, the text within the box takes on the designated attributes.

@ *Row*, *Column* Get *Variable* [Picture *PictureSpec*] [Format *FuncList*] [Color *SayColor*] [Range [Required] [*Min*], [*Max*]] [Default *DefaultVal*] [Color ,*GetColor*]

The variable must be the name of a table column or an initialized variable. The current value will be printed at the specified location. Upon execution of a **Read** command, the user may cursor between all defined @**...Get**s and change the values. You may specify valid ranges and a default value. There are several additional options for more advanced applications. (See the dBASE manual for these additional features.)

@ *Row*, *Column* Say *Data* [Picture *PictureSpec*] [Format *FuncList*] [Color *SayColor*]

Writes the data to the screen at the specified cursor position. This command is typically used with @**...Get** and **Read** to design forms.

Accept *Prompt* To *Variable*

Prints the prompt to the screen and waits for the user to input text to the designated variable. **Accept** converts all data entered to text format (see **Input**).

Activate Screen

If any windows are active (see **Activate Window**), this command allows write access to all portions of the screen. Unlike the **Deactivate Window** command, the windows are not cleared from the screen.

Activate Window *List*

Displays the windows listed in the command, and restricts write access to the last window named in the list. Alternately, you may use **Activate Window All** to activate all currently defined windows. Before using **Activate Window** you must first define and name windows with **Define Window**.

Copy To Array *ArrayName* [Fields *FieldList*] [*Scope*] [For *Condition*] [While *Condition*]

Creates an array from the specified rows and columns of the current table. The array must be defined before **Copy To Array** is used: One-dimensional arrays will hold a single row, two-dimensional arrays are required for multiple rows. (See **Declare** for information on array creation.)

Create Label *LabelName*

Places the user in the label design screen and creates the named label. If a label of the same name already exists, you will be asked if you want to modify the existing label or create a new one (**Modify Label** is synonymous with **Create Label**, but will skip the prompt and immediately load the label).

Create Report *ReportName*

Places the user in the report design screen and creates the named report. If a report of the same name already exists, you will be asked if you want to modify the existing report or create a new one (**Modify Report** is synonymous with **Create Report**, but will skip the prompt and immediately load the report).

Create Screen *FormName*

Places the user in the form design screen and creates the named form. If a form of the same name already exists, you will be asked if you want to modify the existing form or create a new one (**Modify Screen** is synonymous with **Create Screen**, but will skip the prompt and immediately load the form).

Deactivate Window *WindowList*

Clears the named window(s) from the screen, revealing the underlying screen or windows. **Deactivate All** clears all windows and returns to the default full-screen mode.

Declare *ArraySpecs*

Creates arrays based on the listed specifications. Each array may have one or two dimensions: Multiple names are comma delimited. For example, **Declare A[5], B[2,5]** would create an array called **A** with five elements and an array called **B** with ten elements (two by five).

Define Window *WindowName* From *TopRow*, *LeftCol* To *BotRow*, *RightCol* [Double|Pane|None] [Color [*SayColor*], [*GetColor*], [*FrameColor*]]

Creates a window that limits the scroll and write region. The default is a single-line border, though this can be overridden to double, none with inverse video (**Pane**), or none. (See **Activate Window**, **Deactivate Window**, and the example in Chapter 9.)

Display [Fields *FieldList*] [*Scope*] [For *Condition*] [While *Condition*] [To Printer|To File *FileName*]

**Display All** is handy for listing all records to the screen while working at the dot prompt. The scrolling will stop with each screenful of data. By itself, **Display** shows only the current row. In its other forms, you may limit the fields and/or rows displayed, or redirect the output to another device. **List** has a similar effect, but does not pause between each screenful of data.

Display Status [To Printer|To File *FileName*]

Displays the current status of each active work area (tables, aliases, indexes, and locks), current settings, and the function key assignments. **Display Status** is particularly useful for debugging and working at the dot prompt.

Display Structure [In *Area*] [To Printer|To File *FileName*]

Displays the column definitions of a table.

Eject

Sends a formfeed to the printer unless you have set the system variable **_padvance="LINEFEEDS"** (in this case enough linefeeds are sent to move to the next page; **_plength** controls the page length).

| | |
|---|---|
| Erase *File* | Erases the designated file from the disk. |
| Input *Prompt* To *Variable* | Prints the prompt to the screen and waits for the user to input a valid dBASE expression. **Input** converts all data entered to a simple type, e.g., **5+3** converts to the number 8. Dates may be entered in {}s and text in quotes. Note, however, that text entry works better through the **Accept** command. |
| Insert [Before] [Blank] | Opens a new row following the current row (or before the current row if **Before** is specified) and places the table in Form mode. Unlike **Append**, multiple rows may not be entered, and the table must be in exclusive use. |
| Label Form *LabelName Scope* [For *Condition*] [While *Condition*] [Sample] [To Printer\|To File *FileName*] | Prints the designated pre-defined label format for the current table either to the printer or a disk file. The **Sample** option will ask if you want to print sample labels for alignment—the user may then continue printing samples until the paper has been properly aligned. |
| Read [Save] | Activates the **@...Get** commands and allows cursor movement between the defined fields. Control returns to the program when the user moves off the page or sends a termination code (such as Esc or Ctrl-End). Unless the **Save** option is specified, the **@...Get** definitions will be cleared when the **Read** ends. |
| Report Form *ReportName Scope* [Plain] [Heading *Text*] [NoEject] [Summary] [*Scope*] [For *Condition*] [While *Condition*] [Sample] [To Printer\|To File *FileName*] | Prints the designated pre-defined report format for the current table either to the printer or a disk file. You may suppress several portions of a report with the various options: the initial blank page with the **NoEject**, headers and footers with **Plain**, and detail lines |

with **Summary** (i.e., only the summary lines are printed). You may optionally specify an extra one-line header with **Heading**.

Wait [*Prompt*] [To *Variable*]

Program execution is temporarily suspended until the user presses a key. You may optionally include a variable that stores the key pressed by the user.

## dBASE Menus

dBASE menus are more complicated than PAL's. This is, in part, due to the operational differences in the menu systems. Paradox uses a Lotus 1-2-3 style menu with a selection bar that changes with each level of the menu. dBASE menus use a pull-down and pop-up approach in which the previous selections remain visible. Thus, to mimic the dBASE menus, you must use different menu commands for each level. The Initial level that appears across the top of the screen is called the *Menu*. Each item within the menu is called a *Pad*.

First you must define a menu and its associated pads with **Define Menu** and **Define Pad**. Then you must specify a submenu (pop-up) for each Pad with the **On Pad** command or an action to perform with **On Selection Pad**. **On Pad** is followed by a pop-up menu name. **On Selection Pad** is followed by a dBASE command (from which you can activate another pop-up or execute a procedure).

Pop-up menu definition is similar to the main menu definition (**Define PopUp** with a name, size, and location). Selections within the pop-up menu are called bars, and are defined with **Define Bar**. The resultant bar actions are specified with **On Selection PopUp** commands. The Bar number selected is returned via the **PopUp ( )** function.

To create an initial menu (called Main) across the top of the screen with the choices Edit, Report, and Exit, and a variety of pop-ups you could write:

```
Clear

Define Menu Main
Define Pad Edit Of Main Prompt "Edit a table"
Define Pad Report Of Main Prompt "Print a report"
Define Pad Exit Of Main Prompt "Exit to dot prompt"

On Pad Edit Of Main Activate Popup PopEd
On Pad Report Of Main Activate Popup PopRep
On Selection Pad Exit Of Main Do ConfExit
```

```
Define PopUp PopEd From 1,0 To 4,20
Define Bar 1 of PopEd Prompt "Edit Addresses"
Define Bar 2 of PopEd Prompt "Edit Invoices"

Define PopUp PopRep From 1,13 To 3,30
Define Bar 1 of PopRep Prompt "Print Invoices"

Define PopUp PopInv From 3,32
Define Bar 1 of PopInv Prompt "New Invoices"
Define Bar 2 of PopInv Prompt "All Invoices"

On Selection PopUp PopRep Do PopRepAct

Activate Menu Main

Return

Procedure ConfExit
   @1,1
   Accept "Are you sure you want to exit? " To Ans
   If Ans="Y" .OR. Ans="y"
      Deactivate Menu
   EndIf

Return

Procedure PopRepAct

   Do Case
      Case Bar( )=1
         Activate PopUp PopInv
      && If there were more cases for this menu
      && we could add them here
   EndCase

Return
```

Notice that the **Define Bar** command does not require the **To** option; if it is omitted, dBASE will calculate the proper size automatically. In Figure C.3, **Print a report**, **Print Invoices** is selected from the menus defined by the sample program.

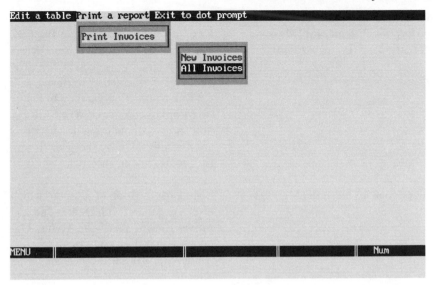

**Figure C.3   A custom menu created with the dBASE menu commands.**

The **Deactivate Menu** command in the exit confirmation procedure removes the menu from the screen and continues program execution on the line following the initial **Activate Menu** command.  The Esc key (when pressed by the user) has the same effect as a **Deactivate Menu** command.

| *Command* | *Description* |
|---|---|
| Activate Menu *MenuName* [Pad *PadName*] | Displays the named menu and waits for user input. The menu must first be defined with **Define Menu** and (optionally) **Define Pad**. |
| Activate PopUp *PopName* | Displays the named pop up menu and waits for user input. The pop-up menu must first be defined with **Define PopUp**. |
| Deactivate Menu | Clears the active menu from the screen. |
| Deactivate PopUp | Clears the active pop-up menu from the screen. |

Define Bar *BarNumber* Of *PopUpName* Prompt *Text* [Message *MsgText*] [Skip [For *Condition*]

Creates selections for inclusion within a pop-up menu (see **Define PopUp**). The **Prompt** specifies the text that is placed within the selection bar. The bar number selected is retrieved with the **Bar** ( ) function via the **On Selection PopUp** command. The **Skip** option specifies conditions for bars that are *not* selectable by the user (if you need to deactivate choices).

Define Menu *MenuName* [Message *Text*]

Begins the creation of a Menu, which is then expanded with **Define Pad** and activated with **Activate Menu**. Optionally, you may include a message, which will print at the bottom of the screen.

Define Pad *PadName* Of *MenuName* Prompt *PadText* [At *Row*, *Col*] [Message *Message*]

Assigns pads to a menu definition (see **Define Menu**). The prompt is the text that appears in the menu bar. The pad name is used by **On Pad** or **On Selection Pad** to specify the associated pop-up menu or action, respectively. You may alter the default position of the pad with the **At** option, and/or print a message at the bottom of the screen with the **Message** option (the message appears when the pad is highlighted and can act as a help prompt).

Define PopUp *PopUpName* From *TopRow*, *LeftCol* [To *BotRow*, *RgtCol*] [Prompt Files Like *Wildcards*] [Message *Text*]

Begins the creation of a pop-up menu that is filled with bar definitions (**Define Bar**), or filenames (the **Prompt Files** option). The filenames may be selected through DOS wildcards, e.g., **A\*.DBF**. dBASE will calculate the pop-up size based on the bar definitions unless the optional **To** command is included.

On Pad *PadName* Of *MenuName* [Activate PopUp *PopUpName*]

By itself, **On Pad** deactivates the current pad. With the **Activate** option, it specifies a pop-up menu to activate from the current pad selection (thus showing the associated pop-up menu as you move from selection to selection). (See **On Selection Pad** to specify an action, rather than a pop-up menu.)

On Selection Pad *PadName* Of
*MenuName* [*Command*]

By itself, **On Selection Pad** deactivates the current pad. If a dBASE command is specified, the command is executed when the user hits the Enter key while the named pad is active (i.e., the command is not executed each time the user scrolls over the pad as in the **On Pad...Activate PopUp** command).

On Selection PopUp *PopUpName*
*Command*

Specifies a dBASE command to execute when a bar from the pop-up menu is selected. This will typically be a **Do** *ProcedureName*, which includes a **Do Case**. The **Do Case** retrieves the selected bar number through the **Bar ( )** function and acts accordingly.

## Query Commands

A few of the query commands listed here are actually **Set** commands that are used to create or activate queries.

*Command*                          *Description*

Create View *ViewName*

Places the user in the query design screen to create the named view. If the query file already exists, dBASE will ask whether you want to modify the file (**Create Query**, **Modify Query**, **Create View**, and **Modify View** are synonymous). The command to use a view is **Set View To** *ViewName*—this will close open tables and clear the work areas, because each view may require several work tables and work areas.

Set Filter To [*Condition*]

**Set Filter** applies only to the work area in which it was activated. Table access will be restricted to those rows that match the specified condition. Restrictions will be removed if a condition is not specified. The filter is not activated until the first movement; i.e., if the initial row does not match the filter condition, it will remain visible until the row pointer is moved with **Skip** or **Goto**.

Set View To *QueryName*

Activates a query created with the dBASE QBE design screen. **Caution:** A dBASE view consists of several elements, including tables, work area assignments, and filter conditions. Open files will be closed and work areas cleared when **Set View** is executed.

## dBASE Functions

## Status Functions

| *Function* | *Description* |
| --- | --- |
| Alias ([*AreaNum*]) | Returns the current alias of the current (or designated) work area. |
| Bar ( ) | Returns the number of the status bar last selected from a pop-up menu. See the menu section in this appendix. |
| BOF ( ) | Returns **.T.** if the last **Skip** command attempted to move the pointer before the first row (**B**eginning **O**f **F**ile). To test if the pointer is *on* the first row, use **RecNo ( )**. |

| | |
|---|---|
| Change ( ) | On a network, returns **.T.** if the row has been changed by another user since it was last read by the program. |
| DBF ([*AliasNum*]) | Returns the name of the table open in the current (or designated) work area. |
| Deleted( ) | Returns **.T.** if the current row is marked for deletion (see the **Delete** and **Pack** commands). |
| Field (*Number*[,*Alias*]) | Returns the name of the *N*th field in the current (or specified) table. |
| File (*Name*) | Returns **.T.** if the named file exists. |
| Found ( ) | Returns **.T.** if the last search operation (**Seek**, **Locate**, **Continue**, or **Find**) was successful. The value will change to **.F.** if any other pointer movement (such as **Skip**) is used. |
| InKey ([*Delay*]) | Returns the ASCII code of the next character waiting in the type-ahead buffer. If no characters are in the buffer, **InKey** ( ) returns 0. Special keys, such as function and Alt-combination keys, will be returned as negative numbers. If the optional delay is included, **InKey** ( ) will wait the specified number of seconds before continuing. If the delay is entered as 0, program execution will pause indefinitely until a key is pressed. |
| IsColor ( ) | Returns **.T.** if the computer has a color monitor. |
| LastKey ( ) | Returns the ASCII code of the key pressed before exiting full-screen mode. Generally, **ReadKey( )** should be used to get the meaning of the last action rather than the last key. |

Network ( )

Returns **.T.** if dBASE is running on a network.

Order ([*Alias*])

Returns the name of the index tag that the table is currently using.

Pad ( )

Returns the name of the pad that was last selected in a pop-up menu. This is typically used within a **Do Case** loop to determine the action based on the last menu selection (see the example in the Menu section of this appendix).

PrintStatus ( )

Returns **.T.** if the printer is online.

Prompt ( )

Returns the text of the prompt from the last menu item selected. (See **Pad ( )** to retrieve the Pad number.)

ReadKey ( )

Returns a code indicating the type of action last performed during a full screen editing session, e.g., the action that ended a **Read** or **Edit**. The code also indicates whether data was altered during the session. (The codes are listed in Chapter 9.) The **LastKey ( )** function returns the code of the key that ended the session.

RecCount ([*Alias*])

Returns the number of rows in a table. The count is not affected by filters, and includes rows marked for deletion.

RecNo ([*Alias*])

Returns the current record (row) number. Although you should try to avoid referencing record numbers, this is particularly difficult in dBASE because the record number acts as a row's primary identifier. Note that the record number does not necessarily reflect the position in the current view; if an index tag is in use, the records may appear out of order.

RecSize ([*Alias*])

Returns the size of the current record (row) in bytes.

Select ( )

Returns the number of the highest available work area. If you must assign work areas dynamically, you should first **Use** tables in the highest numbered areas and work down. If the catalog is open, it will use work area 10.

Version ( )

Returns a string representing the name and version number of dBASE under which the program is currently running.

## String Functions

*Function*

*Description*

Asc (*Character*)

Converts a single letter to the equivalent ASCII number. Thus, **Asc ("A")** returns 65.

At (*SubStr, FullStr*)

Finds the starting position of the first (sub) string within the second full string. If the substring does not occur in the full string, **At( )** returns 0. Thus, **At ("ad","Bradley")** returns 3 since the substring begins at the third position of the full string.

Chr (*Number*)

Converts a numeric ASCII code to the equivalent character. Thus, **Chr(65)** returns "A".

IsAlpha (*String*)

Returns **.T.** if the first character of the string is a letter.

IsLower (*String*)

Returns **.T.** if the first character of the string is a lowercase letter.

| | |
|---|---|
| IsUpper (*String*) | Returns **.T.** if the first character of the string is an uppercase letter. |
| Left (*String*, *N*) | Returns *N* characters, starting from the left of the string. For example, **Left ("Bradley",4)** returns "Brad". |
| Len (*String*) | Returns the number of characters in a string (its length). If used with a text field, **Len ( )** returns the length of the field, rather than the number of characters entered in the field. |
| Like (*Pattern*, *String*) | Returns **.T.** if the string matches the pattern. The pattern is a string that is composed of literal characters: ?s (for matching any single characters) and/or *s (for matching any number of characters). |
| Lower (*string*) | Converts uppercase letters within a string to lowercase letters. |
| LTrim (*string*) | Removes blanks from the left side of a string (**Left Trim**). |
| Replicate (*String*, *N*) | Returns *N* concatenated copies of the string. **Replicate ("ab",5)** returns "abababab". |
| Right (*String*, *N*) | Returns the last *N* characters of the string. For example, **Right ("Stilt",4)** returns "tilt". |
| Round (*Number*, *Place*) | Rounds a number to the specified inverse power of 10 (decimal place). **Round (5.91,0)** returns 6, **Round (5.91,1)** returns 5.91, and **Round (5.91,-1)** returns 10. |
| RTrim (*string*) | Removes blanks from the right side of a string (**Right Trim**). **Trim (*string*)** is synonymous. |

Soundex (*String*)

Returns a four-character string that represents the "sound" of a word. Two such words may then be compared to see if they are perhaps two different spellings of the same word (this is particularly useful for comparing names).

Space (*Number*)

Returns the designated number of spaces (similar to the **Replicate ( )** function).

Str (*Number*[, *Size*][, *Precision*])

Converts a number to the equivalent string. You may optionally include the number of characters in the result (*Size*) and/or the number of decimal places (*Precision*).

Stuff (*OrigString, Position, Length, ReplaceString*)

Returns a string in which the original has been overwritten by the replacement, starting at the designated position and continuing for the specified length. Thus, **Stuff ("Boot Camp", 4,3,"k L")** would return "Book Lamp".

SubStr (*String, Position, Length*)

Returns the portion of a string starting at the designated position and includes the number of characters specified by the length. Thus, if **a="This"**, then **a+" "+SubStr(a,3,2)+" "+SubStr(a,2,3)** would return "This is his".

Transform (*Data, Template*)

**Format ( )** takes text or numeric data and applies the designated template. It works with any data type that matches the template (see the description of the **Picture** specifier in Chapter 2).

Trim (*String*)

Removes blanks from the right side of a string. **RTrim (***String***)** is synonymous.

Upper (*String*)

Returns a string in which lowercase letters are converted to uppercase.

Val (*String*)                          Converts a string of numerals into the
                                         number it represents. For example **Val
                                         ("12345")** would return the number
                                         12,345. If the string does not represent
                                         a number, 0 is returned.

## Time and Date Functions

*Function*                               *Description*

CDOW (*Date*)                            Returns the full name of the weekday
                                         for the given date: "Monday", "Tues-
                                         day", etc.

CMonth (*Date*)                          Returns the full name of the month for
                                         the given date: "January", "Febru-
                                         ary", etc.

CTOD(*DateString*)                       Converts a string, such as "2/1/90",
                                         into date format.

Date ( )                                 Returns the current date.

Day (*Date*)                             Returns the day in number format.
                                         **Day ({2/1/90})** would return the num-
                                         ber 1.

DMY (*Date*)                             Converts a date to **D**ay **M**onth **Y**ear
                                         format, e.g., **DMY ({2/1/90)** would be
                                         "2 February 1990".

DOW (*Date*)                             Returns the day of the week as a num-
                                         ber with Sunday=1 and Saturday=7.

DTOC (*Date*)                            Converts a date to a string in the stan-
                                         dard date format, e.g., **DTOC
                                         ({2/1/90})** would be "2/1/90".

DTOS (*Date*)                            Converts a date to a string from the
                                         most significant portion to the least
                                         significant portion (year, month, date).
                                         This function is intended for dates that
                                         must be combined with string data into

a sorted index entry. The string itself does not have delimiters: **DTOS ({2/1/90})** returns "19900201".

MDY (*Date*)

Converts a date to a month, day, year string with the month spelled in full. For example, **MDY({2/1/90})** returns "February 1, 1990".

Month (*Date*)

Returns the month as a number.

Time ( )

Returns the current time in hours, minutes, and seconds as a string: e.g., "15:22:25".

Year (*Date*)

Returns the year in number format.

## Mathematical Functions

As with PAL, several dBASE mathematical functions are quite specialized and are more useful for scientific and engineering applications. These include the trigonometric functions **Sin ( )**, **Cos**, **Tan ( )**, and their inverses **ASin ( )**, **ACos ( )**, **ATan ( )**. As befits their application, radians are used for angular measurements. Similarly, **Pi ( )**, **Exp ( )**, **Log ( )** (base e), and **Log10 ( )** are of more technical than general interest, so they will not be covered in-depth (though the latter may be of occasional value in financial applications).

dBASE supports three financial functions: **FV ( )** (future value), **Payment ( )** (amortization), and **PV ( )** (present value). However, these functions are limited to regular payment schedules; i.e., they do not operate on a column of irregular payment amounts and/or intervals, and are thus somewhat limited in a database application.

*Function*

*Description*

Abs (*Number*)

Returns the absolute value of a number (negative numbers are made positive).

Ceiling (*Number*)

Returns the next highest integer; i.e., it always "rounds" up (toward positive infinity).

Fixed (*Number*)

Converts a floating point number to a BCD number.

Float (*Number*)

Converts a BCD number to a floating point number.

Floor (*Number*)

Returns the next lowest integer; i.e., it always "rounds" down (toward negative infinity).

Int (*Number*)

Returns the integer portion of the number by truncating any fractional portion.

Max (*Number1, Number2*)

Returns the larger of two numbers. **Max (9,5)** and **Max (5,9)** return 9. This function will also work with strings.

Min (*Number1, Number2*)

Returns the smaller of two numbers. **Min (9,5)** and **Min (5,9)** return 5. This function will also work with strings.

Mod (*Dividend, Divisor*)

Returns the remainder (modulus) of the dividend divided by the divisor. **Mod (5,3)** returns 2.

Rand ([*Seed*])

Returns a random number between 0 and 1. Optionally, you may set an initial seed to start a repeatable sequence. The default initial seed value is 100001 (i.e., each time dBASE is started the seed is set to 100001). If you do not want repeatable sequences, dBASE will generate a seed based on the system clock if you use a negative number, e.g., **Rand(-1)**.

SqRt (*Number*)

Returns the square root of a number. **SqRt (9)** returns 3.

## Miscellaneous Functions

| *Function* | *Description* |
|---|---|
| IIF (*Condition, TrueData, FalseData*) | The **Immediate IF** evaluates the condition and returns the first data item if the condition is **.T.**, or the second if the condition is **.F.** The data may be of any type (string, numeric, date) as long as both items within the function are of the same type. |
| Lookup (*RetField, KeyVal, SearchField*) | Searches the alias and field named in the search field for the key value, and returns the data found in the return field (the alias of the return field should match the alias of the search field, though dBASE won't enforce this). The **LookUp** ( ) function may be used to partially implement foreign keys (see the example in Chapter 9); however, it cannot handle multiple column keys. |
| Seek (*SearchVal* ⌊,*Alias*⌋) | Moves to the record whose key value (based on the current index tag in use) matches the designated value. The function returns **.T.** if the row exists, and **.F.** if no match was found. (See the **Seek** command in this appendix for specific operational information.) |

## Summary Functions

dBASE does not have direct summary functions. However, there are several functions that are used within a **Calculate** command to summarize data over selected rows of a table. The syntax of the **Calculate** command is:

```
Calculate [Scope] Functions [For Condition] [While
Condition] [To Variables|To Array]
```

The functions are any of those listed below. You may use several functions within a single **Calculate** by separating the function names with commas. You also may designate several variables (one for each function) or a one-dimensional array (with one element for each function). The column expression may be a column name, or an operation based on one or more columns.

| *Function* | *Description* |
| --- | --- |
| Avg (*ColumnExp*) | Averages the specified column, which must be a numeric type. |
| Cnt ( ) | Counts the selected rows of the table. |
| Max (*ColumnExp*) | Returns the largest value in the column or calculation. |
| Min (*ColumnExp*) | Returns the smallest value in the column. |
| NPV (*Rate, Column*[, *Initial*]) | Calculates the Net Present Value of the specified column using a fixed periodic rate of return. Each selected row of the table represents a single period. Remember to scale the rate accordingly (e.g., divide an annual rate by 12 if each row represents one month). If the optional initial investment is not included, it is assumed to be 0. |
| Std (*Column*) | Calculates the population (*n*-weighted) standard deviation of the column. This assumes that the column contains all data for the group (the population), rather than a portion of the data (a sample). To convert to sample deviation, multiply the result of **Var( )** by **Cnt( )/(Cnt( )-1)**, and take the square root:**SqRt ( )**. |
| Sum (*Column*) | Calculates the sum of the column. |
| Var (*Column*) | Calculates the population (*n*-weighted) variance of the column. This assumes that the column contains all data for the group (the population), rather than a |

portion of the data (a sample).  To convert to sample variance, multiply the
result by **Cnt( )/(Cnt( )-1)**.

# Appendix D

# Error Handling

## Error Processing in PAL

Error processing and recovery can be a bit tricky in Paradox. For most situations, you should try to avoid errors by checking the relevant status ahead of time; for example, using **IsTable ("Answer")** before using the Answer table or **PrinterStatus ( )** before printing a report. But it is in the nature of programming for unexpected events to occur—overlooking a possible result (sometimes the most difficult problem to find), or simply entering the wrong command or sequence.

Normally, if PAL encounters an error while playing a script, Paradox will present a **Cancel** or **Debug** menu selection. More serious errors may shell out to DOS and ask the user to free disk space and type **Exit** to continue executing the script, or abort Paradox altogether and return to DOS. Assuming the problem is a minor error in your program, you can select **Debug** to try and find the cause, fix the problem, and continue (**Cancel** simply stops script execution and returns you to the Paradox workspace and interactive menus).

Paradox reports the name of the script and the line number at which the error occurred, followed by a copy of the line that caused the error. The message window displays a description of the error. An example appears in Figure D.1. In the example shown, you have several options: type in the correct name of the table and report number (since Paradox left you at the report prompt) and continue with the next step, call the editor and change the line that is causing the problem, create the PASTDUE table and continue with the current step, or abort the process.

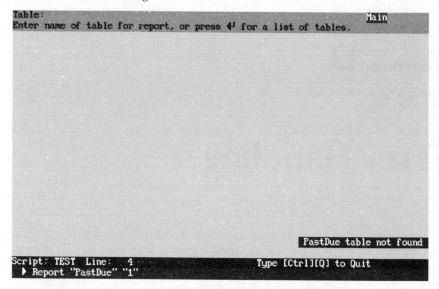

**Figure D.1    Paradox error message and Debug screen.**

There are a few keys (and menu choices) that come to your aid in such a situation: **Ctrl-N** skips the current instruction and moves on to the next; **Ctrl-S** executes the current instruction and moves to the next; **Ctrl-G** starts execution at the current instruction (without stopping at the next instruction); **Ctrl-Q** aborts the script; and **Alt-F10** presents a debugging menu, which gives you these same choices (**Next, Step, Go**, and **Quit**), and more!   For example, if you select **Editor** from the debug menu, Paradox will load the script into the editor and move the cursor to the line that caused the error.

The Debug menu also presents a few choices that can help you figure out what went wrong. The **Value** selection lets you enter an expression and displays the result in the message window.  So, if you're told that the variable Foo has an illegal value, you can display the value by selecting **Value, Foo**.  Of course, if you need a more complicated expression, you may enter any combination of operations that return a value, e.g., **Value, Dow(Today( )+5)**.  The **Value** selection is useful with some of the special debugging functions, too. As soon as you use the keyboard, the message window, which explains the type of error you encountered, disappears. You can get it back with **Value, ErrorMessage ( )**.

The **Miniscript** selection will execute as many PAL instructions as you can fit on a line (and accurately transcribe).  This can be handy for instructions that aren't available from the menus or are easier to type as a command, such as **Index**.  If you make a mistake entering a command, you will return to the

**Cancel/Debug** menu, where you may select **Debug**, return to the debugging menu (**Alt-F10**), and select **Editor**. Rather than placing a miniscript in the editor, you will be returned to the Miniscript entry line (you can use the same process if you mistype a **Value**).

One last note about the Debug menu: It may be called at any time, even when no script has yet been played. This can be a handy utility for short, simple tasks such as **Scan** loops called from **Miniscript**. The menu selections will vary slightly, depending on the current system state. For example, if the menu was accessed outside of script play, the **Debug** selection will appear. **Debug** works much like **Script**, **Play**, but places the script immediately in single-step mode. This is very useful for debugging problems that occur near the beginning of a script (you don't have to try and hit **Ctrl-Break** immediately after execution starts).

You may write a special error-handling function (using **Proc... Endproc**). If you assign the name of the procedure to the reserved variable ErrorProc, PAL will automatically execute the procedure any time an error is detected. For example, if the error-handling procedure were defined as:

```
Proc ErrorDetect ()
     Private ErrorProc ;This keeps ErrorDetect
                       ; from calling itself
        ;Program goes here
EndProc

ErrorProc=ErrorDetect
```

the last line would enable the error handling procedure. Error procedures have three special return values: 0, 1, and 2. **Return 0** re-executes the line that caused the error, **Return 1** executes the line after the error (skips the line that caused the error), and **Return 2** (the default), returns the user to the **Cancel/Debug** menu as if the error handler had never executed.

The following functions are useful within error-handling routines:

| *Function* | *Description* |
| --- | --- |
| ErrorCode ( ) | Returns the error number of the most recent error. These may not always be specific enough for the error-handling routine to use. The error codes are listed at the end of this section. If you need a more specific error return, read |

the text of the error message with **ErrorMessage ( )**.

ErrorMessage ( )

Returns the text of the error message. This can be useful for retrieving the last error with **Miniscript, Value**.

ErrorUser ( )

Returns the name of the user currently using the files that you are locked out of. This function is for use on Local Area Networks.

## Error Codes

The following error list is not complete—it includes only those errors which will call an error procedure. For example, error 40 (out of memory) will immediately halt script operation or drop to DOS, so it is not listed.

| Error Code | Description |
| --- | --- |
| 0 | No Error |
| 1 | Drive not ready |
| 2 | Directory not found |
| 3 | Table in use by another computer on the network |
| 4 | Full lock placed by another computer on the network |
| 5 | File not found |
| 6 | File corrupted |
| 7 | Index corrupted |
| 8 | Family member belongs to a different version (earlier or later restructure) |
| 9 | Record locked by another computer on the network |
| 10 | Directory in use by another computer on the network |
| 11 | Private directory belongs to another computer on the network |
| 12 | Directory not available |
| 13 | Index inconsistent with sort order |
| 14 | Multiuser access denied |
| 15 | PARADOX.NET conflict |
| 20 | Operation not possible in current mode |

| | |
|---|---|
| 21 | Insufficient rights |
| 22 | Table is write protected |
| 23 | Field value does not match restriction (Validity Checks) |
| 24 | Obsolete procedure library |
| 25 | Insufficient image rights |
| 27 | Operation not complete |
| 28 | Too many nested closed procedures |
| 29 | Table is remote |
| 30 | Data type mismatch |
| 31 | Argument out of range |
| 32 | Wrong number of arguments |
| 33 | Invalid argument |
| 34 | Variable or procedure is not defined |
| 35 | Invalid menu selection |
| 41 | Out of disk space |
| 43 | Printer not ready |
| 44 | Low memory |
| 60 | Referential integrity violation |
| 61 | Corrupt multitable form |
| 63 | Link locked (must return from row/column view to the multitable form where modifications were begun). |

## Error Processing in dBASE

dBASE has a very handy debugging environment modeled after the full-screen debuggers used by professional programmers. To activate the debugger when errors occur, you must **Set Trap On** (or place **TRAP=ON** in the CONFIG.DB file to change the default). You may also activate the debugger by interrupting the program with the Esc key. The debugger screen is shown in Figure D.2.

The top window shows the program that is currently executing, and the highlight is on the line that will execute next. Note that the program in the example is an infinite loop: The value of C will not change; you must hit **Esc** to get into the debugger. You may enter variable names in the Display Window—it shows the variable name and the current value. As you step through the program, the variables in the Display Window will continuously update with new values. The Breakpoint Window holds conditional expressions, which will halt program execution whenever one of the conditions becomes true (in the example, **C=20** will never break execution). The bottom

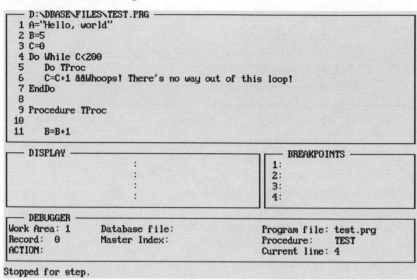

```
─── D:\DBASE\FILES\TEST.PRG ──────────────────────────────
 1 A="Hello, world"
 2 B=5
 3 C=0
 4 Do While C<200
 5    Do TProc
 6    C=C+1 &&Whoops! There's no way out of this loop!
 7 EndDo
 8
 9 Procedure TProc
10
11    B=B+1
```

```
── DISPLAY ────────────────────        ── BREAKPOINTS ───────
                      :                   1:
                      :                   2:
                      :                   3:
                      :                   4:
```

```
── DEBUGGER ──────────────────────────────────────────────
Work Area: 1      Database file:           Program file: test.prg
Record:  0        Master Index:            Procedure:    TEST
ACTION:                                    Current line: 4
```

Stopped for step.

**Figure D.2    The dBASE full-screen debugger.**

window shows various status information—debugger commands are entered here.

When you first enter the debugger, dBASE displays a list of the commands. Some commands move the cursor into the various windows. You may then enter, delete, or change the items:

| *Command* | *Description* |
| --- | --- |
| B | Move into the Breakpoint Window |
| D | Move into the Display Window |
| E | Edit the program (changes appear in the listing, but do not take effect until the program is recompiled) |

To return to the bottom window to resume command processing, simply hit Esc or **Ctrl-End**.

You may step through the program one line at a time to see what is happening, or you may resume execution where you left off:

| Command | Description |
|---------|-------------|
| S | Execute next instruction |
| N | Execute next instruction, but do not trace into a new procedure (i.e., run the procedure completely and stop at the step after the **Do** statement). |
| R | Resumes normal execution |

**S** and **N** may be prefixed by a number (e.g., **5s**) in order to run through several steps at once.

You may call the help screen (which reviews these and other functions) with the **F1** key. And, if you need to see the output screen as the program would appear to the user, you may toggle between the debugger and output with the **F9** key.

To leave the debugger, type **Q** (for quit). If you want to temporarily suspend the debugger, type **U**. This allows you to shell out to the dot prompt, perform some commands (for example, place a table you left out of the program in one of the work areas), and then return to the debugger where you left off with the **Resume** command.

If you want dBASE to run a special procedure or command every time an error occurs, you may use the **On Error** command. For example, **On Error Do Handler** would run the procedure Handler when dBASE detects an error. The error handler could then access functions to determine the cause of the error and possibly remedy the situation.

| Function | Description |
|----------|-------------|
| Error ( ) | Returns the error number. dBASE has several hundred different error numbers. (See the dBASE manual for a complete listing.) |
| LineNo ( ) | Returns the current line number. If this is passed as a parameter to a procedure that handles errors (e.g., **On Error Do Handler With LineNo ( )**), it will pass the line number that caused the error. |
| Message ( ) | Returns the error message. |

| | |
|---|---|
| Program ( ) | Returns the name of the procedure or function that caused the error. |
| Retry | This command is used within an error handler to again try processing the line that caused the error (if the error procedure ends with **Return**, it will simply resume execution on the line *after* the error). |
| Resume | This command will return to the debugger, if the debugger has been temporarily suspended through a **Suspend** command in a program or the **U** command in the debugger. |
| Suspend | This command is used within a program or error handler to temporarily suspend execution of a program and return to the dot prompt. **Resume** will resume execution of the program at the point at which it was suspended. |

# Appendix **E**

# The Paradox Custom Configuration Program

The Paradox Custom Configuration Program (CCP) sets several default options for the Paradox program. These include monitor and display adapter type, screen colors, printer information, and much more. The CCP must be run from the directory that contains the CCP script and library (CUSTOM.SC and CUSTOM.LIB). The changes must be saved to the directory that contains the configuration file (PARADOX.CFG). You should find this file before starting the CCP. In some cases (particularly on networks), there may be several directories that have copies of the configuration file. Paradox will use the first copy it finds in the path. To see your path, type PATH at the DOS prompt—each directory name is separated by a ";". For example, consider the following path:

```
PATH=C:\;C:\DOS;C:\SU;C:\WORD;D:\PDOX35;M:\PDOX35;
 C:\NETWORK;L:\BASIC;L:\ASM;L:\C;L:\U.DOS;L:\UTILSB;
 D:\EDR;D:\EDB;C:\DV
```

Both C:\PDOX35 and M:\PDOX35 have copies of PARADOX.CFG, but C:\PDOX35 appears first, so its copy of the configuration file is used. The system files are located in M:\PDOX35, so the CCP is started from that directory:

```
M:\PDOX35paradox custom
```

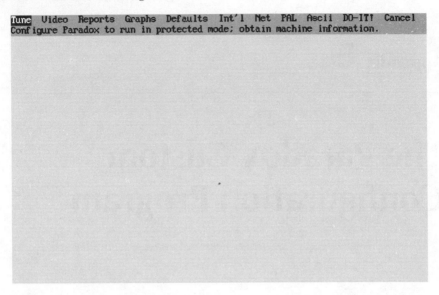

Tune Video Reports Graphs Defaults Int'l Net PAL Ascii DO-IT! Cancel
Configure Paradox to run in protected mode; obtain machine information.

**Figure E.1    The initial Custom Configuration Program menu (Scripts, Play, Custom).**

Figure E.1 shows the initial CCP menu. This appendix will not cover all of the options, just those that frequently require changes. The **Video** menu is perhaps the most important option for working comfortably; it lets you change the monitor type and display colors. It is particularly important if you have a monochrome display on a color adapter such as the CGA or VGA. In this case, the option should be set as **Video, Monitor, B&W**. On very old CGA adapters, you may get "snow" on the screen when it is updated. To eliminate the snow, select **Video, Snow, Yes**.

Under the **Reports** menu, you should probably change the **PageLength** and **FormFeed** options. Many offices use a mix of laser printers and dot matrix printers, so it is useful to have a generic setting, which will work on both. A letter-size page (at standard spacing) has 66 lines—this is the Paradox default— but most page printers (such as laser printers) have an unprintable region, which limits the range to 60 lines. **Reports, LengthOfPage, 60** will create a page length that will fit on nearly any printer.

This is not enough to make the printer support generic, however, because Paradox usually moves to the end of a page by sending linefeed characters to the printer. On a dot matrix printer, a setting of 60 lines will not fill the page. However, most printers in use today can accept a formfeed character, which moves the paper to the next page. To make Paradox send a formfeed character at the end of each page, select **Reports, FormFeed, FormFeeds**.

```
Editing printer setup table.
Press [F1] for help, [F2] when done, or [F10] for menu.
PRINTER          Name              Port             Setup String
   1    StandardPrinter*           LPT1
   2    Small-IBMgraphics          LPT1    \027W\000\015
   3    Reg-IBMgraphics            LPT1    \027W\000\018
   4    Small-Epson-MX/FX          LPT1    \015
   5    Small-Oki-92/93            LPT1    \015
   6    Small-Oki-82/83            LPT1    \029
   7    Small-Oki-192              LPT1    \029
   8    HPLaserJet                 LPT1    \027E
   9    HP-Portrait-66lines        LPT1    \027E\027&17.27C
  10    HP-Landscape-Normal        LPT1    \027E\027&l1O
  11    HP-Compressed              LPT1    \027E\027(s16.66H
  12    HP-LandscpCompressed       LPT1    \027E\027&l1O\027(s16.66H
  13    Intl-IBMcompatible         LPT1    \027\054
  14    Intl-IBMcondensed          LPT1    \027\054\015
```

**Figure E.2** **Predefined printer setup strings available through the Setting, Setup, Predefined menu of the Custom Configuration Program.**

The **Reports, Setups** can be very useful if you must support unusual printers, printer modes, or multiple printer ports. It presents a Printers table (see Figure E.2) that defines the style name, printer port, and setup string. These pre-defined options are available from the report design screen in Paradox (**Setting, Setup, Predefined**). You may change any of the existing setups, or add new entries.

Most of the **Defaults** options are frequently used. **Defaults, SetDirectory** will create a fixed working directory for Paradox. If you want Paradox to access files in a specific directory every time it's started, you should enter the directory name here. If you want Paradox to use the directory from which you started Paradox (the default), this entry should be left blank.

**Defaults, QueryOrder** alters the column order of the ANSWER table. The default (**TableOrder**) places the columns in the same order as they appear in the original tables—the method used since Version 1. However, when this option was first added in Paradox 3.1, the default was **ImageOrder**, and the columns followed the order of the query forms. Thus, if you used **Ask** and then rotated the query form columns with Ctrl-R, the order of the ANSWER table columns would change.

**Defaults, Blank=Zero, Yes** will cause mathematical operations to treat blank numbers as a 0. Usually, a blank number has a distinct meaning (the quantity is unknown) and hence, mathematical operations are invalid. The default, **Defaults, Blank=Zero, No** will return an error if a value is blank. But, when working with large numeric-based tables, handling blanks can become awkward. If you find yourself constantly adding steps to your procedures to treat blanks as 0, it is often beneficial to set this option to **Yes**.

**Defaults, DisableBreak, Disable** is useful when developing stand-alone applications for novice users. It will prevent them from inadvertently hitting the break key and halting the execution of a program. Sometimes, this will add some security to your applications by keeping users' hands off intermediate steps that may contain sensitive information.

The **Net** option is intended primarily for network installations. **Net, Username** sets the name other network users will see for your computer. And **Net, AutoRefresh** sets the number of seconds between screen updates for shared tables. But **Net, SetPrivate**, which sets the private directory, can be useful on individual computers as well as networks.

If a private directory is set, the temporary tables (for example, ANSWER, DELETED, KEYVIOL, and many others) are stored in the private directory rather than the working directory. On a network, it is important that every user have a separate private directory so that one person's ANSWER table does not overwrite another's. But even on a stand-alone system, there may be advantages to keeping these tables in separate directories.

First, if you are using a system with more than one hard disk, you can improve system performance. For example, if a query is reading tables on one drive and writing the ANSWER to another, the disk arm on the reading drive will not need to skip over to the ANSWER table as it works. It is very important that it be a separate physical drive and not just a different drive letter: in the latter case (a single physical drive), the arm may end up travelling more and degrade performance.

Private directories are also useful for organizing template tables (for reports and forms), especially if you are developing applications for use by others. Placing **Privtables** *Tablenames* in your script will access the named tables through the private directory (rather than the working directory). When forms or reports are updated, you can simply copy the entire private directory from one computer to the other, without destroying valuable data by accidentally copying a data table.

It is not strictly necessary to set the private directory through the CCP. Alternatively, you may set it through your own scripts with **SetPrivDir** *Path*. The negative side of this approach is that the person using the application loses control over where the private directory is located.

**PAL, MaintainIndexes, Yes** forces Paradox to update secondary indexes on keyed tables every time the tables are updated. Under the default (**No**),

Paradox updates the indexes only when they are required for an operation (queries, sorting, etc).

The built-in editor for PAL scripts is very minimal; it can't even copy or move text from one location to another. Anyone who works extensively with Paradox scripts should use another editor (or word processor). Fortunately, through the CCP, you can tell Paradox to use your choice of editors for editing scripts. **PAL, Editor** asks for a DOS command to start your own editor. This is essentially the same command you would type at the DOS prompt, with a few additional symbols:

- **!** at the beginning of the command tells Paradox to use **BigDOS** to run your editor. This allocates more memory to the editor: most external editors will require this option.
- **\*** is used in place of the script name (Paradox will place the script name here when it runs your editor).
- **\*\*** may be used for the line number (if your editor supports this feature).

Usually, Paradox moves the cursor to the first line in a program. But, if you call the editor from the Debug menu, Paradox will report the line that caused the error. For example, to use the Microsoft Editor, the **PAL, Editor** command line is:

```
!me /e "BeginGoto \"**\" Goto" *
```

The /e tells the editor to run a macro (in this case, called BeginGoto) that loads a line number (\*\*) and then moves the cursor to the line (Goto). The last item on the command line is the filename (\*).

# Appendix F

# Data Formats

| Data Types | dBASE | Paradox |
| --- | --- | --- |
| Logical | Yes | No |
| Integer | No | Yes |
| Short Real | No | No |
| Long Real | Yes | Yes |
| Calculated | No | No |
| Packed Decimal | Yes | No* |
| Currency | No* | Yes |
| Date | Yes | Yes |
| Time | No | No |
| Text | Yes | Yes |
| Memo | Yes | No |

*dBASE Numeric (packed decimal) and Paradox Currency are both intended for use with monetary figures. However, packed decimal is often the preferred storage method because it can prevent rounding errors. For example, if you perform the calculation 1-.99-.01 in Paradox, the result is 8.67361731E-18. While this number is close enough to 0 for most purposes, if you compare the result to 0 (as you might when balancing financial transactions) the truth value is False.

While the results of such comparisons can produce alarming results, this is a fairly common problem with computer-generated reports (Lotus 1-2-3 will also return False). You can work around this problem by using the **Round ( )** function: **Round (1-.99-.01)=0** will return the logical value True. Packed

Decimal format does not require this extra step:  All numbers are stored with a fixed number of decimal places, so rounding is not necessary.

# Index